The Man *from* Steamtown
The story of F. Nelson Blount

The Man
from
Steamtown

The story of F. Nelson Blount

JAMES R. ADAIR

© 2015 by F. Nelson Blount. All rights reserved.

Trusted Books is an imprint of Deep River Books. The views expressed or implied in this work are those of the author. To learn more about Deep River Books, go online to www.DeepRiverBooks.com.

No part of this publication may be reproduced, stored in a retrieval system, or transmitted in any way by any means—electronic, mechanical, photocopy, recording, or otherwise—without the prior permission of the copyright holder, except as provided by USA copyright law.

The story of F. Nelson Blount, by James R. Adair, was originally published in June of 1967. An update section was added by him in 1988.

Hannah R. Goodman re-edited James R. Adair's version and added another update in 2012.

The Man from Steamtown, (c) James R. Adair (1967, 1988), Hannah R. Goodman (2012) Printed in the United States of America. All rights reserved.

No part of this book may be reproduced without written permission, except in reviews. For information, contact F. Nelson Blount II, 630 Currant Road, Fall River, MA 02720.

Unless otherwise noted, all Scripture verses are taken from the *King James Version* of the Bible (KJV).

Verses marked C. B. Williams translation are taken from that translation of the Bible.

ISBN 13: 978-1-63269-042-5
Library of Congress Catalog Card Number: 2013933505

Dedication

To dyed-in-the-wool steam fans, who, with Nelson Blount, help keep the Steam Age alive.

And to the rail buffs, those who aren't so dyed-in-the-wool but simply like to ride steam trains (the real rail hobbyists call them "daisy pickers").

CONTENTS

Introduction: How This Book Began................ix

1. Steam Discovered 1
2. The Train Chasers......................... 14
3. The Girl from Poppasquash 26
4. A Million from the Sea 38
5. A Telegram and Adventure 58
6. Live Free or Die.......................... 73
7. Edaville's Two-footers 90
8. A Skidding Car 98
9. Steam over Steamtown 107
10. On the Right Track 117
11. A Family Affair 130
12. A Town Steams 168
13. Reluctant Teddy.......................... 181
14. A New Owner for Staghead................. 190
15. Highballing It to Vermont.................. 203

16. Magnificent Steamtown, 1967............... 214
17. Whistle-stopping for the Lord............... 225
18. Caboose................................... 242

Appendix One: An Update, 1988 251
    Nelson's Last Run 251
    A New Home for Steamtown................ 255
    The Blount Family—In Their Own Words, 1988 .. 258

Appendix Two: Another Update, 2012 269
    Steamtown National Historic Site, 2012 269
    Edaville Railroad 271
    The Blount Family, 2012.................... 272
    Blount Seafood, 2012...................... 278

Epilogue: A Personal Word from F. Nelson Blount... 279

Endnotes..................................... 283

INTRODUCTION
HOW THIS BOOK BEGAN

ONE SPOOKY, OVERCAST, icy afternoon in mid-January of 1966, at precisely 3:03 in the afternoon, the *Ambassador* creaked to a stop at the Boston & Maine railroad depot in Bellows Falls, Vermont. I detrained into the near-zero cold, carrying a suitcase and tape recorder. This was my first visit to Steamtown, USA.

I first met F. Nelson Blount, the founder of Steamtown, USA, in Chicago, a few weeks prior to this trip. There we made plans for my visit, after Moody Press editor Robert DeVries, a railfan himself, asked me to write this book.

I looked around the platform. My host was nowhere to be seen, and no one else was there meeting the train. I went into the small, dimly lit depot to wait. The station was deserted except for a silent, gray-haired, little woman who emerged from the closed restaurant, peered outside, and floated back in, followed by her tabby cat.

A man in overalls and a mackinaw coat finally came in, and I thought for a moment that he might be a Steamtown employee sent to pick me up. But he merely exchanged cold-day pleasantries with the gray-haired woman, who he called Margaret.

When I phoned Nelson Blount, I found that there had been a misunderstanding about my arrival time. "I'm down with the flu, or I would have been there to meet you myself. I gave instructions for someone from Steamtown to meet the 3:15AM train, and if you were not on that one, to meet the afternoon train. Obviously, there has been a slip up."

His voice was hoarse as he explained that the sickness had come on him partly as a result of his going too long without sleep. He had left England the week before and flown directly to San Francisco, where he had addressed several gatherings. By the time he got home, he could barely talk.

"Tell you what," Nelson said, "I'll get someone to take you down to Keene, New Hampshire, and you can ride over from there to Dublin with my daughter, Carolyn."

A short while later, I was riding south toward Keene in a pick-up truck driven by the hefty bachelor superintendent of Steamtown, Bob Adams. As we entered Keene, he said, "The Blounts have a couple of cars, and I'm not sure which one Carolyn will be driving, but we'll keep a lookout for her near the bus station where Nelson said to wait." He parked the car and then let the engine idle so the heater could fight off the deep-freeze cold.

Presently, a white, 1965 Cadillac with a Rhode Island license plate, NB 2, turned the corner. I sensed correctly that it was Carolyn.

The Blount home sat on a windswept hill near Dublin, New Hampshire. I was relieved to find that the flu only had Nelson on the ropes, and was not a total knockout. He was dressed and indicated that he would be able to follow the full schedule we had planned.

Introduction

Two days later, he drove me to North Walpole, NH for my first look at Steamtown, USA. I grew up in a railroading family, so the long stretch of steam locomotives and other rolling stock brought back childhood memories. I was especially reminded of a trip I took as a twelve-year-old with my uncle, John Simpkins, a Southern Railway conductor, on his red caboose. I could still remember its clacking at the end of a freight train, pulled by a snorting Iron Horse.

Nelson ushered me into the Steamtown shop and roundhouse, which was once owned by the Boston & Maine. In the shop I saw his grimy, little office. It was quite a contrast to his antique-filled, well-appointed office at Blount Seafood, which I visited later in Warren, Rhode Island.

At lunchtime that day, we drove across the bridge spanning the Connecticut River to Bellows Falls and parked beside the depot. I was surprised to learn that Nelson owned the depot café.

He wanted me to meet his friend Margaret, the woman I had seen two days before. As we swung up on stools at the counter, she greeted us quietly. Nelson introduced us, and then, Margaret took our order.

"A couple of years ago, the Armstrong News Company decided to close this place down, and Margaret, who had been here for years, was to be transferred to Boston," Nelson commented. "So I talked it over with her and finally bought the café to keep her here in the place she loves. Right now, we're losing about $300 a year, but it's worth it."

After lunch, we said "good-bye" to Margaret and drove two miles north of Bellows Falls, where Nelson's steam excursions originated. There we watched earth-moving equipment leveling off a hill and filling in a long stretch of land beside the Connecticut River. "This is the future home of Steamtown," Nelson told me.

As we sat in the car, the operator of the machine shovel stopped his work and walked over.

"Hi, Mike, how's it going?" Nelson greeted the man and then introduced us. Mike appeared to be about twenty-eight. Nelson had already told me that he had pumped money into Mike's operation to help bail him out of financial difficulties.

"How's the flu bug going?" Nelson asked Mike. He obviously was not feeling well and should not have been on the job. "Here," Nelson continued, reaching into his pocket. "Take two of these and get more; they're penicillin tablets—they'll knock it out of you." He pushed them into Mike's hand. "I notice you haven't got that boom fixed. I'd put somebody on it and get it working; you really need it to keep all of the trucks busy that you have here." Mike said he would, and we drove on.

"You know," Nelson said, "I've always been fascinated by machinery of all kinds. After I became wealthy, I bought a steam shovel just to have one. I also bought a crane. When it came in on a low-bed trailer, there was nobody there to operate it, so I climbed into the cab, fumbled around with the controls, and finally got her going. I brought her off by myself."

The next couple of days, I became Nelson Blount's shadow. We drove for miles in Vermont and New Hampshire and into upper New York. I taped conversations relating to his past, present, and future and talked with many of the people who knew him best.

We visited the office of his newest line, the Green Mountain Railroad, which ran between Bellows Falls and Rutland, Vermont. We flew in Nelson's green and blue Cessna 180 to South Carver, Massachusetts, not far from Plymouth Rock, to visit another fascinating Blount enterprise, Edaville Railroad, whose narrow-gauge tracks meandered through cranberry bogs and picturesque, wooded areas.

During my time with Nelson Blount in January, I believe I saw him as he really was. A husky six-footer with hulking shoulders, Nelson moves with long, sure strides, like a tank. His rough-and-ready ways made him a man's man. Dressed in overall pants and a faded, blue denim shirt, he looked like the hardworking railroad engineer that he was. When he was not railroading, he liked to wear a sports jacket and a sporty fabric hat that made him look like a man who enjoyed life. With his charming Boston-like accent, he also talked like a man who enjoyed life, and it was obvious that his mind was alert.

Nelson's lined, outdoorsman's face showed that he must have been handsome in his younger days. He was approaching fifty, but he still had an abundance of masculine, good looks about him. Friendly, deep-set, blue eyes, which had often felt the sting of flying cinders, peered from beneath craggy brows. An enthusiastic smile revealed a flash of white against tan. His brown, once curly hair, thin on his receding forehead and graying around his temples, highlighted his overly large ears, and a lantern jaw added to his rugged appearance.

Nelson's wife, Ruth, was much like Nelson, a New England blue blood. She was an attractive, unusually tall, delicate-appearing woman with an oval face, large, blue eyes, and a slightly turned-up nose. She had quietly backed Nelson in his many projects and interests.

Without a doubt, Nelson's greatest interest in those days centered on a discovery he made in 1962, while on the trail of a lost locomotive. His discovery brought him such peace of heart and mind that he daily sought to share with others what he considered to be the Key to life. This interest went beyond even his passion for steam.

Not everyone appreciated Nelson's zeal. On my last day in Dublin, during that January visit, I observed, firsthand, an incident that classically depicts the seething hatred that some people have for the message of the Man from Steamtown. It happened in a little restaurant on Highway 101, smack in the middle of Dublin, and is recounted later in this book.

As I left New Hampshire, my work had only begun. Ruth Blount had wisely kept clippings and other items for many years. From them, she had compiled eight large scrapbooks. For weeks, I poured over these, seeking further details of how her husband became a millionaire in the seafood business and was involved in numerous other activities, including big-game hunting, deep-sea fishing, flying as a stunt pilot, and, of course, collecting steam locomotives the way some railroad fans collect old timetables, insignia of various railroads, lanterns, and the like. In general, I was trying to piece together the Nelson Blount story and attempting to determine what kept the pressure fired up in his boiler.

The results of my visit and these efforts make up this volume. If he comes alive to you in these pages, then the efforts have not been wasted.

—James R. Adair, 1967

Chapter 1
STEAM DISCOVERED

ALMOST ANYTIME THE small boy in the big, white, two-story house at 11 Wheaton Street, looked from his corner bedroom window, there were fascinating sights to behold. In the railroad yards, a block away, visor-capped men in blue overalls worked along the gleaming tracks, waving heavy-gloved hands as sooty steam engines switched boxcars from one place to another. The mere coupling of an engine to a train was fun to watch. The engineer, his red neckerchief contrasting against his blue overall jacket, leaned importantly from the cab, as below on the ground, the fireman or brakeman measured the distance between car and engine with his hands. Then *ka-whamm*, the coupling would be made, followed by a chain of resounding *ka-whamm*s as each boxcar in the line responded to the jolt.

In Warren, Rhode Island, in those years—the early 1920s—crack mainliners of the New Haven Railroad swept along the tracks, going from Providence to Bristol and Fall River, or streaking back toward the Rhode Island capital,

Providence. At peak times, as many as seventy-eight trains a day, mostly electric, passed through Warren.

The boy who watched this endless drama of power, must have been four, the day he scampered through the hedge surrounding his house with his dog, Bruno, a tan and white mixture of St. Bernard and collie, trotting clumsily behind. Nelson wanted a closer view of the stage and its actors; he could watch from a second-story window just so long.

Boy and dog crossed a wealthy man's yard, and suddenly, they were there. The cinders made pleasant crunching noises beneath the boy's feet, and the sounds and smells of the railroad yards delighted him.

Nelson stood with Bruno, watching an overall-clad man throw a switch. The man smiled, and Nelson smiled back. Then the man hopped on the rear of the wheezing switch engine and waved as he rode past.

The throbbing sound of the steam-driven pistons and sight of the flashing drive-rods quickened the boy's pulse. He had heard and seen it all from his bedroom window, but now, he stepped—in person—into the wonderful world of steam.

Destined to become the "savior of steam" in his adult years, Francis Nelson Blount could hardly have picked a better time to be born or a more accessible area to railroads, for steam was the backbone of New England, and New York was not far away.

It was late evening on May 21, 1918, that the Blount family doctor hurried up the stairs at 11 Wheaton Street with his familiar black bag. "Came as quickly as I could, Mrs. Blount," he spoke reassuringly as he entered Ruth Blount's bedroom.

Tall, sturdily built Willis Blount, concern flashing from his blue eyes, took Dr. Conway's jacket, and the doctor opened his bag, rolled up his sleeves, and went to work.

Later, as a grandfather clock ticked off the anxious minutes downstairs, the doctor held the newborn infant by the feet, and a whack on the rump brought a hungry cry that gladdened the hearts of the proud parents and doctor.

The fact it was a boy—their second son—made the occasion even grander, especially for Willis. The new son, Francis Nelson, and their first son, Luther, would later help at the ice company founded by Willis Blount in 1919 in nearby Barrington. But beyond that, here was another boy to carry on the Blount name, a name associated with heroes and prominent individuals from as far back as 1066. That year, Robert le Blount commanded the invading ships as the French stormed onto the shores of Britain. His brother, William, was general of the foot soldiers. The brothers settled in Britain following the conquest. In 1403, Sir Walter Blount distinguished himself as standard-bearer of King Henry IV at the Battle of Shrewsbury—and apparently he first omitted the prefix *le* from the family name.

The Blounts hit New England soil at about 1635, with the coming of William Blount from England to Massachusetts.

The squalling young son of Ruth and Willis was named Nelson after Ruth's side of the family. She was a Yankee blue blood through and through, for the Nelson family in New England went back to *Mayflower* days and to Colonel John Nelson, Ruth's great-great-great-great-grandfather, adjutant to George Washington during the Revolutionary War. Colonel Nelson, in 1791, also became justice of the peace of Plymouth, appointed by Massachusetts Governor John Hancock. (Nelson Blount prized the time-yellowed document signed by Hancock in making the appointment.)

As owner of the Willis E. Blount Ice Company in neighboring Barrington, Willis Blount was a man of more than average means, evidenced by the big, twenty-room, two-hundred-year-old house in which the family lived. There were always three square meals on the table. Willis Blount, however, seldom dined with the family, except at dinner, for in order to begin his ice deliveries, he was usually up and out of the house at 6AM.

Ruth Blount, a large-framed woman of about 150 pounds, had a strong hand in running affairs at home. She was a hard worker, helping to keep the house in good order and regularly whisking away the soot and dust that accumulated from passing trains.

In her twilight years, Mrs. Blount recalled Nelson as a "good boy," one who remembered her birthday with a small gift bought from pennies he had saved—"even when others would forget."

Nelson was still four when tragedy deprived him of his mother's care and attention for two years. Walking along a street in Providence, Mrs. Blount was struck on the head by a falling part of an electric sign. As a result of her injuries and shock, she lost her unborn twins and was ill for about five years.

With Ruth bedfast, Luther was cared for by the Blount family (who shared the big house with their son Willis's family), and Nelson was hustled off to Lakeville, Massachusetts, twenty-three miles from Plymouth Rock, to live with Aunt Hannah and Aunt May Nelson, aged spinsters. There on the old Colonel Nelson homestead, young Nelson lived until he was six. It was a place of many adventures.

The homestead itself dated back to 1632. Indians had burned the first house, and the British had burned the second. The third house, built by Colonel Nelson after the Revolution, still remained. In that house, Nelson experienced living on a farm with no central heating, no electricity, and an outhouse. In the sitting room on wintry days, a wood fire popped and crackled in the huge open fireplace. By the light and smell of a kerosene lamp, he was tucked into a big, feather bed on cold nights, with a warming pad at his feet that was fashioned from a heated iron wrapped in a towel.

Aunt Hannah and Aunt May kept all sorts of delicious canned fruits, jellies, jams, and vegetables in the big, outside pantry and cookhouse, where they did all the cooking. And in the fourth-floor attic, there were spinning wheels and other relics; those old smells would linger with Nelson always. In the attic, he was allowed to dress in a piece of his grandfather's Revolutionary War uniform and put on his sword.

With his dog, Bruno, who came to live on the farm too, young Nelson explored the fields and woodlands, chasing rabbits, catching turtles, and occasionally standing in awe as a deer streaked through the trees a few yards away. Hired men plowed the farmland, using slow-footed oxen, and Nelson and Bruno ran along behind on the moist, freshly turned soil, looking for worms.

The old Nelson homestead was a place Nelson loved dearly. There he milked cows with his aunts, helped collect eggs, and played with his own treasured toy—an old wagon wheel, about eighteen inches in diameter, which he found in the barn. With it he played truck and bus.

It was around the big fireplace, with its dancing light from the blazing logs, that Aunt Hannah and Aunt May shared with Nelson, thoughts from the Bible. "This is God's

Book, Nelson, and God wants us to hide His Word in our hearts," they would tell him.

When he was four, Nelson learned Psalm 23. At night, his aunts put him on his knees to pray. And on Sundays, with everyone dressed in their finest outfits, his aunts took him in a horse-drawn carriage to the Precinct Church (Congregational).

Back in Warren, Nelson had gone to Sunday school with his parents since he was an infant. Father was a trustee in the lovely, white-spired First Methodist Church of Warren (the oldest Methodist church in Rhode Island), and Mother was the organist. But the Bible seemed even more important to his aunts than it did to his parents.

On vacations in later years, Nelson returned to be with his aunts, swim, sail a boat (when he was in his teens), and hunt. On one occasion, he fell while hunting, and both barrels of his shotgun went off, narrowly missing him. This blast, along with a deafening roar when lightning struck a radio he was listening to in 1934, slightly impaired his hearing.

Back home in Warren after his two years with his aunts, young Nelson kept one eye on the passing trains and romped with his friends through normal boyhood experiences. He spent many happy hours as king of his own castle—a tree house in a big apple tree. Not all his experiences were happy. One cave-digging adventure ended in tragedy for one of his friends. The cave fell in on Nelson and his friend, and they were rescued, but the friend developed pneumonia and died.

Apparently, even in his youth, Nelson had a full head of steam and dashed ahead with enthusiasm—as in when, for example, he crossed streets. In Nelson's early years,

Mr. Blount cautioned him to look both ways. But once, when some boys were chasing him playfully, Nelson darted in front of an oncoming car. A fender caught him, knocking him to the street.

"It only bruised me," Nelson later recalled, "but my father was really mad. He heard about it and went looking for me. I climbed the highest tree I could, but when I came down, my father gave me a licking that was worse than the bruises I got from the car!" His dad packed the wallop of a Missouri mule, as might be expected of an iceman.

Nelson got one licking he thought was a bad deal. A house was being constructed next door to the Blount home and, as normal boys, both Luther and Nelson had a hankering to explore after the workmen left. But Father Blount sternly said "no."

One afternoon, Nelson heard Luther call to him. His older brother had gone into the house and was motioning for Nelson to come in too. "Come on, Dad will never know!" he whispered loudly. The smell of fresh lumber excited Nelson, and it was fun to look out of the second-story window onto the Blount yard.

Suddenly, as if on impulse, Luther jumped out a window in the back, and the next thing Nelson knew, Luther was standing below, alongside Father, pointing up at Nelson: "Dad, look at Nelson up there!"

The hand of Willis Blount was extra heavy that afternoon, and the bottom of Nelson was unusually sore. But the worst part of the whole affair was that Luther, the stoolie, went scot-free.

As a disciplinarian, Willis Blount was excellent but seldom played ball or romped with his sons. He was a good, straight-laced Methodist; he didn't smoke, drink, or swear. He would, however, occasionally load the family into the Flint car and take them to a wholesome movie. Mr. Blount went regularly, once a week, and if he discovered something good, the family would see it later. Nelson's father was also generally a man of refined tastes. He made it a point to acquaint his sons with museums. A trip they took to New York, to the Museum of Natural History, made a lasting impression on Nelson.

When Nelson was twelve, he set out to a rodeo. That day ushered him into a dark experience that he did not soon forget.

"Stay on the bucking bronco for one minute—just one minute—you would-be cowboys, and you'll win fifty dollars! Step right up and ride the bucking bronco," chanted the barker at the rodeo at Camp Joe Hooker, near Lakeville.

Nelson and his buddy Billy Hall figured they would strike it rich; fifty dollars a minute was not bad at all. But first, they would practice at Billy's farm. They cornered a mare, and while Billy held her, Nelson climbed on to ride bareback. All might have gone well, except something frightened the horse. She bolted, and Nelson tumbled to the ground.

"Broken in two places; doesn't look good at all," the doctor announced a little later. Nelson watched his arm glumly as the doctor put it in a cast.

But the matter had not ended. Nelson's arm failed to heal right, and the doctor announced they would start over. Nelson was blindfolded, and his arm was positioned carefully in an apparatus on a table. Sandbags were dropped; the arm popped.

But even after that, the arm did not seem to be healing properly. His hand was twisted toward his wrist, and the doctor decided that an operation was the only solution.

"Oh, Mother, please don't let them operate!" Nelson begged. "I've had all I can stand."

Mrs. Blount told the doctor to wait. The case would have to go to the Great Physician. She prayed fervently, telling God she was leaving the problem wholly in His merciful and skillful hands.

As the weeks passed, the breaks healed. Nelson faithfully exercised the limb. By the end of a year, his arm and hand had returned to normal.

More trying days came upon Nelson as an early teen. In those years, he walked or hitchhiked to school in Barrington every day. It was an eight-mile round trip. He went to Scouts and burned up lots of energy in this and other types of activities. But his battery seemed to be running down faster than he could build it up. He bolted down huge quantities of food that were filling out his large frame nicely, but still he was becoming more tired by the day.

One day at school, he climbed to the fourth floor and collapsed as he reached the top of the stairs. His friends took him home. Nelson made it inside but fell on the couch and went to sleep, still in his leather. Mrs. Blount came home an hour later and woke him.

"I fell at school; I just got weak," he explained. "I just don't have any strength."

Mother felt his head. He was burning with fever. A few hours later, he was delirious.

"Undulant fever," an elderly doctor said solemnly.

It was just what Mrs. Blount suspected. She had read of a Rhode Island case a short while before.

For months, Nelson had remittent fever, pain, and swelling in his joints. Discouraging spells of weakness overwhelmed him.

A family friend, who was a veterinarian, looked at Nelson one day and said, "I have shots that will help." He produced "horse serum shots," and they did the job, so the story goes.

One of Nelson's visitors during his illness was a New Haven railroad engineer named Lewis Jerald—undoubtedly the most marvelous man Nelson had ever met. Mr. Jerald never failed to bring candy, usually crunchy chocolates, and when Nelson felt well enough, Mr. Jerald took him and Luther in his car to an ice cream shop in Providence. The kind engineer would buy a quart of ice cream, and the boys would sit down in the kitchen at 11 Wheaton Street and dig in.

The story of Nelson becoming acquainted with Lewis Jerald is a classic. It was chapter two in Nelson's discovery of steam.

Nelson had continued his visits to the New Haven tracks. Bruno was always at his side or plodding along behind him, his tongue hanging out as he tried to keep up with the young railfan. Then one afternoon, when Nelson was eight, Mr. Jerald spoke to him in a friendly fashion.

"What are you doing, Sonny?"

"Oh, just looking. I like trains and locomotives," replied young Nelson.

Mr. Jerald motioned toward the engine of a work train. "Want to take a ride?"

"Sure. But what about my dog?"

"Well, bring him too."

Jerald helped both the boy and his dog into the cab, and that afternoon, Nelson had the time of his life. For a minute or two, Nelson even held the throttle.

In subsequent rides, he rang the bell, blew the whistle, and shoveled coal.

Jerald explained the various gadgets in the cab. The throttle, he said, had to be eased back slowly to avoid spinning the wheels of the engine and ruining her tires; the Johnson bar was the reverse lever; the hand wheels and valves controlled steam pressure. It was all so mysterious to Nelson, but it was all so necessary to give power to the great Iron Horse.

Jerald pointed out differences in various engines to Nelson. The boy decided he liked the big 1300s and the 1-4s best of all the big, high-wheeled Pacific types, engines that could clip along at eighty miles per hour, pulling ten passenger cars, which carried hundreds of people.

About that time, as his interest in railroading increased, Nelson began collecting pictures of New Haven engines. He ultimately had a picture of every New Haven locomotive.

It was also around this time that Nelson's mother became especially concerned. She had not realized that he had been spending so much time around the railroad yards. Thoughts of possible injuries and crude men pulsated through her motherly mind.

"Nelson, you are forbidden ever to go there again," she scolded. "It's bad enough that you are down there and might get killed, but those railroad men, they swear and are rough, and I don't want you down there with those kind of people."

The "good boy" that he was, Nelson sneaked through the hedge the next day, Thursday, and found his friend Mr. Jerald.

"My mother says railroad men are all rough guys. She told me I can't ever come down here again. And I'm gonna get a spanking if my mother knows I'm here." Tears stung his eyes as he turned to leave his friend, but the boy turned back as a grin flashed across the face of the engineer.

"Well, Nelson, you tell your mother that all railroad men aren't the wrong kind. Tell you what, I'm going to come and talk to your mother. Where do you live?"

Nelson gave him the address and then pointed to the big, white house through the trees.

"You tell your mother that I will be there next Sunday at 2:30."

Nelson bounded home, happy once again, with Bruno panting at his heels.

When Nelson announced that Mr. Jerald was coming, Mrs. Blount patted him and went on about her kitchen chores. "Oh, he's just kidding."

Willis Blount sided with Mama. "Don't get your hopes up too high. And anyhow, you shouldn't be around those railroad men. Like Mama says, they're rough, they swear, and you have no business down there."

The days passed slowly from Thursday to Sunday, but after dinner that day, Nelson took a lookout position in the living room window. He began watching at two o'clock, figuring Mr. Jerald just might be early. But 2:30 came, and then 2:45—but no Mr. Jerald. Nelson continued his watch.

At five minutes before three, a car turned onto Wheaton Street and stopped in front of the Blount home. "It's him!" Nelson shouted. "And he has his whole family with him."

Surprised, Ruth and Willis Blount greeted the Jerald family: Mr. Jerald, a tall, wholesome-looking man; his wife, a most attractive woman; and their son and daughter.

Nelson officially introduced his friend to Mother and Dad, and a lasting friendship began between the two families. In the years that followed, Nelson spent a week at a time during some summer vacations with the Jeralds, and he enjoyed countless hours riding with Mr. Jerald on his engine, all with the approval of his parents (and the road foreman).

Jerald introduced Nelson to everyone from the superintendent on down. One other engineer especially took a liking to the young rail buff. He was a jolly man named Walter R. Fogg, who brought Nelson pictures of various locomotives.

Those early years in Nelson's life were wonderful years of discovery, of the thrilling sounds and smells and the feel of steam power in his hand when he pulled the great throttle of an engine. He made lasting friendships, but the best friend, of course, was Mr. Jerald, who, in his retirement years, was destined to work for Nelson on a railroad he would later buy.

In the years ahead, there would be even greater discoveries. Nelson would even discover a friend his own age with just as intense an interest in steam. He and Fred Richardson eventually would become familiar figures all along New England's Iron Trail.

Chapter 2
THE TRAIN CHASERS

ON MAY 23, 1933, TWO days after his fifteenth birthday, Nelson Blount did not answer the roll call in classes at Peck High School in Barrington. He had a fever—an especially steamy one—that day. The famous *Royal Scot*, a British-built locomotive and train that had dazzled schoolboys as it sped over English countrysides, was going to be on exhibit in Providence that day, on its way to the "Century of Progress" World's Fair in Chicago.

That day in the Providence railroad yards, there were other boys taking one-day vacations from school, plus throngs of adults admiring the gleaming engine and the train it pulled. With his camera ready, Nelson checked the engine and train like a detective hunting for a murder clue. He lingered and talked to the trainmen and snapped pictures of New Haven trains on the move.

Toward late afternoon, Nelson spotted a familiar face among the *Royal Scot* admirers. *Why that's Fred Richardson from school*, he thought to himself. He went over and grabbed his arm. "Hey, what are you doing here?" he greeted Fred.

"Well, I bunked school so I could come and see this."

"So did I."

"Do you like steam engines?"

"Boy, I love 'em!"

And so it was that the two boy "locomaniacs" met. Things happened swiftly after that. Nelson showed Fred a collection of model trains he had started, plus other railroad souvenirs. Fred, in turn, invited Nelson to his home in Barrington and showed him his collection. Fred boasted that he was a B & M fan, and Nelson countered that New Haven trains were greater. Soon, like collectors exchanging stamps, they began trading pictures of engines. They also exchanged background stories that cemented their friendship even more.

"My grandfather was a country doctor, and he rode in cabooses a lot," Fred revealed. "He was very interested in railroads. My grandmother's uncle was an engineer in New Hampshire. I was born in Meredith, New Hampshire, and spent summers there. There was an engineer up there who would take me into the cab and let me ride with him. I took a picture of his locomotive, brought a print to him, and he gave me a ride as a reward."

Nelson, of course, told Fred of his magnificent experiences with Engineer Jerald.

Though the boys spent much time at Fred's home, a two-story house with a steep, pointed roof at 29 Third Street, Barrington, the better part of their leisure hours found them in the big, white house on Wheaton Street. Fred was an only child, the son of a science teacher, and Mrs. Blount accepted him as a son, just as Nelson was received by Fred's mother in his home.

Fred soon became closer to Nelson than his brother, Luther. Ages made some difference, for Luther was two years older than Nelson, and Fred was only eleven months older. But without a doubt, "locomania" was the greatest single influencing factor in their camaraderie.

Luther himself had some interest in trains, and in earlier years, he and Nelson often visited the Warren railroad yards together and went riding with Lewis Jerald. But Luther's fever never quite matched Nelson's, although they did work together to build a complex electric railroad in the Blount basement.

Fred and Nelson spent hours on end, along with their high school friends, operating that miniature rail system. In September of 1936, a *Providence News-Tribune* writer described the railroad in these terms:

> A semaphore drops slowly, and a streamlined express steam train moves slowly up the track, picking up speed at every revolution of the driving wheels. Soon, it is up to cruising speed and pounds down the rails to a crossing, a symphony of steel on steel. Automatic gates lower, green lights turn to red, and the train roars by into the distance along a tree-shaded right-of-way.
>
> On a nearby siding, a freight, sidetracked for the through-express, begins to rumble back to the main line.
>
> Here is one of the most complete miniature railway systems in the East, possibly in the country. Over a maze of tracks, past stations that are exact reproductions of some on local roads, Lilliputian trains speed in the manner of their prototypes.
>
> The road is composed of ten locomotives, sixty cars and a control board. It is operated over 300 feet of track, built by Blount's brother, Luther. The tracks are of wood, covered with a zinc strip to carry the current. The entire layout ... covers a specially built table, half the size of the entire cellar. In the center, a hole is cut to allow the operators to crawl through.... From this point ... the entire system is manipulated by a remote

control unit [made by Luther] from the "insides" of two discarded radios.

During the years from 1933 to 1942, until Fred left for military service, it was Blount and Richardson, Railfans, Inc. Their lives were wholly devoted to the cause of railroading. When Fred, valedictorian of his graduating class in 1935 at Peck High, presented an essay, "The Providence, Warren, and Bristol Railroad," at his commencement exercises, Nelson, of course, was there to applaud.

The boys collaborated later and published in the Warren and Barrington Gazette a challenge for better rail service on the P W & B branch of the New Haven. They verbally lambasted the New Haven Railroad in such words as these:

1. Present train schedules should be speeded up. Commuters do not want to drift along in this age of speed. Present schedules are so slow that engineers have to kill time by drifting in order not to be ahead of schedule.
2. More common sense equipment should be utilized. The New Haven Railroad, which could afford to sink a quarter of a million in the Comet, should be able to rebuild some of its equipment in the style of railroad cars rather than in the style of dump carts.

In his senior year of high school, Nelson made the football team as a 190-pound tackle, even though his father did not want him wasting his time and getting hurt. Nelson was a better-than-average student in school, but it was not obvious from the grades he got in old Mrs. Spangle's (not her real name) class. Nelson had a hunch she just plain did not like him, for the more he tried, the worse his grades seemed to get.

So one day, just to test her, Nelson and a buddy—another football player—put their names on each other's paper. His buddy, seemingly no smarter, always got a higher mark, so they both decided to see if old Mrs. Spangle would automatically give Nelson the lower grade, even though the work was really his buddy's. It was a crazy stunt, but it happened much as they had expected: Nelson actually did get a high grade with his buddy's name on it, and his buddy's work got a low grade with Nelson's name on it.

When Nelson tried another stunt and turned in the work of a professional writer as his own theme, Mrs. Spangle blew sky high.

"But, Mrs. Spangle," he moaned, "I was only trying to see if I could get a decent grade from you."

The teacher marched Nelson to the principal's office. But when Nelson's buddy testified concerning the switched-papers episode, the principal made it hotter for Mrs. Spangle than he did for Nelson.

In 1935, both Nelson and Fred attended the Rhode Island School of Design in Providence, but for both of them, it was a way to go into Providence together on Saturdays to see trains and visit the "main stem" of the New Haven. Classes began at 9:00 AM. on Saturdays, and the boys left on the six o'clock train, which gave them a couple of hours to fondly pat engines and take pictures.

At home, the Blounts and the Richardsons wondered about it all. One Saturday morning, the parents dropped into school to make sure the boys were remembering to report for classes. Unfortunately, on that particular Saturday, the call of the rails was stronger than the call of school, and Nelson and Fred failed to show up.

"Upon arriving home, we were immediately put on the carpet, and that 'pulled the pin' on our Saturday visits to the 'main stem,'" the boys later wrote.

After Nelson graduated from Peck High in 1936, he went on to attend night classes at Bryant College in 1939 and was a student for one year at Brown University, but he never got his college degree.

Fred finished at Brown. Yet his sticking to studies at Brown in Providence did little more than separate the boys physically. In spirit, they were together.

In early days of their friendship, the rail twosome rode bikes to railroad yards as far away as Fall River, Massachusetts. Then in his junior year in high school, Nelson bought a Model A Ford roadster, and the young steam fans were off running. Fred had a paper route, and he worked summers with Nelson in Mr. Blount's ice plant, so they had money for gasoline.

As they roared along, often on a dollar's worth of gas, they challenged each other's retentive powers, seeing who could name the most railroad lines without stopping.

They preferred to hitch rides on locomotives whenever possible, but the roadster took them to remote areas where they could marvel at such rolling stock as the stout little Maine two-footers. All told, they put 25,000 miles on the noisy little car.

The little Maine steam engines were fast disappearing from the scene, and the boys chased from one road to another, admiring and sometimes polishing the engines. They spent much time in the yards and on the rails of the Sandy River & Rangeley Lakes Railroad in western Maine, a road that was abandoned in 1935. They lugged engine bells and other parts to the roadster, to add to their collection of railroadiana.

They felt so bad about the Sandy River road that they wrote Henry Ford about it. It could be purchased for $21,000, and since Mr. Ford was something of a railfan and owned a small road, he seemed the natural person to buy it. The bargain price included 100 miles of track, six stations, and complete shop and roundhouse facilities. The youths almost wept when Mr. Ford turned down the idea, and tears stung their eyes the day they helplessly watched a Sandy River engine go for one hundred dollars. Some of the scrap iron, they learned, was going to Japan.

It was in those days that the idea of Steamtown occurred to Nelson and Fred. What shape it would take, they did not know, but someday they hoped to accumulate enough money to rescue rolling stock from the Steam Age and put it on display for other steam lovers.

About the same time they saw the Maine two-footers vanishing, they planted a seed in the mind of Ellis Atwood, a distant cousin of Nelson's, that would help bring some of the Maine equipment to a railroad center called Edaville that Nelson himself would later buy.

On their trips into Maine and elsewhere, Nelson and Fred made lasting friendships with many—from railroad presidents on down to section crewmen. It was at Bridgton, Maine, that the two steam kids met Edgar T. Mead, who would later become a Steamtown trustee and general partner of O.C. Haas & Co., members of the New York Stock Exchange.

Mead, then an eighteen-dollar-a-week vacation employee of the Bridgton & Saco River Railroad, recalls, "You couldn't forget Nelson. He and his sidekick, Fred Richardson, blew into town one day in a Model A Ford. When Nelson arrived, everything that had been going on tended to become still and small. There was an assertion to his manner and a positiveness, which seemed only heightened by the twinkle in his eye. Nelson had arrived on the scene. He wanted to talk with those in command. He wanted to see everything and do everything."

On their trips, Nelson and Fred snapped literally thousands of pictures of rolling stock. Back in Warren, in Nelson's basement, they developed the film and made prints. But these pictures were not enough. They wrote railroads for handout pictures, hoping to have the most complete collection of rail photographs in the world. They got a few, but often replies were, "Sorry, fellows, we don't send pictures to collectors—only if you are doing something for the cause of the railroad."

In 1936, Nelson got an idea after a few such letters. "Fred, let's write a book! Then we will get all the pictures we need."

Fred grinned. "OK, let's try it."

So they went to work. Both could type, and soon form letters were going out to various railroads. "We are writing a book called *Along the Iron Pike*. Please send us pictures …"

The idea appealed to railroad public relations men. There had not been a book for railfans, and there were an estimated 300,000 buffs snooping about railroad yards across the country. The book had a chance.

Photos began pouring into the mailbox of the Blount home. Moreover, they continued to come for months—piles of them.

Finally, Mrs. Blount and Mrs. Richardson became concerned. "What are we going to do with these boys? They aren't writing any book. This is just a way for them to get pictures."

Then the ultimatum came: "Boys, either write a book, or send all those photographs back to the railroads!"

Nelson looked at Fred, and Fred looked at Nelson.

"We gotta do something," Nelson said.

"Gee, let's get going and see what we can do," responded Fred. "We've got a lot of the material. Let's dig more and get something on paper."

They checked into the history of railroading, for obviously this would be the first chapter. They already knew, of course, that in 1814, ten years after an Englishman named Richard Trevithick introduced a steam locomotive that did not work out, George Stephenson, another Englishman, built a locomotive that had an upright boiler. This ushered in the Steam Age at three miles per hour.

The boys soon discovered facts about the first US built locomotive, *The Best Friend of Charleston*, which pulled passenger and freight trains out of Charleston, South Carolina. It went into service on Christmas Day, 1830, but a few months later, the locomotive blew to smithereens in the first boiler explosion on an American railroad. The South Carolina Railroad replaced it with the equally successful *West Point*, which carried a "barrier car" loaded with baled cotton between the engine and the passenger cars to protect customers against another possible explosion.

Some of these facts went on paper. The boys shared the writing, but Fred, the better student, edited the pages from Nelson's typewriter.

Letters went out for more material, and railroads and railfans alike responded. Then a railroad magazine helped them round up sand house stories and boomer tales. At this point, the boys were about a year and a half into writing their book, though most of the work was done in a four-month period.

Finding a publisher was the big job after the manuscript was ready. A page-one headline in the Warren and Barrington Gazette, dated Friday, August 28, 1936, suggests their next step:

ENJOY RIDE TO NEW YORK IN CAB OF COLONIAL EXPRESS

Nelson Blount and Fred Richardson of Barrington Leave Union Station in Cab of Crack New Haven Road Express. Will Seek Publisher for Book on Railroading.

This article and subsequent news stories made it clear that the boys had a serious work going:

> That their effort is not based on sketchy knowledge of their subject is indicated by the fact that in the last three years Fred and Nelson have journeyed approximately 10,000 miles throughout New England, New Jersey, and New York [visiting engine houses].

Another article pointed this thought up further:

> In all, they made seven trips to New York City, visited Washington, D.C., Philadelphia, Boston, made innumerable trips to New England railroads and have covered the eastern section of the United States in a most thorough manner. They have sat in the offices of railroad presidents ... they have chatted with publicity ex ... and have talked with section hands. And wherever they traveled and with whomever they talked, they were respectfully listened to. For one thing, one railroad man can recognize another by sight, and there was something about the manner of both Fred Richardson and Nelson Blount which indicated that railroading to them was not only a fascinating subject but the only one really worth while talking about.

Though local people applauded their efforts, the big-time publishers had little time for a couple of youthful rail buffs turned writers. But apparently, someone did listen long enough to realize that 300,000 other railfans were waiting for a book on railroading. For back home, the fellows later got wind that one of the publishers they talked with was laying plans for a rail book—one written by a professional writer.

"We'll show them!" the boys boomed.

"We'll go see Uncle Hi Jinks!" Nelson declared.

Uncle Hi Jinks was none other than the editor and part owner of the Greenfield, Massachusetts, *Daily Recorder Gazette*. He sent them to Brattleboro, Vermont, and a publisher there sent them to the Tuttle Publishing Company in Rutland, Vermont. There the boys put up $500 to back the project. In addition, various railroad companies sent monetary donations, and Baldwin Locomotive Company offered thousands of dollars' worth of engravings for the boys to choose from. They chose a total of 250 illustrations for use in the book, including several Baldwin cuts and their own pictures.

Nelson and Fred's book was published in 1938, under the revised title, *Along the Iron Trail*. It became an instant success. Only the war and a curtailment on paper kept it from going beyond approximately 3,000 copies sold. In later years, it became a collector's item, worth up to twenty dollars, even though it had sold for $2.95. (In 1966, it was republished as a paperback at $3.95.)

After the publication of the book, the boys set to work on another volume, *Steam, Steel, and Streamliners*, but even though they spent many hours on it, the war and a paper shortage killed the project.

By this time, they were known throughout the land among railfans, and locally, they were looked upon as greater authorities on railroading than many rail officials themselves. One newspaper writer put it this way:

There is something about their enthusiasm for railroads, which is infectious, even to one knowing little about railroads and their problems. If you have the temerity to dispute a point, you are immediately assailed with facts and figures to show how vital are the railroads in this country; how they should receive every cooperation from national, state, and local authorities, and they quote authorities as you would quote your next door neighbor. They are particularly tender on the subject of highway transportation by truck, claiming that the large trucking companies contribute practically nothing to the communities through which they pass, in comparison with the heavy taxes, which every railroad pays to every town, county, and city through which it passes.

In their book, Nelson and Fred discussed the problem of the trucks and included a cartoon showing an endless stream of trucks on a highway being physically supported by weary taxpayers.

For their contribution to railroading through the book, Nelson and Fred were offered scholarships to Harvard from the New Haven Railroad and the American Association of Railroads. But neither took advantage of the offer.

Nelson and Fred continued their pursuit of trains following the war. In the meantime, there were other interests cropping up in the life of young Nelson Blount, the strapping son of the Barrington iceman.

During his high school years, Nelson seldom dated girls. He was too busy with trains and writing the rail book. He would go to a school dance, once in a while, and sit like a wallflower, watching everyone else. But in his post high school years, he was to become something of a Romeo.

Chapter 3

THE GIRL FROM POPPASQUASH

IT WAS PARTLY because John Simmons Palmer II got tired waiting for a son that he made a tomboy of his fourth daughter. An oval-faced, pretty girl with large, blue eyes, Ruth Richmond Palmer grew up as a gangling companion of her sports-loving father. She spent endless hours on his knee or walking with him, and he delighted in sharing with her tales from his annual hunting trips to New Brunswick for deer and moose.

When Ruth was six, he introduced her to fishing, showing her how to hold a rod and when to jerk the line should a fish strike the bait. To help her keep a healthy tan, Mr. Palmer gave her a small sailboat when she was twelve, a hand-me-down from her older sisters. With her younger brother, Richard, she had merry times sailing in Bristol Harbor off Poppasquash Peninsula, Bristol, a few miles from Warren.

In Ruth's early years, the family lived in Providence, where Mr. Palmer ran the firm Palmer & Capron, manufacturing jewelers. The family spent summers in a rented house, which later became Bristol Yacht Club of Poppasquash.

Mr. Palmer retired relatively early in life, living like an English squire and managing his lucrative investments. Ruth's father also delighted in pursuing his hobby of genealogy. Proud blood flowed in his veins, for he could trace his family back to the *Mayflower* and notables from the time of the Magna Carta and the Crusades of the Old World. He could tell you that the name Palmer came from the custom of the pilgrims of medieval days who carried palm leaves as a token of a pledge of their having been to the Holy Land.

But sportsman that he was, John Simmons Palmer II perhaps most enjoyed spinning tales he had heard of the Palmers who sailed the clipper ships. Captain N. B. Palmer, in the 1830s, had designed sailing vessels for E. K. Collins & Company, one of the enterprising firms of the day, to start a new Liverpool line. He was one of the famous Yankee masters and delighted in winning battles against the sea. Once, as the story goes, he had himself tied to the mast for forty hours as he ordered the crew to win a race against time in heavy seas. Later on a whaling expedition to the Antarctic area, he discovered what became known as the Palmer Peninsula.

Ruth's mother, Abbie, came from equally fine stock, a fact of which Mr. Palmer was proud. John Greene, progenitor of the family, arrived in Boston in June of 1635 and settled first in Salem. He was one of the eleven men baptized by Roger Williams and was one of the twelve original members of the first Baptist church on the American continent, at Providence. He was also the first professional medical man in the area.

John Palmer was also proud of the government leaders in the Greene line. These included Nicholas Easton, deputy governor of Rhode Island from 1670–71 and governor under the Royal Charter from 1672–74.

Thus, it was no ordinary girl that was playing tennis at the Excelsior Tennis Club on Main Street, Bristol, near Poppasquash, that summer day in 1938 when Nelson Blount and Ginger, a railroad engineer's daughter, had a spat. Ruth overheard it all. There was a dinner party that night, and Ginger was angry with Nelson; for her money, he could go jump in Bristol Harbor. So she took her tennis racket and went home.

Nelson, a tall, curly-haired hulk of a fellow by now, smiled in his winsome way, his blue eyes sparkling, and called to Ruth, "Hey, Palmer. What are you doing tonight? Want to go to a dinner party with me?"

Ruth was sixteen, slender, and overly tall but pretty in her white tennis outfit. She had known Nelson casually. She flashed a shy smile, wondering if Mother and Daddy would approve on such short notice. And it was a rebound date at that.

"What do you say, Palmer? I'm not such a bad guy."

"Sure, I'd like to go. But I'll have to ask my mother."

"OK. Where do you live? We'll drive over and ask her."

If his iceman father was moderately well-heeled, Ruth's father was rich, Nelson concluded as he looked at the Palmer layout on Poppasquash Road, which John Palmer had built the year before. There may have been a fishy, low tide smell from Bristol Harbor, but Harbour Oaks, as the place was called, was the kind of place where Cadillacs were expected rather than a noisy Model A. There was a low rock wall surrounding the white-frame twelve-room home. Huge oaks shaded a lush, green lawn that dropped off behind the house on the harbor, where sailboats and fancy yachts added to the enchantment of the setting.

There was one thing Nelson learned later that he never quite figured out: John Palmer never owned a car, and he sent his family places in taxis.

Ruth and Nelson left the roadster at the front door and breezed in on Mrs. Palmer, an aristocratic-looking woman. She smiled at the ruggedly built, young man Ruth had in tow.

After introductions, she said, "Are you Ruth and Willis Blount's son?" As Nelson nodded, she hurried on. "I was in the same high school class as your father and mother."

Ruth requested permission to go with Nelson to the dinner party, and Mrs. Palmer gave her blessing. "But I expect you to mind your Ps and Qs and be in at a reasonable time," she added.

And here another lifelong relationship began for Nelson. He liked Ruth's company, but he did not begin dating her steadily until a year later. He dated others, including Ginger, when he was not chasing trains with Fred. But now and then, he called Ruth, "Hey, Palmer, doing anything tomorrow night? Want to go to the show with me?"

There were times Nelson got Ruth home later than the Palmers thought was proper, and on these nights, to avoid his own dad, he climbed up the trellis to his bedroom on the second floor of the Blount home. Once, his father was waiting for him in the bedroom.

"What are you coming in this way for, Nelson?" his father boomed.

"I didn't want to disturb you."

"I want to be disturbed! You come in through the door from now on and knock on my door when you're in." The elder Blount turned on his heel and left his hulking offspring to ponder the matter and get to bed for a few hours' sleep before arising to deliver ice.

Over the years, working part-time and later full-time at the ice plant, Nelson had developed a physique that girls and fellows alike admired at the beach. At the ice plant, he often demonstrated how he could simultaneously lift two

300-pound cakes of ice a few inches from the floor. When he was filling iceboxes in the Hampden Meadows and Rumstick Point areas of Barrington, he slung 100-pound chunks over his shoulder with his ice tongs.

Nelson was regarded not only as a strong, hardworking, young man but also as a fellow who delighted in showing off his swimming and diving abilities. At the lake near the ice plant, he spent hours a day in the water, perfecting such feats as double somersaults from a high board.

In the summer of 1939, a waterfront accident in the back of Ruth's home in Bristol Harbor darkened the bright, exciting world of Nelson Blount. As they were playing follow-the-leader, a friend playfully grabbed Nelson's legs as he stepped on a piling of an old wharf. Nelson lost his balance and threw himself toward the water. In his twenty-foot fall, he scraped the bank and ripped his right leg on a broken milk bottle, probably a memento of the hurricane the previous September.

A doctor put thirty-six stitches in the wound, leaving a bit of glass in Nelson's leg that remained there the rest of his life. But the worst injury was to Nelson's back. Not until later was it determined that it was broken. Then, a tetanus shot, routinely administered, brought back a siege of undulant fever.

The next months were days away from railroad roundhouses and the gang he ran with. Ruth and others would drop in, to be sure. Even Engineer Jerald popped in now and then. But these were relatively quiet days for Nelson. He had picked up enough musical training from his mother to play the piano, and the fact that his father had, at one time, been a trombonist in a nationally known band, stirred Nelson's musical interests. So he concentrated on music: piano, saxophone, and clarinet. Propped up in bed, he composed a couple of songs that he later used in his own small orchestra.

In the winter of 1939, Nelson went to Florida with his great-uncle and aunt, Willis and Nan Blount, to speed his complete recovery. In St. Petersburg, instead of merely soaking up Florida sunshine, he got a job playing the piano in one of the hotels.

When his money started to run low, the hostess of the dining room introduced him to a coffee dealer, and Nelson asked for a selling job. The man did not need help, he said.

"Look, it won't cost you anything if I don't sell any. You can't lose," Nelson bargained.

"You're a pretty persuasive guy. What's your angle?"

"Just let me have some samples, and I'll show you."

That afternoon, the young Yankee went into the office of a restaurant chain that the coffee dealer had never been able to crack. He told the manager, "Look, if this coffee isn't better than any coffee you've ever had, don't pay me for it. At least try it." He pushed a sample package into the manager's hands. "And let me know when you're trying it, because I want to be able to know that there's going to be some change in your coffee."

When Nelson found out which restaurant in the chain would be testing the coffee, he persuaded hurriedly-made friends to go in and tell restaurant help how good their coffee was. Soon enough, the manager told Nelson, "Boy, I didn't notice any difference, but that must be real good coffee, for we've had a lot of compliments."

Thus, the result of Nelson's attempt to sell the coffee was that the chain split the business between Berry Coffee Company, the firm Nelson represented, and the company with which they had been doing business.

From then on, Nelson got into several other restaurants, and his commissions sometimes were as high as twenty dollars a day—not bad for 1939.

Wearing a brace for his back but otherwise back in shape, Nelson returned to Warren in the spring of 1940, rejoining Fred, Ruth, and the gang. The fellows at the ice plant welcomed him, and he showed that he could still hoist ice as before. Dad Blount was especially glad to see him. By this time, Nelson was becoming his right hand man, even though he was paying some others considerably more than his son. (This would cause problems later.)

Things thickened with "Jimmy," as he had begun to call Ruth (Everybody in the gang in those days was "Jimmy"—including Nelson!). In the fall of 1940, Ruth went off to Stoneleigh College in Rye, New Hampshire, a solid New England girls' school, with an enrollment kept at one hundred and forty to "insure individual guidance for each student in a two-year program of academic or technical study." That Ruth chose to specialize in home economics was gratifying to Nelson.

When Ruth was not at home weekends, Nelson was often at Stoneleigh. At the Christmas formal on Saturday, December 14, 1940, each student received a booklet in which to record the names of those with whom she danced. Ruth scrawled "Nelson" across each page.

When they were home for Christmas vacation in 1941, Ruth and Nelson attended the Yacht Club dance, and orange, green, and yellow straws went into her scrapbook.

But before wedding bells would ring, it appeared that the well-known, long arm of Uncle Sam would claim Nelson. World War II, of course, was now well under way. As much as he hated leaving "Jimmy," Nelson "wanted like everything to wear a uniform and help keep the US free."

In the spring of 1942, it appeared he would soon be seeing the world aboard a Navy ship. He was a little surprised that he was being accepted, for his broken back was still somewhat of a problem, and Undulant fever was still in his system, though dormant. To get in, he had withheld certain information. But for all practical purposes, he was in the Navy.

In Providence, waiting for Ruth to come down from New Hampshire, he visited a fortune-teller—anything for kicks while killing time. Looking into her crystal ball and then studying the lines in the palm of one hand, she announced, "You think you're going to war, but you're not."

"Oh, I'm going to war, all right. But am I going to get killed? That's what I want to know."

"You're not going to war."

Nelson brushed back his curly hair from his forehead. "OK, I'm not going. What is going to happen?"

"You're going to get married."

"Is that so?"

"Yes, as a matter of fact, you're going to marry a very wealthy young woman. Not only that, you're going to become very rich in your life. You're going to have lots of children. You're going to have a wonderful life."

Laughing aloud by this time, Nelson took out his train ticket that the Navy had sent him. He said, "Look, I'm already accepted into the Navy and am on my way to Norfolk, Virginia, for my training."

Nelson and Ruth went to the movies that evening. Then the next morning, Nelson got a call at home from recruiting headquarters. They said, "Come back in; we want to make some more tests. It appears you haven't told us everything."

At the recruiting station, he leveled with them and got his discharge before he ever wore a uniform. The draft board refused him, and he was given a 4-F status: "Unfit."

On April 4, the day before spring vacation, Ruth got a telegram she would never forget:

Been refused. More vital to defense here. Will meet you.
Love Jim.

This set the stage for the love match that started at the Excelsior Tennis Club and would end in matrimony. But a few months prior, a dark cloud had hung over the whole affair.

Even though Ruth was still in college, Nelson decided that time was wasting and they should at least become engaged. In proper fashion, Nelson went to Mr. Palmer, who sat alone in the living room, reading, to ask for his daughter's hand. The scene shook Nelson to the extent that he considered ending the relationship.

Nelson said, "Mr. Palmer, I would like to marry Ruth."

Mr. Palmer lowered *The Wall Street Journal* he was reading. Then in his austere way, the thin, slightly stooped man looked at Nelson over gold-rimmed spectacles, his high, bushy eyebrows raised more than usual. His close-cropped mustache wiggled ever so slightly before he spoke: "No." Then he put the paper up again and resumed reading.

Nelson walked out on the porch where Mrs. Palmer sat with Ruth and her sister, Jane. He could hardly talk.

Mrs. Palmer had a session with her husband that evening, for the next day, Mr. Palmer came to Nelson and apologized in an offhand way. Then he made matters somewhat worse, so far as Nelson was concerned.

Mr. Palmer said, "You're of good stock, but I want to tell you one thing: if you're marrying Ruth for her money, you'll never get a nickel!"

Nelson allowed that he was as good as the Palmers—not as rich, but just as good.

Mr. Palmer did not bat an eye. He had meant what he said, and he now admired Nelson's fortitude. "I'll be glad to have you as a son-in-law. You're all right. Just as long as we understand each other man to man, we'll have a good relationship."

Nelson hocked his alto saxophone to buy an engagement ring. Then the engagement was announced in hotdog rolls at a wiener roast on June 27. But before the wedding, Nelson met with Mr. Palmer's attorneys and signed papers that indicated to Mr. Palmer's satisfaction that Nelson would in no way rely on the Palmer family for cash. He was on his own. It was simply the John Palmer method. (Until the preparation of this book, even Ruth was not aware of this transaction between Nelson and her father.)

Nelson, in turn, made it clear to Ruth that, sink or swim, she would have to live in his way—even in a cellar, if necessary. "You'll have to learn to live simply; no going out charging a lot of fancy clothes that I can't afford. With your dad, you could do it, but not with me, for a while yet," Nelson warned with a twinkle in his eye.

But underneath, Ruth knew he was serious.

When she graduated in June from Stoneleigh, Ruth applied for a teaching job at Lincoln School, a private girls' school in Providence, to teach sewing and cooking. She had gone there, grades six through twelve.

The wedding was held October 10, 1942, in St. Michael's Episcopal Church, across Bristol Harbor from Poppasquash. Fred Richardson served as Nelson's best man. The wedding would have been held in Providence, at Central Baptist Church, where the Palmers had attended many years, but gas rationing dictated a church near the Palmer home.

The bride was "exquisitely gowned in Alencon lace, in rose and leaf pattern. It was on Princess lines and was cut entraine," raved a society reporter. The reporter continued:

> It had long, tight sleeves, and from the tiny Peter Pan collar, it was buttoned down the front to the hemline with ball-like buttons of the lace, the only relieving note. Her veil of tulle, fastened to a cap arrangement with a sweetheart brim, cascaded down the entire length of the train. Tiny clusters of orange blossoms peeped from either side of the tulle brim of the cap, and flowers she carried—gardenias and bouvardia—were arranged in shower-style. Accompanying her was her father, John Simmons Palmer, 2nd.

As might be expected, the honeymooners took a train trip to Montreal via Niagara Falls. Instead of a cellar, the iceman and his "Jimmy" moved into a five-room, forty-dollars-a-month apartment, upstairs at 28 Broad Street, Warren.

On October 14, 1943, a son was born to the Blounts. They named him Frederick Nelson Blount. However, because Fred Richardson, for whom the new son was given his first name, kept popping in and out of their home, little Frederick soon became Teddy.

A daughter, Carolyn, was born in June of 1946, six months after Mr. Palmer's death. Three other sons came along later: Bobby, Steve, and Billy.

But that's getting far ahead of the story. Nelson had some proving to do. He had to show Mr. Palmer that he too had the Midas touch. Chasing trains had been the big thing in his life, but that had been mainly for fun. Now he had to get ahead, make a name for himself, and find that wonderful spot in life spoken of in the haunting lines of one of two poems he learned in old Mrs. Spangle's class in high school, a poem he quoted to Ruth on one of their first dates. Edgar Allan Poe wrote "Eldorado," but Nelson Blount was now beginning to live it:

> Gaily bedight,
> A gallant knight,
> In sunshine and in shadow,
> Had journeyed long,
> Singing a song,
> In search of Eldorado.
>
> But he grew old—
> This knight so bold—
> And o'er his heart a shadow
> Fell as he found
> No spot of ground
> That looked like Eldorado.
>
> And, as his strength
> Failed him at length,
> He met a pilgrim shadow—
> "Shadow," said he,
> "Where can it be—
> This land of Eldorado?"
>
> "Over the Mountains
> Of the Moon,
> Down the Valley of the Shadow,
> Ride, boldly, ride,"
> The shade replied—
> "If you seek for Eldorado!"

Chapter 4
A MILLION FROM THE SEA

WITH HIS BARREL chest, sinewy arms, and brute shoulders, Nelson Blount might have heaved ice for his father until the Willis E. Blount Ice Company melted into a puddle with the coming of electric refrigerators into every home. But young Nelson was indeed more than a brawny iceman.

Just how much the idea of "proving something" to his father-in-law, the straight-laced squire of Poppasquash, played in Nelson's gallop toward financial success cannot be measured. The thought was there—like a stinging whip—but he was a thoroughbred from the Blount stables and was showing it even before he played peek-a-boo with Mr. Palmer and his *Wall Street Journal*.

Nelson exuded driving energy in handling important business matters for his father, who early on recognized that Nelson was a boy with business acumen. Willis had been able to get Luther through college (with courses at Massachusetts Institute of Technology and a degree from Wentworth Institute), but Nelson had only a look inside schools of higher learning; nevertheless, the elder Blount knew he had a runner in his chief iceman.

There were times when it appeared that Mr. Blount, conservative old Yankee that he was, thought Nelson was going too fast, and Nelson had to fight him for progress. With an eye for more business, Nelson finally talked Dad into taking out a loan for $25,000 and buying a cold storage plant to double his business.

And it paid off. For with the building up of army camps in the area in the early forties, Nelson began knocking at the doors of army brass and coming back with contracts for an avalanche of ice. It was the beginning of his own contribution toward the war effort, as the Blount firm supplied more than forty million pounds of ice annually for two years to Camp Edwards and Camp Standish, as well as, to other army posts on Cape Cod.

Nelson worked like an army mule of earlier wars. "I'd be up and at the plant by 3:30AM, loading ice on our trailer," Nelson later recalled. "I'd unload it on the Cape, be back at Barrington for a second Cape trip at 9:00AM, then make two trips to Boston to pick up ice that we bought from another supplier. Lots of nights, I'd sleep in the cab at the Middleboro traffic circle. During warm weather, I delivered ice to camps seven days a week until I was twenty-three."

Even prior to beginning to bring ice to the Army, Nelson had another big deal sizzling. In the spring of 1941, with wisdom ahead of his day, he tried to arouse Barrington city fathers to the need for obtaining a town-owned water supply. Water, he argued, could, in future years, become a major problem with increasing population demands, and there was no time like the present to make a move.

The solution, which he strongly suggested in rousing town meetings, was the water supply owned by the Willis E. Blount Ice Company. In a Citizens' League gathering in May, he said that the firm's Echo Lake could supply up to four million gallons a day, with the addition of six more artesian wells to the four then on the property. Bristol County consumers, he pointed out, were using some 3.5 million gallons daily. He happily offered to sell the town the ice plant, with all equipment and other assets, for $100,000, with the Blount's company reserving the right, at a rental of $5,000 annually, to make ice for its customers.

This well-thought-out proposal only served to cause the Bristol County Water Company, then supplying water from a distant source, to lower its rates from a minimum metered charge of eighteen dollars a year to fourteen. Except for young Blount and a handful of other foresighted taxpayers, everyone applauded, and the matter rested.

Nelson did finally negotiate the sale of the ice firm in 1944 to the Saltsea Fish Corporation of New Bedford, Massachusetts. His father and mother were planning a lengthy rest, Nelson told the press.

But before this transaction, and even before the ice contracts with the Army had expired, Nelson had other thoughts about making a living. This was in late summer of 1942, a few months before his wedding.

"Look, Dad, I've got to have more than the twenty dollars and board I'm getting," he spouted one day. "I'm marrying Ruth."

"All right, Son, I'll knock off the room and board and raise you to thirty dollars."

It was a nice thought, but some employees who had less responsibility than Nelson were getting more than sixty dollars. In the middle of September, Nelson walked out. With winter coming, he figured Dad could manage.

Before the wedding in October, Nelson was helping the war effort in another way. This time, he was feeding soldiers. The hurricane of 1938 had wrecked oyster businesses in the area, destroying oyster beds and inundating plants. But Nelson gambled that he could scare up oysters for the Army if the brass would put oysters on the menu.

Uncle Byron Blount, who had lost everything in the hurricane but his shirt and know-how in the oyster business, gave Nelson a little encouragement. "At the moment, I can't get you any oysters, but I can give you some clams to tide you over until oysters come in."

The Army said, "OK," clams it would be until Nelson could get oysters. Even the few clams he delivered felt like big money for Nelson then—$5,000. He did not have sufficient money himself to deal direct, so at first, he acted as the middleman. He was paid a hundred dollar bill for this first deal, plus payment for trucking.

"Boy! This is for me," he told himself.

In the ensuing weeks, Nelson got orders for oysters from camps and then made a deal with the American Oyster Company in Providence, putting the firm back in business. He bought oysters at $1.85 a gallon and sold them to Uncle Sam for $2.30. The first shipment of thousands of gallons was being put on chow plates about the time Nelson and Ruth were hurrying out of St. Michael's. The $1,000-plus he made that week, helped ensure first-class hotels on the honeymoon.

Things continued at a fast pace in the fall of 1942, as the army business continued to grow. Nelson got a corner on a huge supply of oysters, one of the first beds to produce again after the hurricane. Old Eddie B. Blount, Nelson's grandfather, who had started the Blounts in the shellfish business back in 1880 in Barrington, would have been proud of his grandson. He was working alongside Uncle Byron, who had taken over the E. B. Blount Oyster Company in 1923, and this new activity was putting the firm back on its feet.

Early in the game, Nelson bought a $5,000 truck. He put one thousand down and then leased it out. He had twenty-eight trucks bringing in money within a year. So, he was in the trucking business as well as working as a food supplier.

Nelson took his biggest step in 1943, when what was left of the Narragansett Oyster Company captured his interest. It was on Water Street and was one of the last of some thirty oyster houses that once had lined the Warren River. The big storm had wrecked the plant, drowned one of the company leaders, and put the firm into receivership.

Nelson offered $10,000 to the mortgage holder, even though the Narragansett firm had once spent perhaps half a million to transform it from a cotton plant to an oyster house. Then someone removed a couple of items of equipment, and Nelson hollered. The owner deducted $144, so the cost was $9,856.

Painters slapped a dark-green coat on the outside of the awkward-shaped, two-story building, and plumbers and carpenters began making changes in the old oyster shop to fit it for the shucking and quick freezing of quahogs (pronounced *kwo-hogs*—an Indian name applied by shell fishermen to thick-shelled clams of the area).

Huge quantities of these marine, bivalve mollusks had come to Nelson's attention through his uncle, Harold Gibbs, commissioner of fish and game for the state of Rhode Island. He had visited Ruth and Nelson one Sunday night, and Nelson, puffing his pipe thoughtfully as they sat in the living room, asked, "What do you think is the greatest untapped resource in the ocean? I've got this new plant, I'm supplying army camps, and I'd like to pull out all the stops."

Uncle Harold leaned forward. "Well, I'll tell you. It's interesting that you ask. This week, we've been out looking on an experimental basis, and we just found a tremendous bed of clams out in the ocean."

"Out in the ocean? How much water?"

"Oh, one hundred ten feet."

"You found clams at one hundred ten feet? How'd you get them?"

"Dredge. We had a little kind of a thing we rigged."

"Gee, I'd be interested." Nelson emptied his pipe and began refueling. "Can I see some of these clams?"

The next day, Nelson went with Uncle Harold and watched as his men brought up clams from the mud, miles out in the ocean off Newport. Eagerly, Nelson opened a clam, but disappointment swept him as he saw dark rather than white meat.

"These are black quahogs," he pointed out to Uncle Harold, "and I'm not sure if they'll be marketable. But if they're here in abundance, I'm going to see what I can do."

Later, Nelson roared over to Camp Edwards and challenged a Colonel Hamilton, who had been buying oysters from him, to try some of the new quahogs.

Officers' mess made up chowder, and the Colonel admitted it tasted good. "But," he said, "I can't buy them. Black quahogs aren't on the approved list. As far as the Army is concerned, such an animal doesn't exist. But tell you what, Nelson, go down to Washington and get the quartermaster corps to approve it, and we'll get it on the menu."

It wasn't the first time Nelson had been to Washington. Rhode Island Senator Theodore F. Green, head of the Senate military affairs committee, had helped him put ice in camps, and now Nelson knocked at Senator Green's door again.

"Senator, you can do a lot to help the shellfish business back to good health if you will get the Army to give a good look at our quahogs. They don't look as good as bay clams, but they're as tasty and nutritious; you can bet on that."

As the quahogs underwent exhaustive tests in Washington, Nelson continued shoveling oysters into military camps. For a young man, he was doing all right. But a bigger opportunity presented itself six weeks later, with the approval of the off-color clams. It was better than anticipated; they were on the list for training camps everywhere—not only for the Army but also for all other branches of service. The demand went from nothing to thousands of tons.

Almost overnight, Narragansett Bay Packing Company was in full operation, with about one hundred men on the payroll—mostly cripples, men over military age, and waterfront bums. The plant operated around the clock, seven days a week.

Nelson got together a small fleet of boats and sent them out to dredge about every place they could reach, and they brought in tons of clams. In addition, Narragansett bought the catches of probably another twenty boats. As many as ten trailer trucks hauled clams to camps and elsewhere. One trailer actually broke in two at Newport, Rhode Island; thirty-five tons was just a mite too much.

"We were short on all kinds of equipment in those days. We couldn't buy it, though we had the orders," Nelson recalls. "It was a real thing to try to start a business from scratch with all the War Production Board rules and regulations. It was a real test of endurance, let me tell you, to start from nothing, to build a big business during the war years, but I did it with little outside help. Fred Richardson wasn't with me then. He was in the Coast Guard. All my men helped, to be sure. But I worked night and day to put this thing together.

"Food became very important, of course. The government was issuing steel to me, and I built a lot of my own equipment. We had to develop a lot of new machinery that was absolutely one of a kind, first of a kind, to do this job. There were nights when we would land as much as two hundred [and] fifty tons of clams in one night, and I had men shucking clams and sending them through the processing system."

Even with the business at such a high pitch, there were times of merriment for Nelson. For example, he tried out his black quahogs on fellow Rotarians and their wives, at the same time showing off his modern machinery and new plant. According to a news article, his "modern machinery, could hold its own with any 'hot stones, sand bags, and tarpaulin' bake ever cooked in the county, in the opinion of the Rotarians."

Uncle Byron Blount, bakemaster, took advantage of the "natural resources" of the plant, the article stated, converting the big, eight-by-five-foot sterilizer into a mammoth "pressure cooker." He used a steam pipe hookup with the plant's heating system, and in went "succulent ears of summer corn, clams, fish wrapped in cheese cloth, whole potatoes, white onions, sausages, frankfurters, and the all-important kettle of butter."

But there were more problems than times of merriment for the hard-driving, young industrialist. The OPA insisted on 1942 ceiling prices on oysters, for example, but labor costs mounted, wages of shuckers jumping from thirty to thirty-five to fifty cents a gallon. Draft boards and other industry snatched men one by one, and replacements were almost impossible to find. So Nelson, innovator that he was, turned to steam to open clams, converting a steam boiler from an old oyster steamer to meet his needs at his Warren plant.

In the meantime, shipping problems plagued him. The first carload of clams he shipped by train to California went bad; someone connected with the railroad had neglected to ice them! And to make matters worse, the shipment lost three or four days because of a series of routing mistakes. The Army was hollering for clams, and Nelson needed money from the shipment to meet certain obligations. He said he considered himself lucky when a bank loaned him "a bunch of money to go back into the same thing all over again. We had the order from the Army, and it had to be filled." All of this was to tide him over until he could get a settlement from the railroad.

There were times in those turbulent days that, without a spoiled shipment, Nelson had to scrape to meet the payroll. But a bookkeeper recalled that even then he had a generous spirit about him. Once, he ordered her to put an extra ten-dollar bill into the pay envelopes of a crew of a certain group of his clammers.

"But we can't afford to do this," she objected.

"We can't afford not to," he countered.

One of the best things that happened to Nelson during the war days was Jim Milne, who left a top job with a brand-named shirt company to work at the packing company. He was divorced; his only son was in the Air Force (killed during Jim's time with Nelson). Jim just preferred helping out an up-and-struggling, young firm. More than once, when Nelson had a payroll of as much as $4,000 a week to meet, Jim Milne loaned him the money. "Pay me when you can," he'd say.

During this period, Nelson never once went to his father-in-law for help, even though he had become something of a favorite of the elder Palmer.

Being constantly under pressure and naturally given to a blustery temperament, Nelson could be generous and smiling one minute and thundering the next. One veteran employee remembered that Nelson fired one particular man "at least once a week" and then rehired him.

An executive of the firm recalled his first day on the job. "I was a 124-pound kid, and Nelson scared the daylights out of me. He handed me a bucket and asked me to get some oil. I brought it back full—five gallons. Actually, he had wanted only a little oil but didn't make it plain. He fairly exploded at the amount of oil I brought, and I thought I'd be seeing the paymaster."

Another man remembered something else about Nelson: "If anything went wrong, it was always somebody else's fault, even if it was really Nelson's own idea. He was proud of his accomplishments, but if anyone suggested that he was egotistical, he'd get very upset and deny it up and down and try to prove he wasn't."

Despite the fact that he was about as unpredictable as April weather, and seemingly egotistical about his accomplishments, by and large, Nelson Blount was a big, likeable fellow, easier to live with than isolated incidents might indicate.

Nelson went to church on Sundays at the white-spired First Methodist Church of Warren. He tried to keep on speaking terms with God and generally tried to make it a better world in which to live or let live. He was public spirited, joining clubs, hosting dinners, and fighting generally for a better Rhode Island. He ran for city council and campaigned as a Democratic candidate for state senator, but he lost both times.

One of his finest contributions came in the mid-1940s, when he headed the Pollution Abatement Committee of Rhode Island. As a shellfish leader, he was vitally concerned that domestic sewage and industrial waste were killing the shellfish business in the area, as well as generally spoiling beaches along the Rhode Island shore. Pollution had begun as early as 1900 and, coupled with overfishing, had wiped out many natural oyster reefs; in more recent years, pollution had made vast oyster grounds unsafe for shellfish cultivation.

Spearheading the drive of the Pollution Abatement Committee, Nelson signed correspondence and a series of full-page newspaper advertisements, seeking to arouse public opinion and encourage legislation to correct the menace. Then in 1947, in a surprise move, the Senate passed five bills that finally led to establishment of the Blackstone Valley Sewer District and a giant stride toward a solution to the problem.

In the meantime, Blount enterprises were growing and becoming more complex and diversified. In the early days of the firm, E. B. Blount Sons Oyster Company, headed by Uncle Byron Blount, became a division of Narragansett Bay Packing Company, buying and selling oysters while the parent company kept clammers busy unloading huge quantities of clams at the pier in back of the plant. A cannery was added in 1944, when Marcus L. Urann, head of Ocean Spray Cranberries Inc., phoned Nelson and suggested that Nelson join him in an operation at his Plymouth plant, which needed work. Seeing the end of the war in the distance, Nelson knew his army business soon would disappear. For that reason, he agreed and began canning clams for civilian use. In addition, he developed the first canned oyster stew in the United States.

On October 17, 1946, all of his firms were reorganized as Blount Seafood Corporation, altogether employing approximately 300 people. Nelson Blount became president and treasurer; Byron Blount, vice president; and Fred Richardson, secretary. (To Nelson's relief, his boyhood sidekick joined him immediately after completing war duty with the Coast Guard.) Marcus Urann, whom Nelson credits as sharing with him a considerable amount of business knowledge, became a member of the board of the new firm.

All looked like smooth sailing until a slick, high-pressured lawyer slithered into Nelson's office one day and suggested that he sell his clam business to the lawyer's client; a steam roller who wanted a free course in selling clams. This actually occurred in 1945, but the resulting problems continued on into the Blount Seafood days.

"We've got the outlets, the advertising; we can snow you," said the lawyer.

"What's your proposition?" Nelson asked, biting his pipe.

"We'll give you a quarter of a million; you can keep that other thing."

"What other thing?" Nelson boomed.

"Plymouth Packing Company. You keep it, and we'll give you a quarter of a million for the rest. But I want $30,000 put aside for me for putting this deal through for you."

"Are you out of your mind?" Nelson puffed furiously on his pipe. "I wouldn't sell this thing for a million dollars. And I wouldn't give you even five cents commission. Get yours at the other end! What do you think these people want this business for? I developed it. I got control of this clam thing. You want to walk in here and threaten me. Get out! I won't even talk to you unless it's on my terms."

After that, everything seemed to go wrong. Somebody somewhere had some connections; someone was pushing buttons. Food and Drug Administration investigators descended on the clam company like flies, or so it seemed. Quality ratings were high. Methods were wrong.

One man at the Plymouth company, tired of overtime work caused by the added pressures, sent out a shipment of three or four railroad cars that should not have gone out. The government put a stop on the cars. Later, the following news item appeared in a local paper:

F. Nelson Blount of Barrington, president of the Plymouth (Mass.) Packing Company, yesterday was fined fifty dollars and the company two hundred fifty dollars in Federal Court at Boston on a charge of violating the Federal food, drug, and cosmetic act . . The charge: 4 1/2 ounces of drained weight instead of 5 ounces.

Blount, reached at the Blount Seafood Corporation in Warren, said the fine was imposed for an act of negligence, rather than willful violation. "This incident happened about two years ago," he said. "At the time, we were having difficulty obtaining a supply of the local product. We bought soft shell clams from Long Island and mixed them with ocean quahogs, to keep the plant operating, with the idea that when you cooked the clams, the same amount of drained weight would result. Under heat and pressure, the clams broke down into water more quickly than quahogs. But, before we realized this fact, shipments had gone out.

"Naturally, the Government felt that anyone processing food should know what he is doing. We bought back the shipments at full price, when we learned what was happening, and relabeled them, selling them at a greatly reduced price. At the time, we were very busy at some of our plants ..."

As it turned out, continued pressure from various sources caused Blount and Urann to toss in the towel, and they folded the company, taking tax losses. Until then, Plymouth had been a big, promising operation, so this was a crushing blow. Nelson not only had to go through the ordeal of a court case but also was on the verge of bankruptcy.

Later, the Food and Drug chief for Massachusetts ran into court problems involving, among other things, bribes, and he served a prison term. He was the man Nelson believed was pushing buttons against him. This judicial whipping suffered by his alleged tormentor helped only slightly. The lawyer who started the thing remained at large.

As his wounds healed, Nelson began supplying clams rather than canning under his own label.

About this time, he convinced the Campbell Soup Company that he knew his clams like few people did in those days. It happened along these lines: Nelson, one of several suppliers for Campbell's, had a hunch that the soup people might be searching for clams during the winter season ahead, so he bought them by the ton, processed them, and froze them.

"That winter, we had the severest freeze I've ever seen," Nelson later recalled. "You could walk across Narragansett Bay. Boy, it was tough. You couldn't buy a clam; you couldn't buy anything. The Campbell people went through all the stuff they had. I was chuckling. When they ran out of clams and their plant was about to shut down, I called up and said, 'How would you like to buy a whole month's supply of clams at last summer's prices?'

"'Are you kidding?' came the voice on the phone.

"'I was afraid this shortage would come, and I got you backed up. But first, you've got to give me some of your processing business.'

"'I can't do that,' the voice groaned. 'But come on down here to Camden and see me.'"

The Aeronca, used by the company at times for patrolling oyster beds, heated up, and soon Nelson and Fred Richardson were flying to a conference that would result in a lasting and profitable friendship for all concerned.

But it did not come at once.

At the conference, Nelson continued to insist that he wanted to pull out all the stops as a Campbell clam processor. But this was too much like putting all of Campbell's clams in one basket. Policy would not allow it.

Nelson was down on the street, about to hail a taxi, when the Campbell's man rushed out to catch him. "OK, you win," he said to Nelson and Fred.

"What do you mean? Upstairs you just said 'no dice,'" Nelson boomed, flicking the ashes from the cigar he was smoking.

"The boss said that your request is logical and reasonable, so we'll deal with you."

In a short time, Blount Seafood Corporation, in effect, became part of the Campbell family. The May, 1957, issue of *Campbell People*, the firm's employee's magazine, stated:

> Campbell's buys substantial quantities of its quahogs from the Blount Seafood Corporation ... By far the largest quahog processing operation in New England. Quahog meat and juice from Blount's are used in the production of our heat processed Manhattan Style Clam Chowder and our Frozen New England Style Clam Chowder at all of our major plants. Campbell's assisted Blount's in building up its clam handling capacity and has constantly maintained a close working relationship ...

Getting clams in desired quantities had Nelson fighting to keep his business in Rhode Island from the early days of the firm. Blount felt that antiquated state laws held down mechanized clamming to protect the hand clammers, whose numbers had dwindled and who couldn't produce enough clams to satisfy the demand. Thus, Blount's was forced to buy clams from as far south as North Carolina.

Even back about the time Blount's and Campbell's joined forces, the apparent quiet, peaceful waters of Narragansett Bay had become the scene of what newspapers called a "tong war," involving clam supply. The battle, reflecting a difference in ways of life, pitted tongers and bull rakers (the skilled hand workers plying a trade generations old) against the dredgers (the fishermen who used huge mechanical scoops to bring up quahogs from the bottom of the sea).

The tongers and bull rakers did not object to dredgers fishing in the open sea. It was the bay over which they clashed. The boys with their hand tools (large, heavy, curved-tooth rakes about thirty feet long and instruments like ice tongs up to twenty-feet long) argued that dredgers would ruin the bottom of the bay and kill off clamming forever.

To keep employees busy at Blount's, Nelson naturally backed the dredgers. As president of the Southern New England Shellfish Dealers Association, he spearheaded a movement to get legislation through, threatening at one time to take his business to some other state unless quahogs became more plentiful. But ultimately, he liked Rhode Island too well to leave.

In 1949, Nelson tried a "first" as a means of needling Rhode Island officialdom to do something to increase clam production. With a local newspaper reporter along, Nelson flew to Maine to begin improving that state's clam production.

During low tide, across great stretches of mud flats of Casco Bay near Brunswick, Maine, Nelson piloted his firm's silver-winged plane and dumped nearly 250,000 young seed quahogs that were garnered for him by local fishermen from the two major quahog-producing bays in Maine. He hoped the then barren Casco Bay would become a major source for quahogs by 1951.

Actually, the venture was only a mild success, but Nelson got news coverage that once again pointed up the need for new legislation to keep the shellfish industry alive in Rhode Island. The reporter who accompanied him on the history-making flight quoted Nelson as saying he would go in for aerial sowing in Rhode Island in a big way if it were not for "those laws." He told the reporter, "Thousands of bushels of quahogs in polluted areas could be transplanted by air to clean waters, but you just batter your head against the wall if you propose such a thing."

At that time, he was said to have bitter critics in Rhode Island because some felt his startling and unpredictable maneuvers were indicative of a desire for greater personal gain. He admitted it to this extent: "After all, I buy quahogs. I'm worried about a diminishing supply. If I can help increase the quahog resources, I will ultimately benefit, and so will others."

In the late forties, Nelson got himself arrested in the tong war, but he found the courts as hard shelled as the quahogs. He had leased oyster beds from the state off Mill Gut, Bristol, intending to use them for clams. He planted quahogs there in 1946, but the state objected, maintaining that he use them for oysters or not at all. To bring the matter to a head and get a test case, he dressed in a bright red shirt and blue trousers and ordered a crew to take him clamming in the good ship *Eddie B*.

When he returned from Mill Gut, a game warden and a blue-uniformed policeman were waiting for him and came aboard to remove bagged quahogs. He had notified authorities that he intended to clean his oyster beds with dredges and keep any quahogs brought up for commercial purposes. Thus, the welcoming pair was no surprise.

Nelson was tried in a District Court in Warren and was found guilty of taking quahogs illegally, something he also anticipated. It was his contention that the lease had been changed after he made the agreement. But in an appeal to Superior Court, he lost again and paid a fine of fifty dollars and costs. On the way out, he told reporters it was worth it all if he in any way aroused public opinion toward the need for "an up-to-date program that would permit Rhode Island to maintain its natural advantage in shellfish production."

Later, Blount tossed in the towel for the time being, hoping for new blood in the legislature. It was then that he turned to other states for a large portion of his clams. In 1966, he was still hoping for a change in Rhode Island laws, but union pressures and other factors continued to suppress the dredgers, relegating shellfish activity in Rhode Island waters largely to hand-to-boat operations.

Running a large firm and locking horns with legislators would be a full-time job for the average executive, but those who knew him attested that the president of Blount's was hardly average. He developed surf clam strips used in many restaurants and operated a surf clam plant for a while on Long Island. He helped his brother, Luther, get started in big-time boatbuilding with the opening of Blount Marine Corporation and was a member of the board of his brother's Hustad Marine Corporation.

Nelson, at one time, owned a weekly newspaper and was chairman of the board of B & M Aviation Company, New England distributors of new airplanes. He also once backed a diamond-mining venture in South America, but that left him holding the bag when his prospector failed to produce and ran off with his money. Then an effort to launch an oyster business in Florida lost $150,000 when thieving fishermen raided the Oyster beds under cover of night and got only light fines for their acts. One of the fishermen drowned when his overloaded boat sank.

Soon after World War II, Nelson purchased an old DC-3 and two torpedo bombers, and for a time, the Blount Corporation flew Maine lobsters to the South. It was a joint venture with a Maine lobster firm. "We lost too many cargoes because of bad weather," he recalls. "But I came through about even. Oh, I've lost an awful lot of money and have started a lot of harebrained enterprises—some I've forgotten, I guess."

It was Nelson's eagle eye that eventually put him in to the tuna business in 1961. In 1950, while flying his plane, he spotted schools of bluefin tuna off the southeast New England coast. In 1955, he bought a ninety-foot Coast Guard cutter, named it *Stormy Weather II*, and personally went tuna fishing and found them by the ton. The tuna project marked time until the late fifties. Then Nelson converted the cutter to a clam dredge and gave it to the state of Rhode Island to transplant clams from polluted waters into areas where clamming could be done commercially. This was his most marked victory in his battle to improve the shellfish industry.

In July of 1957, in a fifty-seven-foot boat christened *Aphrodite*, Nelson turned to tracking tuna again. Personally designed by the owner, the yacht used her arsenal of electronic devices to prove to Nelson—and later to others—that Atlantic tuna were worth going after.

Hence, in 1961, Cape Cod Tuna Corporation was formed, with Blount owning twenty-three percent of the stock and serving as chairman of the board for a time. A sardine packing company was leased in Eastport, Maine, and a small fleet went to work. One of the ships, a sixty-four-foot clipper launched from the Luther Blount shipyard and using a 30,000 dollar nylon net, was named the *F. Nelson Blount*. Director Blount's daughter, Carolyn, christened the all-steel boat. A feature of the vessel was its forty-six-inch controllable pitch propeller that could be adjusted to a silent pitch setting for close approaches to schools of tuna.

The *Blount* caught 290 tons of tuna, or an average of 8.3 tons a day, during a five-week fishing period soon after she was launched. In 1962, poor air spotting and the invasion of the waters by West Coast tuna fishing companies kept the tonnage of the fleet of four ships down below expectations, and the progress had been slower than desired after that. But

Cape Cod Tuna remained a promising venture, supplying as it did a number of private-labeled accounts.

To say that Nelson Blount's business career was exciting would be an understatement. Few men have been involved in so many projects. There were certainly men in the East who were wealthier, but if John S. Palmer II were still alive, he would have been mighty proud of his son-in-law. With a head for business and an eye for opportunities, Nelson, as early as 1948, was able to do a bit of calculating and come up with the satisfying fact that he was a millionaire before reaching his thirtieth birthday. By age thirty-five, he had joined the multimillionaires' club.

With his wealth, Nelson had gained a measure of popularity, his colorful, exuberant personality overshadowing some of his blustery ways and winning him more friends than enemies. He was a man known throughout New England. Newspapers saw to that, for when Nelson Blount opened his mouth—and that was always—it usually made news.

But what never made the news pages was that intangible something that kept Nelson Blount stirred up inside. He had everything he wanted that money could buy. As he often said, "I started out with a tricycle, then got a bicycle, a Model A, V-8 Buick, Cadillac, and finally had two Rolls-Royces." Nevertheless, a haunting void screamed to be satisfied.

> And o'er his heart a shadow
> Fell as he found
> No spot of ground
> That looked like Eldorado ...

Chapter 5
A Telegram and Adventure

O N THE EVENING of October 10, 1953, a Western Union boy hopped off his bike and knocked at the red front door of the white house at 1 Manor Road, Barrington. Ruth Blount laid aside the book she was reading and hurried to answer. This was their eleventh wedding anniversary, but their celebration plans were off since Nelson was in Newfoundland hunting. The office had called earlier in the day to tell her that he had been delayed because engine trouble had grounded his plane.

She stiffened a bit as she opened the door and looked in the face of the young man in the olive uniform. She took the yellow envelope from the boy's extended hand, signed a form, said a quiet "thank you," and closed the door.

In the dimly lit hallway, Ruth ripped open the envelope and unfolded the message. Half aloud, she read:

> Sorry this trouble keeps us apart on our anniversary. I am thinking of all. I hope we have many happier years together. I have shot my trophys [sic] and am awaiting

the engine. I hope you get this in time. I am sending this by messenger to the telegraph office. I love you. JIMMY

Being married to the dashing, young millionaire she called Jimmy because he often called her Jimmy, a carry-over from earlier days, was not all moonlight and roses—even at anniversary time. For Nelson Blount's boundless energies and thirst for action and adventure frequently took him far from the lush, green lawns of Country Club Manor and the comforts and love of the first house on Manor Road.

Most red-blooded men enjoy sports activities. The average loving husband and father, lacking extra cash, ventures no farther on a regular basis than a local golf course, bowling alley, or nearby lake. But that was not the case with Nelson. Money, of course, was no problem. It was just a matter of his pinching Ruth on the cheek and saying, "You know, Jimmy, I've got to get away from it for a day or two. Bailey, Balfour, and I are going to fly up to New Brunswick and bring back venison. Heat up the oven, and we'll feast when we get back."

He might have said Newfoundland, home of great herds of caribou and coveted, hot-tempered moose. Or it might have been a mere jaunt to British Columbia to hunt grizzlies, elk, mountain sheep, or moose in the rugged reaches of the Canadian Rockies.

If it was not a hunting trip, it was a fishing trip. Often, however, Ruth herself went with Nelson after swordfish, entering wholeheartedly into the drama of catching a huge sword from the time the dorsal fin was spotted breaking water to the moment the defeated behemoth was hoisted tail first from the water into their yacht.

It was in the Flathead Valley area of British Columbia in 1954 that Nelson shot his first grizzly bear. However, in this case, it turned out to be two—the second one was a mistake!

"We were high on a mountain, hunting mountain sheep and goats in the middle of the day," he later recalled. "I looked down with the binoculars while my guide and I were killing time, and I saw a great, brown grizzly bear maybe two or three miles below us. Realizing we could always get plenty of sheep and goats, we headed down, and about an hour and a half later, spotted three grizzlies turning over rocks, looking for rodents. One would push on the rocks, and another with a huge paw would catch rodents as they scurried out.

"I took aim at the biggest grizzly and shot it in the neck. Growling and yelling, he stood on his feet; my next shot hit his paw and then his body. He took a tremendous leap and disappeared. A few minutes later, I thought I spotted him limping and fired again at the huge brute from about three hundred yards. We waited for half an hour and, since all was quiet, went to investigate. When we got there, we found not one but two grizzlies. We took the large one, which weighed about seven hundred pounds."

For a different approach to hunting, Nelson, from time to time, laid aside his rifle or shotgun and hunted Indian-fashion, with bow and arrows. In 1951, he killed a bull caribou weighing about eight hundred pounds. He used three arrows to make the kill.

But he was glad for his .30-06 Remington rifle the day a bull moose attacked him in Newfoundland. He and Arthur "Cooky" Cooke were stranded after Nelson's plane developed trouble, and they were walking out to civilization. Coming upon seven or eight moose, Nelson shot a calf for survival meat. As the animal went down, he squealed for a moment, and Nelson, to save ammunition, began finishing the calf with his hunting knife.

Suddenly, Cooky screamed, "Look out!"

Nelson straightened and, in a flash, grabbed his gun. A bull, his eyes flashing murder, crashed toward him from the nearby brush. Nelson only had time to fire from his hip, without taking careful aim. The bullet slammed into the bull's nose and came out an eye. He stopped and Nelson fired two more times. Seemingly only dazed, the bull walked away. Another shot killed him. The two hunters gutted him, severed his head, and covered it with brush. A few days later, they returned and brought out the head to be mounted.

When Nelson took his first plane ride in a 1929 Waco when he was ten, little did he know that planes would someday take him into countless adventures. On that first flight, he flew with a pilot named Everett King from King's Field, Taunton, Massachusetts, and it was King who checked out Nelson for his license in 1944.

After leasing planes for two years, Nelson got in line early to buy the first new, postwar, private plane delivered to a Rhode Islander, a 1946 Aeronca Champion, a two-seater similar to a Piper Cub, except with more room. Later, Nelson wished he had waited for production bugs to be worked out; allegedly, inferior engine parts caused the engine to blow up, and he made a forced landing on a farm near Putnam, Connecticut, some months after he got the plane.

With his fever for collecting, Nelson went on to buy various types of planes, including military fighters, trainers, and sports models. At one time, he owned as many as five, and all told over the years, he had some thirty planes.

Just after World War II, Nelson put his flying ability to practical use, serving as captain of the Bristol County AirSea Rescue Unit of the Civil Air Patrol. He and members of the Bristol National Guard unit made news headlines, as Nelson became a flying target for those practicing with antiaircraft guns. On a one-time United States Navy Stearman N2N-5 trainer (*Yellow Peril*), he flew a course between the head of Rhode Island's Bristol Harbor and Hog Island for an hour, his plane sometimes fluttering like a falling leaf while gunners theoretically shot him out of the skies with their 40 mm. cannon and quadruple mount .50-caliber machine guns. The only thing lacking—since combat veterans fresh from European and South Pacific battle areas manned the weapons—was the actual boom of cannon and the stutter of the machine guns. Nelson flew at altitudes ranging from 500 to 2,000 feet, varying the straight flights with evasive tactics to sharpen the gunners' eyes.

All of Nelson Blount's flying was not quite so practical. Air shows, which brought bug-eyed boys and their almost equally awed fathers to flying fields in droves in Nelson's boyhood, got a new daredevil in the young sportsman from Barrington.

Nelson specialized in loops from the takeoff, a foolhardy stunt, combining engine power with a skillful touch that meant the difference between life and death. "If I had a 4,000-foot runway, I could do it," Nelson later recalled. "I would roar down the runway until the plane's speed hit one hundred sixty miles per hour. Then I'd begin a series of short loops immediately after takeoff. At the bottom of the loop, I'd be doing one hundred sixty; at the top, I was doing maybe sixty or seventy. I came pretty close to the ground—this was part of the act. I'd do it ten times, and the tenth time, I did what is called a half-snap fat. At the top of the loop you are upside down, thus a half-snap brings you level again; then I'd shut the engine off and make a circle, and come in right on that line. If the engine had quit as I went into the loop, I would have crashed. Nobody had ever tried it that I had heard of, and in those days, I lived to do things no one else would do. I loved the thrill and excitement."

In 1960, Nelson had an experience that helped him decide to quit stunting. It involved "Whitey," a Navy commander who frequently teamed with Nelson in a simulated air fight. Whitey flew an SNJ, a 600 horsepower, fighter trainer, which looked like a Japanese Zero. Nelson fought him in an old biplane, usually outclimbing, outturning, and generally outmaneuvering the larger plane.

With some 10,000 people looking on at Edaville, near South Carver, Massachusetts, on a Sunday afternoon, Commander Whitey took his SNJ up to about 8,000 feet and went into a power dive. Nelson's biplane stayed on the J's tail for the first 3,000 feet, and then the larger plane pulled away.

Nelson trimmed the plane back and pulled out of the dive, afraid the wings would rip off. Just as he trimmed it, he was over the crowd and gasped as the fabric panel on a lower wing tore loose and fluttered earthward, scattering spectators.

"The airplane had a lot of lift on one side and only a little on the other, and it was all I could do to keep it from flipping over," Nelson later remembered. "I finally got the thing down, and I've never flown in a show since. For one thing, Ruth had been trying to get me to quit. The fellows who looked at the plane and rebuilt it for me couldn't understand how it stayed together under such extreme conditions."

Back in the fall of 1947, Nelson nosed his Stinson northward across Massachusetts and Maine and on into the unspoiled New Brunswick woods. Aboard were some close friends of Nelson's, H. Bailey Mason of Barrington and Balfour Bassett of Barnstable, Massachusetts, and a *Providence Journal* photographer, Edward Hanson. It marked the first time Blount had taken to the air to hunt deer, and the trip proved successful. Photographer Hanson later presented a photo story of the results. The pictures published in *The Providence Sunday Journal* on November 30, 1947, showed that the hunters, dressed in rough outdoor clothing, enjoyed a Saturday night community dance perhaps as much as trailing deer by air. The feature picture showed a smiling Nelson Blount and his two buddies, all leaning on rifles, standing beside the Stinson on whose wing struts hung two of the three deer killed on the hunt.

A level head and know-how born of experience (and mostly God's grace, said Nelson) kept the flying sportsman alive in numerous narrow squeaks. One time in Newfoundland, with four companions, he gassed up his seaplane with fuel that he later found contained liquid latex. It caused exactly nine engine failures. He was circling a moose when the difficulties started. He landed on a lake, took off, and scrambled to get to another lake as he lost altitude; this happened repeatedly, until he finally got to the coast. He made a dead stick landing in ten-foot waves in White Bear Bay. At the time, the waters were being whipped up by the advanced winds of Hurricane Carol.

In 1951, skillful flying of a crippled 1932 open biplane off Martha's Vineyard brought Nelson Blount and a friend, Johnny Mayhew, through a memorable experience. Another friend, Harry Bellas Hess, merchandising czar, asked Nelson to fly out and spot swordfish for him and another fisherman as they fished from a yacht. For about twenty minutes, Nelson flew the plane in the vicinity of the yacht, indicating the best he could, the area where he had spotted a swordfish. But Captain Frank Cyganowski, at the wheel of the yacht, could not seem to find the critter.

Finally, Nelson turned to Johnny. "D'you think we can land this thing and put them on the fish?"

Johnny did not say "yes" or "no," so on impulse, Nelson put the plane down and landed near the fish. The yacht pulled over, and Nelson decided to take off. He yelled to Captain Frank to make a wake for him in the rough water, and moments later, he gunned the engine for takeoff. But it did not work.

Next, he tried another trick that to him seemed logical. He waited for a big wave and tried to ride it into the air. One wing dipped and hit the wave, ripping off the lower part of the wing. But the plane was airborne, and that was the important thing at the moment. In the dual controlled plane, Nelson and Johnny, flying in a semi-stalled condition, got back to Martha's Vineyard, thankful that they had not only survived but also not even gotten wet.

Harry Bellas Hess gave him a Napoleon sporting rifle, worth a fortune, for this act.

In the early fifties, Nelson wrecked his 25,000 dollar Cessna when he had to make a forced landing in White Bear Bay, Newfoundland. The seaplane struck a submerged rock and sank. Nelson and a companion, Francis Manchester, jumped into a dory and escaped without injury. Over the years, Blount was in accidents that wrecked four planes totally or partially.

The experience that resulted in his sending the "I'm-stuck-in-Newfoundland" telegram on his wedding anniversary in October 1953, started out as a pleasant hunting trip. From the air, Nelson and Arthur Cooke drooled as they spotted as many as five hundred caribou at a time. They set up camp some thirty-five miles inland, in a promising wilderness area, and then to refuel, Nelson nosed his Aeronca Sedan to Burgeo, on the coast, on what was to be a routine flight. But fog shrouded the little village, and he had no other choice but to head back up the White Bear River until he saw smoke coming from a cabin.

His problem seemed solved when a game warden offered him gasoline mixed with oil—all that he had. This was better than no gas at all, so Nelson ordered his mechanic to put the mixture into just one tank, and he would use it only in an emergency. The plane was hardly off the water when Nelson knew the mechanic had disregarded orders and mixed it in both tanks. A series of detonations shook the plane, and the engine began to heat and smoke badly. Nevertheless, Nelson managed to nurse the plane back to the Island of Ramea, where he drained both tanks and refueled, at the same time obtaining twenty gallons to repay the game warden.

After delivering the gas to the warden, Nelson headed toward camp, since the engine now seemed to be functioning normally. He flew up the river downwind to save gas. On either side were canyon walls less than a half-mile apart. Nelson's hands gripped the stick tighter as the plane climbed with its heavy load of gas and the two men. The engine was heating up; the detonation damage had started to take, and though the engine was running full power, the plane was losing altitude. He saw no place to turn and perhaps had less than sixty seconds to make a decision. He could not dump the gas. He was clearing huge rocks below by one hundred feet or less.

"Cooky, if you've ever prayed, now's the time," Nelson said. The usual booming, jovial voice could not have been more serious.

Suddenly, hoping against hope, Nelson banked the plane, just making it as the narrowing canyon wall loomed frightfully close for comfort. Now he was flying into the wind again. He adjusted the throttle, and the engine began to run more smoothly, enabling him to keep altitude until he got to the first open water. As he touched down, the engine blew apart with a frightening roar that echoed through the wilderness.

The game warden, who had supplied the gasoline, heard the explosion and arrived a short while later in a skiff. The next day, the warden boated Nelson and his companion thirty-five miles to Ramea, to a fishing boat, and Nelson had a radio message sent to Warren. Ruth got the word that

A Telegram and Adventure

the anniversary celebration was off, and arrangements were made for another engine to be flown in.

Two weeks later, Nelson had the Aeronca flying again and landed in the Ramea harbor on a test flight. By this time, a fierce gale was churning the waters. Nelson was relieved that he did not have to fly farther in such adverse conditions

Then he was approached by a Royal Mountie. "You're Mr. Blount, aren't you?" He had been directed to him. "Mr. Blount, you've got the only way of saving the life of a woman who's dying. Would you take her in your plane to a hospital twenty miles away?"

"Man, it's blowing over fifty miles an hour!" Nelson bit his lip and then lifted his head. "OK, we'll do it."

After the woman had been placed inside the plane, Blount breathed a prayer as he checked the instruments. Then, nosing the plane into the gale, he eased back on the stick. The plane climbed skyward, and a crowd cheered below.

Minutes later, the plane sat down in the harbor of Burgeo, where over twenty men, who had been told of the trip on the radio, grabbed the plane on the beach and held it in the wind and dashing waves. The woman was removed and rushed to the hospital. The quick action saved her life. Nelson, who spent the night in the hospital for convenience, later received a citation from the Canadian government for his deed.

Summers with the family, fishing from the *Aphrodite* off Martha's Vineyard, held some of the most pleasant experiences for Nelson Blount. Actually, there were two yachts named *Aphrodite*. In 1954, Hurricane Carol destroyed the first, a seventy-four foot yacht once used by Franklin D. Roosevelt. *Aphrodite II*, a sleek, white, fifty-seven-foot yacht—the one used to track tuna—then became the pride of the Blount family.

THE MAN FROM STEAMTOWN

While writing for the *Vineyard Gazette* on June 19, 1953, Shirley Mayhew gave a blow-by-blow account of a successful sword foray led by Nelson the year before *Aphrodite I* went down in the hurricane. Here is the thrilling episode:

> We got underway at about 7:00 AM on what promised to be a good day for swords. The sea was glassy calm, and a hot bright sun was already bearing down. Johnny Mayhew was at the wheel of the seventy-four-foot *Aphrodite* and with both engines turning at 1500, we were clipping off a good steady twelve knots. Nelson and Bill were checking the warps and darts, and moving the kegs forward in high anticipation. Nelson's wife, Ruth, was below making up sandwiches. She wanted to be on deck when we were looking for swords.
>
> Soon we were rounding the can off Gay Head, cutting for the green bell, running in the tide between Noman's Land and Squibnocket. We set our course from the green bell, south by east. Nelson, Bill, and I climbed aloft and began scanning the water. One hour from the bell, we shut down one engine. I was told that, whereas we had been in swordfish waters since the bell, from now on we should be especially alert, as we were getting into the rips where the swords are most often found.
>
> Pretty soon Nelson spotted a fin just ticking the surface, and we swung over to have a look. Just a hammerhead shark, so Nelson said. Now I knew what to expect. Just a part of a fin cutting through the water, leaving a small wake behind. Soon, I spotted a fin and we swung again. The fin was quite sharp and small, and was moving fast. I was quite excited but was told it was just a "skilly" or a marlin. We passed him close enough to see his bill. "Almost," said Nelson. Then Johnny saw some bait skipping out of the water and said some fish must be driving it.
>
> We turned to get a better look. Then down through the clear water we could see a school of tuna. They are

A Telegram and Adventure

a beautifully proportioned fish and Nelson said they are fast and powerful for their size. He said the ones we saw would go ten to fifteen pounds. We were anxious to get our sword and so we didn't put over a feather to try for the tuna.

Nelson had his binoculars out and was scanning the water in slow arcs. I almost fell out of my perch when he suddenly hollered at the top of his lungs, "That's him! Port! About eleven o'clock. Way off! He looks like a two-masted schooner!" We strained our eyes in the direction Nelson was pointing, but couldn't see a thing. I wondered if it was another false alarm.

"Steady!" Nelson said. "You're heading right for him now. Check your compass and hold her steady." He was in the stand forward now, and held the pole pointing towards the fish, which we finally all saw, just lazily swimming along, both fins high out of the water.

"With the sun where it is we'll have to come up on him while he's going to port," Nelson said. "Back her down as soon as I throw the dart so he won't get in the wheel." The kegs were on the starboard side. By now we were coming close, and the fish looked tremendous. I aimed my camera. I wanted, if possible, to record the very instant the dart hit home.

Down went the pole. The fish gave a mighty thrash with his tail, turned, and was off! Johnny threw the wheel hard to starboard without backing down, as the fish didn't go under the boat. The line was now zipping and singing out of the tub where it had been neatly coiled. Over went the keg.

"Nice going, Nelson! Do you think you hit him square?" Johnny was exuberant.

"I got him right next to the fin," Nelson said. "I think he's buttoned. You put me on him fine. He's a good fish too."

"How big?" Johnny asked, and Nelson answered, "Oh, about two hundred fifty dressed, I'd say! He's a 'keeper' all right. You put me on him fine!"

At that moment nobody could do anything wrong, it seemed. Big smiles and grins dominated the scene.

"Man, look at that keg travel," Bill said. Spray was flying over the keg now, making rainbows. That fish certainly was going somewhere in a hurry.

We circled the area, keeping the keg in sight, hoping to spot another fin, until the keg slowed down. I was told that if you get a swordfish, it's quite likely several others will be in the same area. Our search was fruitless, however, so we came up near the keg and lowered the dinghy over the side. Nelson climbed in and we cast him off.

"Now's my chance," Johnny said. "Find me a swordfish, and let's see if I can make it two."

We tried for more than an hour and saw several fins too, but they all proved to be sharks. Then we saw Nelson raise an oar—the signal for us to come alongside. Johnny swung the helm over and started the other engine. Nelson threw us the painter and Bill made it fast to a cleat, then swung the stern davit outboard and lowered the block with the hook in it.

Nelson held the fluke rope, which was around the fish's tail, with one hand, and reached for the block with the other. He had the hook almost through the loop in the fluke rope when the fish apparently "came to." Nelson had to let go of the block to hold the fluke rope with both hands. The fish was thrashing wildly now, and water was flying in a drenching spray. Harder and harder it fought.

"You better let him go, Nelson," Johnny yelled. "He'll smash the dinghy if you don't."

"Let him go!" I thought. Not after having him so close. That would be heartbreaking.

Johnny apparently read my mind. "The dart is still in him," he said. "We won't lose him. But we may spot another fish and we'll need the dinghy to tend him—the dinghy in one piece, I mean."

"I think I can hold him," Nelson said. But the fish settled the matter with a mighty thrash that threw Nelson almost out of the dinghy. The fish was gone again, but the keg was still in the dinghy and Nelson slowed him down.

Once again, we came up alongside as we saw the fish was up again. The fluke rope was still around his tail! This time we hoisted him aboard, and I got a picture of him as he hung head down in defeat, in all his sleek, powerful beauty. His coloring was breathtaking. Well over half his sword was still in the water. It was a glorious moment.

I could see now where the dart had entered. Just as Nelson said, he'd been ironed alongside the dorsal fin, and the dart was deep in his body.

It was getting time to head back, so Johnny headed the *Aphrodite* for the green bell.

"I figure we'll make the bell in two hours and twelve minutes at this speed," he said, "give or take a half hour or so," he added with a grin. "These tides tend to foul up a man's dead reckoning." The visibility was very poor due to a thick haze. I had been wondering how Johnny was going to get us back.

"You never know for sure," he said. "You just try to keep track of all the zigs and zags, estimate your position, then hope. Those bells and hooters sure sound sweet when you're headin' home in a heavy haze or fog. When you don't hear them quite as soon as you figured, you begin to think someone must have moved them. But somehow it doesn't usually turn out that way. They're almost invariably where they should be."

And sure enough they were, and we were soon entering Menemsha Bight on a boiling fair tide. Johnny eased her alongside the dock in front of Herb Flanders' Store, where quite a crowd was gathered to see if we'd had any luck. I felt very professional when I heard some of the questions that were being asked by the sightseers.

When I told Mr. Flanders some of the questions I'd heard, he said, "Why that's nothin'. Lady come in the other day. Seems as how she wanted to know how many swordfish she should buy to serve a family of five!"

As busy as Nelson was hunting, fishing, and flying, plus making money by oyster barrelful, he did not quite feel at peace within himself. For one thing, he was becoming nauseated with what he called "codfish aristocracy" and the empty, vain life associated with the pleasure-mad group of New Englanders of which he and Ruth were a part. To be sure, they had many warm friends among them, but they all seemed to be dancing their way to hell—if there, indeed, was such a place.

> And o'er his heart a shadow
> Fell as he found
> No spot of ground
> That looked like Eldorado ...

Chapter 6
LIVE FREE OR DIE

IN 1774, A PLUCKY band of patriots removed powder and guns from Fort William and Mary at New Castle, New Hampshire. This was the first aggressive act of the Revolutionary War. Later, New Hampshire troops played a leading part in the fighting at Bunker Hill, near Concord, using the captured munitions. Then the victory of General John Stark of New Hampshire, at the Battle of Bennington, brought independence closer. Finally, on January 5, 1776, six months before the Declaration of Independence was signed in Philadelphia, legislators in New Hampshire proclaimed that state's independence from Great Britain.

New Hampshire's motto, "Live Free or Die!" (from a message that Stark sent to be read at an anniversary of the Battle of Bennington), expresses the spirit of Nelson Blount in the early 1950s. He turned his eyes to the state of New Hampshire as a place to take his family to escape the incessant social and business pressures that seemed to be taking them to a slow but sure death.

"You know, Fred," Nelson confided to his business associate one day, "I've had it up to here! This is all nothing but a phony existence. Make more money to do more. To go faster is just for the birds! I'm sick of simply spinning my wheels. Get up in the morning, work, and go to bed at night—all for the purpose of basic security. But what is basic security? What is there security in? This is what gets me!"

Fred muttered a few consoling words to try to bring Nelson back on the main line. Nelson was never satisfied with today. He was always looking for tomorrow; what was up ahead interested him, not the passing scenery.

In one conversation with Fred Richardson, in about 1953, Nelson, sure that an ulcer was eating away at his stomach, broke down and wept. Nothing completely satisfied, and there seemed to be no answer to his dilemma.

Among other things, world affairs perplexed Nelson. Even though fighting in Korea had ceased in June of 1953, that year marked the start of the eighth year of fighting in Indochina. Israel and the Arab powers continued to squabble, and efforts to organize a European army came to a stalemate. To make matters worse, the rumblings of atomic bombs in Russia, in September, made the Cold War colder. Then in October, Vice President Richard M. Nixon left on a nine-week goodwill tour of the Far East.

But to Nelson Blount, there was little or no goodwill left in the world, unless it was toward those who would scratch your back just the right way—with dollar bills. Where on the earth did kind feelings exist? They were seldom found among nations or employees and employers. Maybe there were some between fathers and sons and husbands and wives, but not a great deal. If they were there at all, they might disappear tomorrow.

To Nelson, the world was in a mess. There was no hope and no way out.

One day back in 1946, hope had glimmered as Fred Richardson introduced Nelson to the goals of technocracy (government by technical leaders). The philosophy had sprung up in the depression years of the 1930s, among a group of engineers, scientists, and technologists. They believed that since machines had brought about overproduction, new ways had to be found to organize and control industry. They urged industrial planning for the future and government management.

Nelson had gone for technocracy like a late commuter grabbing for the 7:06. But by the 1950s, technocracy had already had its run, and there were few riding that train anymore. Yet, it still looked good to the man who was always thinking about tomorrow, and he got out his checkbook to contribute regularly to Technocracy, Inc., a foundation in Pennsylvania. He also attended meetings, crammed on the subject until early morning hours, and even let someone fly his plane with a streamer advertising, "Join Technocracy Now."

In June of 1953, Nelson spoke to the Bristol Rotarians at the White Rail Riding Club, expounding on the benefits of the philosophy. A news item reported the event in these terms:

> Chiding our present economic system of wholesale deficit spending, Blount told his audience ... that under Technocracy we would have an economy which would give every person over twenty-five years of age an annual purchasing power equivalent to $20,000 in 1929 money for working three hours a day three days [a week]. At the age of forty-five, the workers would automatically [be] forced to retire.
>
> Blount said that increased use of machinery [and technology] is doing away with manpower and purchasing power. He said Technocracy would bring a

readjustment in the present price system whereby the tools of industry would be used for the "good of man instead of to his detriment."

Wherever he got a chance, and to whomever would listen, Nelson championed the cause of technocracy. "We've become morally deficient," he told a reporter for the *Providence Evening Bulletin*. "The real things in life are being neglected. We've neglected religion. We're all for ourselves. We're on the verge of the Garden of Eden, where machines will do all the work, but we may destroy ourselves because of selfishness."

"Money! Money! What's money?" he remarked to the reporter with scorn. He indicated that he would like to do away with money entirely and issue "energy certificates." Then to show his regard for money, he showed the label inside the jacket of his suit. It had been manufactured by a maker of inexpensive clothes.

As was mentioned earlier in the book, in the late forties, Nelson added cranberries to his many interests, as he invested heavily in Ocean Spray Cranberries Inc., which led the way in putting cranberry sauce on Thanksgiving and Christmas tables.

Marcus L. Urann, Ocean Spray president, had had his eye on Nelson for years and continued expressing his admiration for Nelson's ability in operating their joint venture, Plymouth Packing Company, in the mid-forties. In 1946, Nelson had joined him in British Columbia in a company called Cascade Foods, an Ocean Spray subsidiary. Then in 1948, Urann had further business ideas.

"Look, Nelson, why don't you give up on clams and come on over with me," he challenged. "Your business is peanuts compared to Ocean Spray."

"Look, Mr. Urann, you've made your way in life. I've got to make mine. I don't want to hang on your coattail."

"All right, Nelson, do both. Come with Ocean Spray, and run Blount Seafood on the side. How about it?"

Urann had been almost like a father to Nelson. It was not easy to turn him down. "Look, you'd better talk to my wife. If she says 'yes,' then I'll consider it."

One day, Urann appeared with his secretary at the Blount home. Ruth had a good idea why they were there. Urann painted a glowing picture of added wealth and prestige, but it only made Ruth see red—cranberry red, if you please.

"Look, Mr. Urann, you are kind to make us such an offer. But Nelson has a family, and we never see him now. If he takes on more and goes with a company with plants all over the United States, well, that would be it! I think I'd divorce him."

Hearing this news, Nelson gave Urann a positive "no." Then to show his appreciation, he began pouring more and more into Ocean Spray stock. By 1953, he was one of the largest individual stockholders in the firm.

This, together with his other industrial interests, meant more money and more pressures. The social whirl went faster and faster, like a runaway train heading for disaster. The Blounts were on "top of the social pile" those days in Barrington, hobnobbing with codfish aristocrats, the well-to-do, goodtime crowd.

The week's schedule left both Nelson and Ruth dizzy and breathless, breathless like a "belly puffer" nearing the end of a mile-long grade. Nelson went to Rotary on Tuesday nights, and another night, there was usually some other meeting. The other nights, Ruth would usually join him for dinners with friends or perhaps dancing or cocktail parties at the country club. Both Nelson and Ruth drank very little, as alcoholic beverages were not to their tastes. Usually, it was a matter of just standing and chatting jovially while holding a glass.

"I played poker a little," Nelson later remembered. "A gang of guys would come over and play poker once in a while, but I'd slip off to bed at about eleven o'clock. One night Ruth was standing watching, and they set her up with some chips, and she won everything around. She bought a war bond for Ted with her winnings."

In their years at 1 Manor Road in Barrington's Country Club Manor section, Ruth delighted in holding parties and showers for the "girls." One get-together was for Penny Richardson, Fred's wife. The Richardsons were routed from their apartment by fire in early 1954, and Ruth held a shower to help Penny replace the personal articles and household linens that were destroyed. That evening, the Blount home took on a festive appearance.

Ruth especially remembered the New Year's Eve parties she and Nelson threw. "Everyone looked forward to our New Year's Eve parties because we served open oysters and little necks on the half shell. We had champagne punch. I didn't have anything to do with spiking it. I made all the hors d'oeuvres. I never was happy at these parties. I had not been brought up that way. My family had money, but we lived simply. But Nelson had gotten to the point where he was in business and was with these people all the time, and we felt this was a good time to pay them back by having a New Year's Eve party."

In 1966, with no malice toward any of his old Country Club Manor friends but rather feelings of goodwill, Nelson fairly exploded when he discussed the "phony existence" of the former days. It simply did not satisfy.

Nelson said that all of his old friends were solid, community-minded citizens, people with blue blood in their veins. Like most Americans in the pressure cooker of the modern age, they had their frustrations, tensions, and problems. They were seeking answers to life and attempting to find fulfillment and satisfaction in materialism and a social whirl.

Sometimes Nelson mentally condemned them, but the next thought was, *Look, you are no better. You're doing the same thing. You've got everything money can buy, and still you aren't happy. You don't know why you're here or what life's all about!* Then he would look at his growing family—four children in 1953 and one on the way. *Why you're raising a bunch of kids who are going to be nothing but a bunch of spoiled adults when they grow up. They're living too soft a life, following in the footsteps of the rest of us. But what's the answer?*

Many of the Blounts' problems in Country Club Manor were the same as those experienced by any parents. A note from a schoolteacher, dated May 18, 1953, illustrates this:

DEAR MR. AND MRS. BLOUNT,

Mr. Reid asked me to tell you that Teddy scratched two circles with his scissors in the surface of his desk. He also made another hole in the surface. His desk was new this year. Mr. Reid says [he] must refinish the top, and hopes you would make him earn the money himself to pay for this. For particulars get in touch with Mr. Reid.

When Nelson began talking seriously of leaving the charming Country Club Manor neighborhood for wide-open spaces somewhere "to get away from it all," a few people raised eyebrows, to be sure. But none went higher than Ruth's, the day Nelson steamed in and pinched her cheek, announcing, "Jimmy, I've got a big surprise for you. Just closed a deal for a nice little farm up in Massachusetts. I've got it all furnished and everything. It'll be quiet, for there are no other people around; we can get away from it all and get to know each other as a family. It's got—"

"Nelson Blount, you listen to me. I'm all for moving, but it won't be a completely isolated place—not with you traveling. You aren't going to leave me on a lonely farm with the children."

And so a memorable little episode began. Like the average husband might thoughtfully go out and buy a bunch of flowers for his spouse, Nelson had bought a little farm "up in Mass." But whereas the average wife throws her arms around her husband and kisses him when he brings roses, Ruth, as tired as she was of the codfish whirl, wanted that isolated farm like she wanted the Boston & Maine clattering through the living room.

Nelson got the point quickly and rented his most recent investment, but only after Ruth looked the place over and stuck to her original decision regarding it.

But the incident had its good points. The right kind of farm in a nice area near people—this Ruth would consider. And the more they talked as a family, the more it seemed that New Hampshire, where they often had enjoyed visiting, could help revitalize the jaded Blounts.

Thus New Hampshire, with its rugged mountains, 1,300 shimmering lakes, and winding rivers beckoned enticingly. Tens of thousands of tourists and sportsmen flocked to the popular winter sports areas to enjoy skiing, winter carnivals, and dogsled races. And with the melting of the deep snows, the noisy cog train hauled sightseers to the top of 6,288-foot Mt. Washington, the tallest peak in the northeastern United States.

Through a friend, Nelson learned of a place he thought had possibilities. It was near Dublin in the Monadnock region, long known as the Currier and Ives Corner, covering southwestern New Hampshire. In this appealing up-and-down country, fifteen peaks towered more than 1,500 feet high. Its Early American atmosphere would make Ruth feel at home: venerable homes; splendid lawns and giant shade trees; picturesque, covered, and stone-arch bridges; wide, lush village greens; and gleaming frame churches with majestic, pillared steeples.

Dublin itself, Nelson discovered, was a snug, old village that received its town charter from King George III in 1771. As the state's highest village (elevation, 1,493 feet), Dublin catered to many of the well-heeled of New England; its summer population swelled considerably over the approximately 1,000 permanent residents.

The village was on State Highway 101, between Keene to the west and Peterborough to the east. Peterborough was home to the first tax-supported, free, public library, which opened in 1833. Perhaps Dublin itself was best known as the home of *Yankee* magazine and the *Old Farmer's Almanac*.

Outside Dublin, four miles to the south, Nelson sniffed the sparkling mountain air and viewed a country estate owned by a chain department store executive. The Cape-Cod-style main house was built in the late 1700s. The property had once been owned by the Boston Cabots and used as a summer home and grazing land for their cattle.

About 1939, a Cabot had spent an estimated $300,000, adding on to the main house to give it a total of seventeen rooms. He also built a farmer's house, a chauffer's house, a gardener's cottage, and a guest house.

The department store executive had taken it over in the early forties. He built an automated chicken house, and, at one time, had as many as 60,000 chickens. During the war, he made money, but hard times hit afterward. Now, after a heart attack, he had the place up for sale. At this point, Nelson appeared on the scene and made him a firm offer.

Nelson surveyed the slopes of majestic, old Mt. Monadnock, which looked wisely down at the two dickering men. "I don't doubt that you've spent plenty on it, but I've made my offer. It's as high as I'll go. I don't especially want this place. I know of a nice farm I can buy for $20,000 that will satisfy me. The only reason I would consider this place is that my wife likes it, and there are houses around. The other place she'd be by herself, and she's been telling me she doesn't want to live in the sticks by herself. This really is the only reason why I'd even talk to you about so large a place."

Nelson turned confidently on his heel and left the owner simmering over the offer.

Two days later, Nelson returned. "What about it, Mr. W?"

"Mr. Blount, you drive a hard bargain, but I'm going along with your offer," the owner began. "You're a young guy, and I like your family. I love this place, and I'd like to see somebody really get some mileage out of it. Go ahead. It's yours."

That is how New Hampshire got the Blounts.

Ruth received the news regarding the purchase with delight. So did the children.

"Look," Nelson announced gleefully, "we'll move up there, and we'll live in the mountains in the winter, and we'll go on the yacht in the summer. Summers we'll swordfish, and we'll be up here in the winter. We'll really have a great life together. I haven't been much of a father, but I'll start being a real father. I'll put the business second and really turn over a new leaf, and we'll get with it."

"Now you're talking!" Ruth exclaimed. As if he had suddenly produced a bouquet of roses, she kissed him warmly on the lips.

There were people to say "good-bye" to. Most chuckled and bet the Blounts would be back in Barrington within a year.

In a way, it was hard to say "good-bye" to the house at 1 Manor Road. And it was not easy to pull up stakes and leave lovely, old First Methodist Church of Warren. For thirty-one years, Nelson had attended the white-spired church, and only a few years before, had donated a Maas vibrachimes carillon system. He chuckled as he remembered the reactions to the chimes. Though the church and even the town council had accepted the chimes gratefully, townspeople during the first three weeks were not so sure they appreciated Nelson's gift. A news item asserted:

> People living nearby ... claimed the loud ringing was getting on their nerves. Some couldn't go to sleep and others were awakened by them during the night. The chimes will have not only their volume cut from four to two amplifiers, but they will sound forth only between the hours of 7:00 AM and 10:00 PM, according to the donor.

Respected layman that he was, Nelson was invited to deliver the sermon at the eleven o'clock service on May 16, 1954, a short while before the move to New Hampshire. One story said, "Mr. Blount took as his subject, 'This I Believe,' and he was listened to very attentively."

An admirer wrote: "I just want to congratulate you on the fine sermon you delivered yesterday. Your sincerity and humility made your views most impressive. It takes a lot of courage to testify openly to one's beliefs and I know that you did it voluntarily."

The church later honored the Blounts at a farewell reception, and the family left the Barrington-Warren area smiling over the skit detailing various events of Nelson's thirty-one-year membership in the church.

The Blounts arrived in Dublin, and Nelson soon began putting Staghead Farm together. In the months ahead, he built up a herd of eighty registered Holstein cattle, including Dawn Fascination, an artificially bred two-year-old from the University of New Hampshire, which he bought for $3,550. He added 3,000 laying hens and a horse for each of his five children. The original farm consisted of about 400 acres, but ultimately, he expanded it to nearly 1,000 acres.

Neighboring estates were owned by people whose names were well-known in American industry and politics. Especially for Ruth's sake, it was nice to have these neighbors relatively near (At least the farm was not isolated!). There were also several homes on the farm itself that could be rented out. If they did not like the occupants, the Blounts could ask them to move (and they ultimately did ask a couple of families to leave).

For Nelson, just being 110 miles from jangling phones and office pressures made the move well worthwhile. But beyond that, the smells of the farm brought back nostalgic memories of his boyhood days at the old Nelson farmstead. As a result, he delighted in walking in the fields and working right alongside the farmhands.

Once, a visitor observed a worker energetically operating a manure spreader and commented to the dairy foreman, "Look at that guy work. Good help like that is hard to come by nowadays!"

"He's no hired hand; that's Nelson."

Nelson loved stripping to the waist and letting the warm New Hampshire sun tan his back as he worked. Mountain breezes played tag with his hat as he rode mightily over his rolling farmland on a red tractor.

But even on a quiet farm, things can happen that make a man realize just how uncertain life is from one moment to another. Nelson shared about an incident his first year at Staghead: "We were haying on the farm. We have one hill that is very steep, and I was driving my tractor, cutting hay. I made a circle as I went up the hill, and as I turned the tractor, it started to tip with me on it. So I turned the wheel and jumped and landed a few feet from the cutterbar. The tractor was going about two miles an hour, and as I jumped, the tractor righted itself and headed past me. The cutterbar took off most of my clothes as I lay on the ground. I still have the clothes that were ripped off. Fortunately, I was not hurt—only a few scratches. It was just a miracle. The tractor continued on until it ran into a tree. I was badly shaken by this event, because I could have had both my arms cut off, or been killed, but the Lord was with me."

Though Dublin was home, and Staghead was the big thing of the moment in Nelson's life, there were flying trips to Warren to Blount Seafood. Nelson concluded that Executive Vice President Fred Richardson was doing a better job running the place than he himself had. So though Nelson kept on top of the business affairs and did selling, trips became less frequent as time went on.

Summers, at least July and August, were still given over to swordfishing off the *Aphrodite* in Cape Cod waters, just as Nelson had promised the family. During those weeks, Staghead Farm flourished under the capable direction of Farm Manager Donald Burnham.

By the summer of 1955, there were seven Blounts aboard the *Aphrodite*, including two young, future swordfishermen—Steve, born in 1952, and Billy, born in 1954. Ted and Carolyn helped Ruth mind the small siblings, including seven-year-old Bobby, permitting Ruth to join in the fun of landing some of the challenging monsters of the sea.

But as much fun as it was to ply the sparkling blue-green waters off Martha's Vineyard and scan the surface for a sunning swordfish, the family always whooped when they returned to Staghead. They were anxious to talk with Donald Burnham and hear the latest stories about happenings on the sprawling farm. Small Bobby especially loved returning to the farm, for he was to be the farmer among the children.

Probably the most exciting time at the farm, so far as Nelson was concerned, was spring. At Staghead, it was ushered in by 5,000 clanging pails—this, long ahead of robins and crocuses, the traditional harbingers that in many sections of the land announce the early demise of winter and the coming of the good months. Staghead became an attraction to visitors as one of the largest producers of maple syrup in the southwestern section of the state. Annually, in March and April, Nelson and his farmhands would hang buckets, often bucking seven-foot snow drifts to get into the sugar bushes.

Wearing a red cap, a black-and-red-checked jacket, and olive work slacks, Nelson excitedly fired up the big evaporator in the sugarhouse and boiled the sap in the syrup-making process. "It's like running a steam engine," he often told visitors as he turned various valves. He had innovated unconventional preheaters to heat sap using smokestack exhaust.

Back in Rhode Island, he would crow of the good life on the farm, telling skeptical friends who had predicted an early return to Country Club Manor that there was nothing quite as satisfying as early spring at Staghead. He would pound ears seemingly for hours about syrup-making experiences, until the listener wished for a sample of the product.

"Really, we're having a great time!" Nelson would boast. "Some of the greatest and most enjoyable days of my life have been making maple syrup with all my kids helping. We all work. We have horse-drawn sleighs out picking up the sap, as well as three Caterpillar tractors involved in the operation."

Then he would wax eloquent on other details of syrup-making: "Cold nights and warm, clear days during which the sun warms the trees, with the wind blowing gently out of the northeast, gets the sap running and makes the syrup sapping good. For about eight weeks, we're making syrup almost daily. In some cases, it's necessary to boil as many as sixty gallons to get one gallon of syrup. It averages about thirty-five to forty gallons of sap to get a gallon of syrup. Say, you ought to taste some of our syrup from Staghead! I'll send you some."

And he did. Those that got it agreed that syrup from Staghead was, indeed, superb—excellent with flapjacks on a cool, New England, spring morning.

As the years passed, Nelson Blount became increasingly known throughout the southern section of New Hampshire, his many interests making him something of a legendary figure. His farm continued to attract visitors; stories were written about his hunting, fishing, and flying adventures; and everyone knew how he had made his million before he was thirty and of his reputation as a champion of the vanishing breed of great, snorting Iron Horses.

Traditionally a church-going family, the Blounts became pillars in the Dublin Community Church, whose white spire made it the tallest building in the town. That it was not a Methodist church bothered Ruth and Nelson at first. It was especially hard for Nelson, since he had been Methodist for so long. Baptist-Methodist Ruth also had to make a few adjustments.

Nelson once asked the minister why they did not have communion, and he explained that the church had people with varying views and, therefore, communion was not observed to avoid offending anyone. Jesus Christ was recommended as an example to follow, but even at that, He was seldom mentioned, for dissertations from the pulpit usually concerned social issues and had little or no biblical content.

In reality, the church was Unitarian rather than nondenominational as the name seemed to imply. However, Nelson was not one to quibble about labels. After all, were not the Unitarians just another branch of the Protestant Church?

In his quiet, comfortable hideaway in New Hampshire's peaceful hills, F. Nelson Blount continued to fret. His move had not made much difference. His children were still growing up as products of a spoiled society. There were still new business problems as close as the telephone. And national and international affairs seemed to be going from bad to worse.

Nelson often admired rugged, old Monadnock as it smiled benevolently upon Staghead. "Monadnock is a mountain strong," Ralph Waldo Emerson had declared in his famous poem named for the grand, old peak. It stood tall and majestic, like a king. When in ages past, water and winds wore away surrounding mountains, Monadnock had remained.

What would it take to keep Nelson Blount's chin up and for him to remain tall and strong in a world being flattened by the eroding winds and waters of life? Nelson did not know, but he did know he was not made out of the same stuff as Monadnock. He had come to dwell under the shadow of the mountain to escape the social whirl. However, behind the facade of the man whom most people thought was a stalwart, secure citizen, there lived a somewhat melancholy, frightened millionaire who kept hoping his next venture would satisfy longer and give a measure of peace to his heart and mind.

There was one lifelong ambition he had not fulfilled, despite his affluence: to be a railroad engineer. If only he could have his own railroad. Then when he wanted to get away from the pressure of life, he could go out and run an engine. Maybe he could even load up his problems in a gondola and dump them far, far away!

> [He] had journeyed long,
> Singing a song,
> In search of Eldorado …

Chapter 7
EDAVILLE'S TWO-FOOTERS

TALL, PLEASANT-FACED ELLIS D. Atwood, a distant cousin of Nelson Blount, seethed every time he thought about what was happening to the two-foot-gauge railroads that had survived the 1886 agreement of most roads to adopt a four-foot, eight-and-a-half-inch "standard gauge." The colorful Maine two-footers—among them the Bridgton & Saco River Railroad; Kennebec Central Railroad; Sandy River & Rangeley Lakes Railroad; and Wiscasset, Waterville & Farmington Railroad—had long before the turn of the century hauled logs and slate and people. In 1941, the last of the stout, little engines and wonderland cars were being scrapped, and the impersonal but efficient diesels were making the "Midget Steam Empire of the North Woods" only a memory.

Old-time railfans would always remember them, but children of the modern age would never have the thrill of watching or riding behind the Lilliputian locomotives that whistled while they worked.

Edaville's Two-footers

Ellis Atwood, owner of the largest one-man cranberry plantation in the world (1,800 acres) at South Carver, Massachusetts, thirty-two miles south of Boston and near Plymouth Rock, boldly took matters into his own hands in 1941. He decided to bring the midget engines back to Massachusetts, where seventy years before, the very first American Lilliputian had been built and operated. He began buying two-foot equipment, but World War II hindered his transporting it to South Carver until 1946. Then he began setting up a little railroad to meander through his cranberry bogs. Using his own initials, E.D.A., he named it Edaville Railroad and dubbed it, The Cranberry Belt. Eight little engines—four steam and four mechanical locomotives—went to work hauling cranberries harvested from the bogs.

A kind man, Atwood invited children to coax Mom and Dad to come to Edaville for a five-and-a-half-mile ride on his exciting narrow-gauge road. At first, the rides were free. Then when high costs caused his freight line to bow to trucks, passengers began buying tickets. Thousands flocked to Edaville, and it became a major tourist attraction in the Bay state.

But then in November of 1950, tragedy struck Edaville, leaving the future of the little railroad a big question mark. A heating unit in the cranberry screenhouse exploded, taking the life of Mr. Atwood.

Soon, offers to buy the equipment came to Elthea Atwood, his widow, from such well-known figures as Gene Autry and Walt Disney, who wanted to take Edaville's little engines and cars out west. But for five years, Mrs. Atwood faithfully kept the railroad running, even though profit-and-loss figures matched the color of the cranberries in the Edaville bogs.

In September of 1955, thirty-five miles away, Nelson Blount's ears, which had been tuned to the faint, faraway whistle of approaching trains when he was a boy, heard what sounded like the mournful, departing whistle of Edaville. It appeared that the Lilliputian engines and cars would soon leave Massachusetts.

Nelson picked up the phone on his desk at Blount Seafood Corporation and put through a call to Mrs. Atwood. He identified himself. Then he could feel the hard steel of a throttle in his hand as he announced, "Mrs. Atwood, Edaville simply must not close; it belongs to New England, and I think we should keep it alive for Mr. Atwood's sake. Tell you what I'll do: I'll buy the road and run it myself . . ." He slouched back in his chair and talked Edaville for another ten minutes.

The price settled on was in the tens of thousands of dollars, and for Nelson Blount, a boyhood dream had come true: he, at last, owned a railroad!

Actually purchased in the name of the Blount Seafood Corporation, Edaville became Nelson's number one interest in the middle and late fifties. He fired up the boiler of his imagination and went full steam ahead with plans for developing Edaville. At home, Ruth both encouraged him and cautioned him. At the plant, confidant Fred Richardson applauded the move, but like Ruth, he also tried to keep Nelson on the mainline.

In early December of 1955, wearing topcoat, a bow tie, and an engineer's cap, Nelson was at the throttle of a midget engine as he escorted some fifty newsmen on a tour. Typically, before haranguing the men with the wonders of Edaville, Nelson would put on a feast: clams and oysters on the half shell, clam chowder, roast beef, ham, candied yams, relishes of all kinds (including pickled cranberries from the nearby bogs), sliced onions, crackers, cheese, cakes, coffee, cranberry juice, and cranberry sherbet for dessert.

Officers were introduced: F. Nelson Blount, president; Frederick H. Richardson, vice president; and Dalton K. Stratton, treasurer.

Then like a politician full of promises, Nelson addressed the gathering, asserting he would continue practically the same schedule as his predecessor to "give everyone an opportunity to enjoy the only two-foot-gauge railroad east of the Mississippi and probably in the United States." He announced that he would expand the railroad museum and add his antique automobiles and his collection of Kentucky rifles, the largest of its kind anywhere.

A little later, Nelson called in his foghorn voice: "Boaaaard!"

The men climbed on the little train with its red, yellow, green, and orange wooden coaches. Nelson took his place in the cab of the high-stacked, little puffer, and moments later, with a *toot, toot, toot*, eased open the throttle.

Some of the men rode in the special-built, open-air observation car. Others strolled the length of the train, from caboose through the observation cars and the coaches, bringing back memories of a more leisurely way of life.

At each crossing, the little engine sounded its plaintive whistle, and black smoke billowed from its stack. Old-timers broke out with goose bumps.

The excursion whipped through Cranberry Valley and roared past Rusty River and the Golden Spike, where the last spike on the Edaville Railroad was driven in 1946. Then the train tooted by Reservoir, Sunset Vista, Ball Park, Mount Urann, Plantation Center, Eda Avenue, and finally chugged back to Edaville. Peacedale was also a station, with its miniature New England village of the 1850 era. Memorial Whistle Post was later added. There the engine would blow twice in memory of Edaville's founder, Mr. Atwood.

The long, green ticket the rider purchased at the ticket window was, like the train, reminiscent of days gone by. "Notices" had good logic behind them: "Parents, please watch your children at all times;" "No one allowed on the roofs of the railroad cars;" and "Tobacco chewing allowed only on observation cars or cabooses."

At Edaville, five engines took turns pulling trains. They were made between 1913 and 1924. Four were from Maine, and one was from a Louisiana sugar plantation. Their steam boilers rated at 150 to 175 pounds a square inch.

At Edaville, tourists and railfans flocked to the engines on exhibit just beyond the station platform. Among them was the original *Flying Yankee*, a Boston & Maine diesel locomotive, New England's first streamliner, which was placed in service in 1935 and ran up 2,737,735 miles before being retired to Edaville in 1957.

The museum contained 1,000 items to thrill rail buffs and others interested in Americana. Those who had seen a retired, railroad brakeman with one or more fingers missing could find an explanation in the museum: Included among the many displays was a model of the old coupling system known as the link-and-pin. Before automatic couplings came into existence, a steel, oval-shaped ring was used to hitch two cars together. As the cars came together, the ring was slipped into place and a steel pin dropped through to hold the link. A safety tool to hold the ring was issued, but because it was often awkward to use, many men ignored it. Once in a while, the cars crashed together too rapidly. Men whose reflexes were too slow were painfully sorry for ignoring the safety tool!

Countless other items, such as contemporary, colored pictures of mile-long trains and conductors' watches and signaling devices, told their story of the wonderful Steam Age.

Added to railroadiana were countless other items of the past. For years Nelson Blount collected vintage automobiles and antique, fire trucks. He owned more than forty fire trucks, many of which made their way to Edaville, along with some that were loaned for exhibit. Of special interest were completely equipped stores, just as they appeared in the 1800s, from the general store to the old. And there were scads of toy and scale-model trains and locomotives, most of which were from the Blount collection.

Almost worth the thirty-five-cent ticket of admission was the gun collection, something that Nelson perhaps cherished next to his collection of railroadiana. It was no ordinary collection by any means and had items that many other museums could not match.

Nelson remembered the day a repeating flintlock pistol fell into his hands. A Mr. Rooke, a Briton, noticed a display of Blount guns in a bank window in Providence. He walked in and announced: "I have a gun that's probably the most valuable gun in the world today. Maybe Mr. Blount would be interested."

After a phone call from the bank, Nelson later contacted Rooke. His father was a wealthy man in England at one time, he told Nelson; he himself was an inventor who had lost everything, and the gun was his last possession of any value.

"He hadn't had a meal for a couple days, and his clothes were terrible looking," Nelson later recalled. "I didn't recognize the gun, but I knew it was a rare piece. I gave him a meal and bought him some clothes. I took the gun and told him I would have it appraised.

"I found out that the gun once belonged to the King of England and was built by Grice in 1710. It had gold and silver inlays with the crown of the king on it, and I was told you could not put a value on it in dollars and cents.

"When I went back to talk to Rooke, I learned that he had died and had no relatives. So I bought the gun for a mite of what it was worth. It's probably worth at least $10,000 today. The Tower of London has offered me a number of other pieces in exchange, pointing out that there were only eight known in the world like it and that this one was the best of the eight."

Besides this gun and more than 500 Kentucky rifles (only a portion at Edaville), the Blount collection boasted several Wyatt Earp guns and clothes worn by Earp. Nelson also had the "greatest" powder horn, made by Paul Revere for General Lord Howe, commander of English forces in America, twenty years before the Revolution. Then there was an eight-foot rifle, believed to have been the first gun made in America. It was marked "#1 Plymouth." And there was Sitting Bull's rifle, with its twenty-eight brass tacks, indicating the number of whites he had cut down.

The dueling pistols once owned by the Duke of Sussex attracted their share of attention too. To get them, Nelson had to bid against King Faruk of Egypt.

"I started this collection of guns in 1945," Nelson said. "A man on the street offered me a gun, which I recognized as a rather rare piece. It was a Colt Dragoon. Though it's a pistol, it's heavier than most hunting rifles; it weighs about ten pounds and is a tremendously awkward piece. He offered it to me for fifty dollars and told me it was worth much more. He was right, for today I could sell it for over $1,000. My entire collection would bring a small fortune."

An interesting sidelight item on Edaville: Blount hired Lewis E. Jerald, the engineer who in Nelson's boyhood talked Nelson's mother into letting him and his brother, Luther, visit the railroad yards. Jerald, who in 1955 had just retired at age sixty-nine from the diesel engine that daily hauled the *Mayflower Express* between Boston and New

Haven, proudly served at the throttle of Edaville engines for three years.

All told, as many as 250,000 people visited Edaville each year. Some 80,000 of those came in December, when the pint-sized engines fired up to haul dazzled, pink-cheeked children and their equally fascinated moms and dads through the often snow-covered, cranberry bogs. At night, 50,000-plus Christmas lights made Edaville a breathtaking sight, probably unequalled in all of New England and probably the entire United States.

But even after he bought the little railroad, Edaville, with all its festive lights did not bring "peace on earth and goodwill" in the heart and life of Nelson Blount.

> And, as his strength
> failed him at length,
> He met a pilgrim shadow ...

Chapter 8

A SKIDDING CAR

MONDAY, JANUARY 12, 1959, became unseasonably warm in New England, as a bright sun challenged the snow on the ground. In southern New Hampshire and on into Massachusetts, tiny rivulets trickled here and there into busy highways, and passing cars splashed through puddles, forming a brown slush along the roadside.

In Boston, in early afternoon, three women from Dublin removed their coats and carried them as they walked with anticipation to Raymond's on Washington Street. Passersby, in some instances, looked twice at the threesome, for it was not every day a woman as tall and pretty as Ruth Blount marched through a busy shopping district shouldering eight-foot skis, with attractive, shorter women flanking her.

"Other women can put their gifts in boxes or bags and exchange them," Ruth said, chuckling to her companions, Mary Rajaniemi and Harriet Gillespie. "But not Ruth Blount—her Christmas gift can't be hidden. Nelson insisted that he wanted me to have just what he ordered, and I know of no better way than to exchange them in person and get just the right skis."

Their mission accomplished, and with the new skis resting across the seats in the back of the 1957, green, Ford station wagon, the women, with Ruth at the wheel, drove out of Boston at about two o'clock on Highway 2 and stopped for refreshments at a Howard Johnson's restaurant in Concord.

The conversation was girl-talk—about people they knew, parties, husbands, and children. And Ruth said she could hardly wait to try out her new skis on a family outing at the Mittersill at North Woodstock, New Hampshire.

At about 3:30, Ruth, Mary, and Harriet were on their way again, laughing and talking. They had their coats on, for it was colder now that the sun was leaving.

Though it was more than two weeks away, Ruth was looking forward to the annual game supper in the church vestry. Nelson was to furnish moose, caribou meat, and cranberries, and she was general chairman of the affair. Mary and Harriet were working with Ruth. Tickets were only $1.50, and there would be movies of some of Nelson's hunting trips and of Edaville Railroad.

But Ruth wasn't going to be able to attend the event, for now, at nearly four o'clock, tragedy was about to strike.

On Highway 119, just south of the village of Groton, Ruth, an excellent driver, kept the station wagon at a slower-than-usual speed, about forty miles per hour, since here and there the highway was wet.

As she was rounding a turn, the vehicle suddenly lurched crazily and spun toward the opposite side of the highway. Ruth fought to control the wheel. Her two companions, without safety belts, screamed as they were thrown against the door on the right side. The door opened, and Mary and Harriet were thrown clear of the spinning car onto the highway, and the station wagon plowed into a tree. The impact shoved the hood through the windshield opposite Ruth, where her companions had been sitting. A ski shot through the windshield.

For Ruth, everything went black.

In Walpole, Nelson was talking with a salesman about tractors in the John Deere establishment. The phone rang. "Someone wants you, Mr. Blount," a man said, handing Nelson the phone.

"Mr. Blount? Your wife has been seriously injured in an auto accident near Groton ..."

The caller, a state highway patrolman, who had called Staghead Farm and was told where to find Nelson, gave hurried details. Ruth would soon be on her way to the Ayer Community Hospital, about eight miles from the accident scene. Ruth's two companions were being taken there too, but they seemed to be less seriously injured.

A state police lieutenant had gotten the call about the accident on Highway 119. As he went barreling into the same curve where the station wagon had skidded, the patrol car suddenly went out of control momentarily, but the lieutenant skillfully stopped. He had hit ice, which had formed from the melting snow. It was the same ice that had caused Ruth's station wagon to slam into the tree.

"You couldn't see the ice there; it was dry everywhere else," he later told Nelson. "So don't blame your wife. If other drivers hadn't been flagged by those who discovered the accident, she probably would have been killed by other cars smashing into her!"

As Nelson raced toward Ayer, police and a wrecker crew worked desperately to free Ruth. She was pinned against the door and left side of the instrument panel. Her right knee had jammed into the ignition key. Her left knee had slammed into the door handle. As the men worked, Ruth was bleeding from her eyes, nose, and mouth. She came to from time to time, calling for water and murmuring, "Why did I have to do this to you girls?"

Ruth's passengers, though hurt, were able to walk and were waiting anxiously for Ruth to be freed.

A motorist got into the back seat of the car and tenderly put his hands on Ruth's shoulders and held her to let her know someone cared.

After they finally extricated her more than an hour after the accident, ambulance attendants lifted her gently onto a stretcher.

"Don't give me morphine," Ruth gasped in a semiconscious state. "I'm allergic to it."

Ruth was being wheeled into the hospital emergency room as Nelson arrived. He said he would never forget his reaction and the events that immediately followed. He explained, "When I saw Ruth, I felt as if I had been hit with a sledgehammer. I had never been moved by the sight of blood before, having on numerous occasions dressed wild game—moose, elk, deer, bear. But to see my wife in such a bloody mess was almost more than I could take.

"She had a broken nose, a concussion, a fracture around the front of her right eye. In addition, her jaw was injured to the extent that she could hardly open her mouth; she had broken ribs; her right hip was broken in several places; both knees were smashed, one broken in more than fifty places.

"It was like a nightmare that wouldn't go away; yet I did not sleep at all that night. I kept telling myself this was not happening to me. But it was. You know, you never miss the water till the well runs dry. And I sat outside there with my head in my hands, as the doctor told me that they didn't think my wife would make it through the night. And if she did, she'd never walk again or be much good physically.

"She simply couldn't die, I told myself. How would I ever face my five children? Couldn't I write a check? Couldn't I call a lawyer? Usually I got out of jams this way, but in this case, I could do nothing.

"You know, they say there are no atheists in foxholes; I never was in a foxhole, but I'll tell you, there are no atheists in hospitals under conditions like this. I waited for five hours while they worked on her. You look to God, and you ask him to help you.

"But, you know, as I asked God to help me, I recognized that I had no reason, no right to ask God to do anything for me; yet I kept asking for the sake of my children. I said, 'Lord, save my wife for my children!'

"But I wasn't so sure that God would hear me at all in this jam. I had called on Him in the past—flying in fog at night, while running out of gas in my plane; or when the engine began to sputter, I'd pray, 'Lord, help me get down!'

"After I got down, I'd recognize God for a time, but it wore off. I'd go to church on Sunday and tip my hat to God, as it were, and then leave at noon and say, in effect, 'All right, God, nice seeing You; see You next Sunday.' I wanted to remain on speaking terms with God, but I didn't want Him to come too close unless I needed Him.

"This night at the hospital, in the hours I was in the room they gave me next to my wife, I realized I desperately needed God—needed Him as never before. Finally, I said, 'God, I mean business this time. I don't know all that's involved, but I'll really try to live for you. Please, just save my wife.'

"And, you know, I could almost feel then that she was going to make it. A peace stole into my heart."

But just the same, there were tense days ahead—many of them—for Nelson and the children, and certainly for Ruth.

Nelson's friend Dr. Jim Ballou, who later came to see Ruth, recommended that she be moved closer to home, to

A Skidding Car

the Peterborough Community Hospital, about five miles from Staghead Farm. Dr. Harold Lee, a bone surgeon from Boston, would begin putting Ruth back together in Peterborough.

Special consideration had to be given to the matter of moving Ruth from Ayer to Peterborough, about fifty miles away. Patrick McGinnis, then president of Boston & Maine Railroad, kindly offered a special train, but an ambulance was chosen since there would be minimal transfers of the patient. The trip saw Nelson preceding the ambulance. When his car hit a bump in the highway, the ambulance would slow down. Even though Ruth had been given sedatives and a frame had been built around her body to reduce the shock, Nelson and the ambulance driver wanted to take every possible precaution.

For three months, Ruth could move only by pulling on an overhanging bar and inching herself into a new position in her bed. Nelson came every day. One operation followed another, until she had a total of seven. A metal plate held her hip together, and a bolt in her knee enabled the injury to begin healing.

During the early weeks, little, three-year-old Billy broke his collarbone and was hospitalized near Ruth's room, but this news had to be kept from her.

At home, thirteen-year-old Carolyn grew up overnight, it seemed, and took charge, looking after the younger children.

In early April, Ruth was strong enough to be pushed about in a wheelchair, and a family reunion was planned. A table with a linen tablecloth, flowers, and place settings for seven was set up in a lounge on the first floor of the hospital.

As Nelson wheeled Ruth into the lounge, she saw Teddy and Carolyn, but for the moment, she did not see her younger children. Glad tears filled her eyes. Then she smiled as she saw her younger children too and the table set for seven.

It was indeed a happy occasion. There had been countless letters and "I-love-you-Mother" cards, most of them printed and colored by small hands. Little Billy had learned to write his name and signed some cards.

During the meal, Billy remained silent. What went on in his three-year-old mind, Ruth could not quite know. But when time came for Nelson to wheel Mother back to the room, Billy blurted out, "When you coming home?"

It was late April when Ruth came home the first time between operations, accompanied by her special nurse, Joan Pasquale. Ruth went back to the hospital twice after coming home in April.

Finally, the difficult days of therapy began, so important if Ruth was ever going to walk again. Sandbags were put on her legs, and she had to lift them. Rain or shine, she went into a cold lake, helped in by her nurse. There Ruth would tread water until she could take it no longer.

Even so, some of the best therapy was simply being back at home with her family. She had one meal with the family out on the porch every evening. Either Ted or Nelson came and lifted her into her wheelchair and wheeled her out.

However, one evening after dinner, Nelson went to the barn with the children, and Ruth was forgotten. She sat there shivering as the cool evening air settled over the countryside.

Finally, she screamed for help; only then did the family remember poor Mommy there all alone in her wheelchair. When Nurse Joan, who left each day at 3:00PM heard about it, she scolded Nelson, and thereafter, she called each evening to make sure Ruth was being well cared for.

In midsummer, Ruth returned to the hospital for a final operation. The plate was removed from her hip, and the bone was scraped. A blood clot resulted from the ordeal, and for several days, Ruth was bedfast, with one leg elevated. In the meantime, Nelson was going swordfishing for the remainder of the summer with two of the children, and Ruth began to beg to be allowed to return home when the blood-clot danger passed.

Undoubtedly, Dr. Edward Twitchell, assisting Dr. Lee on the case, saw an angle here. No, she could not go home until she began to walk.

Spunky Ruth accepted the challenge. The head nurse brought her a cane, and the supervisor and several nurses came to watch. Her pathetic efforts sent everyone away except the doctor and Joan Pasquale.

Three times Ruth tried and fell back into her chair. Then, finally, on her fourth attempt, she took a few wobbly but successful steps. The doctor's face brightened, and Joan squeezed Ruth's arm. But neither was happier than Ruth; she had walked! And she was going home!

In August, Ruth joined Nelson at their rented cottage in Menemsha on Martha's Vineyard. There her legs continued to grow stronger, and her confidence increased. She was determined to lay down her crutches and walk from the cottage to a little coffee shop about 300 yards away, and she did—slowly, courageously. This was a big milestone. Day by day, she attempted more exciting feats, and she conquered.

Within a year after her accident, Ruth was well on her way to being her old self. Although, even in 1966, she still tired from walking, had to carefully guard against falling, which could have reinjured her frail knees, and bore scars from the tragedy that nearly took her from her family.

As she recovered, both Nelson and Ruth believed God had smiled on them. They had had faith, and Ruth had come through. Together, they searched to know God better. But how did one find God outside of a church service?

They kept searching as they read books on various faiths. Maybe the churches they had been attending did not have all of the truth. They looked into Bahaism and sent donations to the headquarters. Jehovah's Witnesses called, and they seemed so earnest. Together, Ruth and Nelson read books on Mormonism and Christian Science. But all of those groups seemed far out. There was something missing.

As the months passed, Nelson particularly became more and more confused. In a sense, he had come in contact with God at the hospital. But where was He now?

One evening, Nelson heard Billy Graham preach on television, and the famous evangelist made startling statements. "You are born separated from God," he thundered. "You must be born again. You must receive Jesus Christ. That's all you must do to be saved. Jesus is the way to God. He paid for your salvation in full; you can't earn it or buy it. It's free."

Nelson sat alone in the beige, upholstered reclining chair in the living room of Staghead Farm, thinking about the message long after the program was over. Billy Graham made salvation sound so easy. Surely there was some catch. Surely a person was expected to do something to earn God's favor.

In despair, Nelson cried out, "Help me, God. If this is the truth, I want this. I don't know much about it, but Billy Graham talked from the Bible, and I believe the Bible—though I don't know what's in it. But if you're God, and I know You are, I want the truth. Help me!"

The Bible says, "Seek, and ye shall find." Nelson was seeking. Someday he would find.

Down the Valley of the Shadow,
Ride, boldly ride ...

Chapter 9
STEAM OVER STEAMTOWN

IN THE EARLY fifties, Nelson Blount had qualified as a locomotive engineer on the Boston & Maine, passing the traditional writing-of-the-rule-book test that involved 750 operating rules committed to memory. Somewhere, sometime, he wanted to be a railroad engineer. Even though he bought the Edaville Railroad in 1955, and he frequently handled the throttle on his narrow-gauge line, deep down within, he wanted a standard-gauge railroad.

Nelson knew he had to act fast if his dream was to come true. With the end of World War II, railroads had begun a move toward total dieselization. Even before the war, taps had blown for the Maine two-footers and other narrow-gauge stock, and now snorting standard-gauge Iron Horses were being scrapped by the hundreds.

In 1956, a year after Nelson bought Edaville, Boston & Maine President Patrick B. McGinnis signed papers donating the Edaville B & M's No. 1455 (a Mogul-type, 2-6-0 engine), a tender, a combine, and three coaches. It was Nelson's first standard-gauge stock. But getting it to Edaville found

Nelson reaching for aspirins and the yellow pages. A spur connecting with the New Haven near Tremont had been considered as the means for rolling the equipment into Edaville, but this idea was abandoned as impracticable. It would have required crossing a major state highway and a swamp. Thus, flatbed-transport trucks hauled the heavy, bulky equipment, with four big cranes being used for loading and unloading.

Acquisition of the stock whetted Nelson's appetite for more. And as he once had collected photographs of rolling stock, he began to beg and buy standard-gauge steam equipment from roads the country over. But where to put these monsters became an acute problem. It certainly did not make sense to take them to Edaville.

For a time, it appeared that the answer might be the Disneyland-like parks of Pleasure Island in Wakefield, Massachusetts, and Freedomland in the Bronx, New York.

Operators approached Nelson about his running a narrow-gauge train in each amusement center, and he signed an agreement, which also brought stationary steam equipment to each location. But extensive vandalism in Engine City, the imminent bankruptcy of Pleasure Island, and financial problems at Freedomland sent Nelson searching for solid ground for his standard-gauge stock.

And here began an episode that produced enough colorful characters and suspense to make good script material for a Broadway show, as one magazine writer termed it. As far as trains were concerned, it developed into the steamiest period of Nelson's career.

Terminal facilities of Boston & Maine at North Walpole, New Hampshire, on the Connecticut River (opposite historic Bellows Falls, Vermont), purchased in December of 1960, got the drama rolling. There, in a ten-acre railroad yard, he could display stationary stock and build a museum (400 by eighty-five feet for $288,000, he announced). In addition, he could start an excursion line for tourists and rail buffs. Equipment could be serviced in a five-stall roundhouse with a turntable, a coal chute, and a sand house.

Interestingly, the village across the river, Bellows Falls (the population was 3,831), where steam and smoke from Rutland trains had warmed hearts for a century, gave Nelson's Steamtown project the most encouragement at first. For on the evening of January 27, 1961, villagers gathered in the armory and generally cheered the move of the up-and-coming tourist attraction to the area.

Earlier, Nelson had told leaders about two locomotives he wanted to buy, and in the meeting, plans were presented to purchase the engines for $25,312.50 for Steamtown—if the museum project got off the ground and if Bellows Falls was mentioned in advertising.

Some felt it was illegal to appropriate monies for a project in another state (though only a whistle toot across the river), and there were objections to Blount's taking the floor because he was not eligible to vote. But when the smoke cleared, the good people of Bellows Falls voted 140 to eighty-five to donate the locomotives to show Nelson they were for him.

However, Nelson finally had to buy the two engines. For the drama took a sudden turn away from the Bellows Falls/North Walpole area. In early 1961, New England's number-one rail buff strolled into the State House in Concord and approached New Hampshire officials with a proposition. "Let the state build a railroad museum, and I'll donate twenty steam locomotives and certain other equipment," he suggested, puffing importantly on a cigar. "In conjunction with the museum, I would operate an excursion line."

Until then, few people downstate as far as Concord had heard of Steamtown, but at this point, Blount's million-dollar offer began making hot headlines throughout New England. Because State Highway Route 12 was slated to cut into the newly acquired property at North Walpole, Nelson suggested to state officials that he preferred a site at Keene (population 17,562), twenty miles southeast of Walpole. Governor Wesley Powell appointed a seven-man committee that began studying the matter during the spring of 1961, inspecting the museum site, talking to architects, and of course, talking with Nelson Blount.

In June of 1961, they made their initial report, stating that the project would cost at least $775,000, just for two buildings—a roundhouse and a station of traditional style with ticket window, waiting platform, and restaurant. Money for the Steamtown project would supposedly come from a $10,000,000 state recreational bond issue that had just been approved.

In the meantime, Nelson gabbed with the press. He wanted Granite State folks to get the vision of a "cavalcade of steam" and tried to excite interest with such statements as these:

> "[I have] in excess of forty steam engines and over fifty cars, which if placed end to end would be nearly two miles long."
>
> "I have one locomotive that was made famous because it pulled Roosevelt's special train from Worcester, Massachusetts, to Rockland, Maine, for a meeting with Winston Churchill in 1943."
>
> "I have had offered to me a portion of the Pennsylvania Railroad's famous collection, 'Locomotives on Parade,' that was on exhibit at the New York World's Fair in 1940." (This never became a reality for Steamtown because political steam kept the project in the dream stage so long.)

"We have one car that belonged to Mrs. Guggenheim, the copper heiress, a beautiful car later bought by the Boston & Maine for the president of the B & M. It's *The California*, listed in the Palace Cars of America, of which there were less than one hundred built."

In addition to some of this equipment, Blount announced that if New Hampshire would agree to build the museum, he, in turn, would reach down in his bag of railroad goodies and produce perhaps another locomotive or two, plus a miscellany of fire engines, steam rollers, and other steam engines of various types.

How would all of this help the area? As a guest editorialist in the *Keene Evening Sentinel* on June 29, 1961, the would-be donor put it this way:

If Steamtown U.S.A. is built in this area, Keene will be known in the future as the memorial city of steam, just as Plymouth is known for Plymouth Rock. Millions of interested tourists will come in the future to view these preatomic relics and ride behind the belching, hissing, puffing iron monsters. Children of the future will not be deprived of the enjoyment that we had in our youth of hearing, seeing, and riding behind these Iron Horses.

Blount had this to say in the same editorial regarding his offer:

As for the proposed Steamtown U.S.A. museum, it would be a state run and owned project, separate from the railroad except as to working jointly, promotion-wise, to make both a success.

The National Museum of Transport in St. Louis is already displaying twenty-six locomotives and other items of historical interest. It has recently been given one million from a bond issue to help construct new quarters.

The only difference is that St. Louis will not own, control, or receive revenue from the museum because it remains in the hands of the foundation.

You may ask why, then, did St. Louis spend this money? The answer is very clear: because it expects the museum to be a tremendous tourist attraction. My own offer to the state of New Hampshire is a much better one for the state. It would receive the revenue the museum produces, and within a few years pay off all building costs and add to the state's surplus.

Moreover, there is a big difference in public appeal between Steamtown U.S.A. and St. Louis. The museum here would boast operating trains, pulled by an old Iron Horse and would be alive and colorful.

As the Yankee politicians at Concord continued to study and debate the matter, the steam man readied equipment at North Walpole for the 1961 excursion season. Trains would chug along the Cheshire Branch of the B & M as far as Westmoreland. In 1962, if the museum went through, the runs would originate in Keene. But union problems and ICC red tape forced a delay, at least for 1961.

So Nelson highballed it to the office of the Claremont & Concord Railroad, a freight line, and arranged to use the C & C tracks from Bradford to Sunapee (a thirteen-mile stretch northwest of North Walpole). In July, the mournful wail of a steam locomotive's whistle echoed across that strip of New Hampshire countryside for the first time since 1945.

Many gathered to see old *No. 47*, a 4-6-4 T built in 1912 and formerly owned by the Canadian National. Rolling stock included four bright yellow, wooden passenger cars, plus a fire-control car, which followed the train to douse any fires that might be ignited along the tracks. Some children cried, reportedly afraid of the great hissing and puffing machine so different from the roaring, sophisticated diesels.

Tickets were $1.99 for adults and $0.95 for children. All-day tickets were available at special rates. Passengers were scarce, except for those from the immediate area, since North Walpole (not Bradford) had been listed as the terminal in advance advertising.

But interest picked up as the word spread, and by mid-August, the operation had settled into a routine. Then a villain appeared: an ICC inspector turned thumbs down on the locomotive. He pointed out only a few minor discrepancies in the condition of the engine. It had passed all necessary state tests. The main problem involved a long list of federal forms that had not been filed and certain papers that had not arrived from the original owner.

During the next days, Nelson haggled with Washington and finally announced, "We do not cross state lines, nor do we engage in interstate business; yet the ICC demands that we conform to their regulations. I refuse to place myself in the straitjacket that American railroads find themselves today—at least not voluntarily. So rather than submit, I have ceased operations."

The fourteen employees of the road, accompanied by a dog mascot, proceeded to picket the State House, carrying signs that said, "Save Our Jobs," and, "Save the Steam Train." Governor Powell indicated he would go to bat on the matter.

But it was all to no avail, and the firebox of *No.47* remained deathly cold while a leased C & C diesel pulled the yellow coaches on a few more trips. But, as Nelson had guessed, scenery without steam was not sufficient attraction. So before the end of September, all of the equipment rested back in the yards at North Walpole. Nelson kept the employees on the payroll, hoping that better days were ahead.

In early 1962, the ICC and Nelson made up. Nelson did all the conceding, as he recognized that ICC regulations affected all operations, not strictly those on private tracks.

Work began on a small 2-8-0, *Rahway Valley No. 15*, for use on runs from Keene to Westmoreland on the Connecticut River, after B & M approved use of its trackage. More passenger cars, including a steel parlor-diner, were also reconditioned. For the first time, the road became known as Monadnock Northern, "Steamtown &" being omitted. The shorter name sounded better, Nelson and associates agreed. (Although later, the longer name was often used.)

About 400 people, mainly children and railfans, welcomed *No. 15* as she rolled into Keene with eleven cars. "We put $10,000 in the engine," Nelson told a reporter. "Only the shell is left; the crew had to strip it down and rebuild it. We have to do that every five years because of ICC regulations, whether it's needed or not."

On the first run out of Keene, there were 375 paying passengers and forty guests who thrilled to the hissing steam, the plaintive whistle, and the noise of the huffing and puffing machine. No one aboard seemed to mind the acrid smoke, not even the group of theatrical players dressed in old-fashioned garb, who were appearing in, *The Streets of New York,* in the Keene Summer Theatre.

The run that summer was a mild success, with some 20,000 passengers, but the Steamtown issue still was being kicked around, and Nelson himself felt he was getting most of the bruises.

In a public meeting in Keene, one man was bodily carried out shouting and kicking. Blount considered suing him for slander but dropped the action. An Inquiring Citizens Committee rose up after townspeople voted 630 to eleven in favor of $100,000 toward the purchase of the site—which was later worth millions. There were some who objected to smoke. Others feared Blount was bringing another Coney Island to cheapen the staid old Monadnock area and thought property values would go down.

But around Keene, there were far more supporters than Inquiring Citizens, and the growing enthusiasm for the project had supporters on the verge of singing, "I've Been Working on the Railroad." The governor's survey committee's latest reports had been encouraging. And Russell Tobey, son of the late Senator Charles Tobey, as director of the Division of Parks, appeared to favor the project.

Finally, on June 28, 1962, the governor and his council of five met and unanimously approved the project "in principle," directing Tobey to prepare the agreements involving the state, Blount, and the city of Keene.

Newspapers, that had tried to blow the whistle on the state's getting into the Steamtown project, pulled the whistle cord angrily now. The track ahead seemed indeed rough for Blount and company as far as New Hampshire was concerned. Among the sharpest critics were Paul Cummings, Jr., outspoken editor of the Peterborough weekly *Transcript*, and William Loeb, crusading publisher of the *Manchester Union Leader*. They were still saying such things as:

> If the Governor and Director of State Parks Russell B. Tobey want to play P. T. Barnum, let them buy their own uniforms and get their own circus.
>
> LOEB

> Keene and Monadnock Region interests have been in ... a rush to carve up for themselves one million dollars ... from the ten million state recreational bond issue.
>
> CUMMINGS

Both newspapermen and others, contended that the Steamtown project should be developed by private enterprise.

Nelson countered that taxes on a private museum would be prohibitive.

Some opponents hinted that Nelson wanted the state to build the museum so he could get richer running the excursion line.

He pushed back his engineer's cap and moaned, "I've got all the criticism I can stand. If they think Blount's going to make a lot of money, I tell them what I'll do; I'll give them the rights to the railroad now. If they think running a railroad is easy, let 'em go to it."

Amid the steam and smoke over Steamtown, a gubernatorial battle also was taking place. Governor Powell lost out in the primary, which meant the new candidates would have to speak out concerning the issue.

In the meantime, licking his wounds, Nelson was looking across the river toward Vermont. The Rutland was going out of business. He would talk to Vermont Governor Philip Hoff.

But, for the first time in his life, there was a growing peace in the heart and mind of Nelson Blount—all because of something that had happened to him during the stormy months in which he had tried to give away the equivalent of a million dollars and could not.

"Over the Mountains
Of the Moon ...
Eldorado!"

Chapter 10
On the Right Track

CIRCLING HIGH ABOVE Staghead Farm, the little, brown and tan 260 Super Bellanca glistened in the October sun that morning in 1961, as Nelson Blount looked down on the beauty of the scene below. Bright reds, yellows, and browns graced the rolling countryside, and Mt. Monadnock to the west wore a dazzling autumn dress with a dozen hues. She seemed to smile protectively on the maroon and white buildings of Staghead, where Nelson had come eight years ago with his family to begin a new life.

Seemingly, he had everything that a man would want. A lovely wife, four sons and a daughter, wealth, prestige, two railroads—Nelson had them all. Yet deep within, there was an ache, a vacuum that would not be filled.

Since Ruth's accident, he had tried harder to fill the void with religion. He had tried to read the Bible, but it remained silent to him. Many commandments did not seem geared for a man living in twentieth century New England, and even commandments that seemed good were difficult to keep. His and Ruth's studies of certain current religious groups and their beliefs had not helped. If anyone had the answer, maybe Billy Graham did. Certainly, Christian Science, with its mind over-matter philosophy, seemed far-fetched to two people who had felt pain, especially Ruth after her fateful accident. Mormonism, with its golden tablets of Joseph Smith, could not make a latter-day saint out of an egotistical, swashbuckling codfish aristocrat. The major world religions all had weaknesses, so maybe after all, the little, white-spired church he and the family attended in Dublin had as much to offer as any other church or religion.

These thoughts had long disturbed the pilot of the plane that streaked toward New York City on that sparkling autumn morning. Little did he know that on that trip, a series of events would result in his finding peace of heart and mind.

As Nelson's plane left the splendor of the New Hampshire woodlands behind and crossed over the Massachusetts line, dark clouds loomed ahead. Soon, rain began splashing against the windshield, and the pilot, a master at quick decisions, turned the plane and nosed her northward toward blue skies. The weather forecaster radioed that a high-pressure area existed over the north to Montreal—good weather. Business in New York would wait. Nelson had seven locomotives in Canada that he had bought, so he would spend the day in Montreal, preparing papers for them to be brought across the border.

The events of the next few hours were described by the man Nelson contacted, Al Weaver, then special assistant in the office of the vice president, Operations, Canadian National Railways:

> In the course of Mr. Blount's visits [he had been to Montreal several times, negotiating in regard to the locomotives he wanted], we engaged in discussion more

than once as to why he was so determined to preserve a fleet of steam engines—what was his real motivation in this, and where would it lead? It was inevitable that these talks developed, at times, into somewhat philosophical discussions, and we approached, skirted, but never got right to the core of Christian faith, much as I hoped we would.

Mr. Blount had visited Europe about this time as part of an official fact-finding team. What he had seen, not only of life in Europe but also of the questionable conduct of some officials from America, seemed to shake his confidence in the future of the American way of life and raised questions: Why? Why? Why should these things be?

One morning in October [of] 1961, Mr. Blount made a visit to Montreal and dropped in to discuss the movement of the locomotives he had purchased. Involved in this meeting was another CNR representative, and as in previous visits, the discussion eventually turned to why people behave the way they do and what can be done to correct this.

Mr. Blount stated that he was keenly interested in technocracy and was contributing to a foundation carrying on studies in this field. He indicated that the foundation, through scientific study, determines why people do the things they do, then recommends steps to change their actions from an improper or bad course to one that is proper and good. I stated my conviction, as a Christian, that this approach is not sufficient and that the life of the individual must be changed by God; this transformation would change the purpose and motivation of his life.

Time at this point was running out, since I had some work, which had to get out before noon. Furthermore, I was outnumbered, humanly speaking—two to one. In view of this, I said to Mr. Blount, "Look, Nelson, I'd like you to meet some folks who feel the same way I do about these things. There is a convention of Christian businessmen going on at the Queen Elizabeth Hotel. I'll get one of the men to have lunch with us, and we'll talk these things over." Mr. Blount agreed to meet me in the hotel lobby at 12:30.

Everything went wrong that morning after our discussion, and it was with difficulty that I finally broke loose from the annual convention of Christian Businessmen's Committee and hurried over to the hotel, wondering whom the Lord was going to produce out of all those at the convention to join us for lunch. As I went up the escalator to the convention floor, I saw one delegate whom I knew and told him my quest. He was a senior executive of a large Canadian firm, and I thought surely he was the man. However, he said he had some other commitments, and I'd have to get someone else. I then met Ashley Kimber, of the Montreal Christian Business Men's Committee, and he went right to work.

In the next minutes, Kimber contacted Bob Woodburn, a Washington, D.C. banker. He, in turn, went to a luncheon table and asked Ted DeMoss, a Chattanooga, Tennessee, insurance executive, to meet Weaver and the "lost" millionaire. Eyeing the steak that had just been put before him, DeMoss, a man of Greek origin, sat his slender, six-foot, two-inch frame well back in his chair and flashed a smile at the man standing over him. He knew Woodburn well.

"Good friend," he said, "if you are so concerned, why can't you talk to him? As you can see, I'm just starting my meal, and it isn't every day that I have steak for lunch."

Prematurely gray, slender Bob Woodburn smiled. "Ted, I would in a minute, but there's no need in my going, because I can't spend much time. I've got to preside at the meeting here just as soon as the meal is over."

God's insurance man agreed to go and, after taking a hasty bite of his steak, pushed back the plate and went to the lobby. Al Weaver had been described as a tall, ruggedly built fellow, wearing a Gideon pin. DeMoss had no trouble spotting him.

A few minutes later, Weaver and DeMoss were seated with Nelson Blount at a table in the Beaver Club of the hotel, chatting together as they awaited their orders.

As successful businessmen, Blount and DeMoss hit it off nicely from the start, especially after it came out in conversation that DeMoss, an ex-Navy pilot, also often flew in connection with his business.

However, after their meals were served, Nelson felt a bit ill at ease as DeMoss thanked God for the food. To say grace at home was one thing, but it seemed a bit ostentatious to pray over a meal in public.

As the three men ate, the conversation quickly turned to the issues that had brought them together.

"Mr. Blount, are you a Christian?" DeMoss asked forthrightly.

Somewhat abashed, Blount asserted, "Why, yes, of course I am."

"Where are you going when you die, Mr. Blount? To heaven or hell? Do you know?"

Without hesitation, Blount exploded with, "I'm going to hell, of course. I'm going there with all the other sinners I know." The New Englander's eyes flashed his resentment. He had never been talked to like this. "I've never met anyone good enough for heaven. Maybe my wife or my mother, but certainly no one else. Just exactly where do you think you're going when you die, Mr. DeMoss?"

DeMoss answered quietly but confidently. "I have no doubt about it—I'm going to heaven when I die."

Blount put down his coffee cup. "On whose authority are you going to heaven?"

DeMoss pulled from his jacket pocket a New Testament and placed it on the table. "On the authority of this Book right here."

"And what Book is that?"

"The Bible."

"That's not a Bible. I've never seen a Bible that little. Bibles are big books."

"This isn't a whole Bible—just the New Testament and Psalms," DeMoss explained.

"You mean to tell me it says somewhere in there that you're going to heaven when you die?" Incredulity wreathed Blount's face.

"Yes, sir." DeMoss still spoke like a man who was sure.

"All right, show me where you get your authority."

The meal finished, Ted DeMoss opened his New Testament, and with his finger, he pointed to verse after verse as he read them to the obviously bewildered Blount. Some Bible verses that he read were:

- "But as many as received him [Jesus Christ], to them gave he power to become the sons of God, even to them that believe on his name."

  —John 1:12

- "[Christ said,] Verily, verily, I say unto you, He that heareth my word, and believeth on him that sent me, hath everlasting life, and shall not come into condemnation; but is passed from death unto life."

  —John 5:24

- "If thou shalt confess with thy mouth the Lord Jesus, and shalt believe in thine heart that God hath raised

him from the dead, thou shalt be saved. For with the heart man believeth unto righteousness; and with the mouth confession is made unto salvation."
—Romans 10:9–10

Obviously impressed, Blount nevertheless countered, "That's all very good, but these are just some isolated verses."

A three-way conversation resumed, with DeMoss and Weaver referring Nelson to other verses relating to personal salvation: Revelation 3:20; Ephesians 2:8–9; Romans 5:8 and 10:13; John 3:16; and 1 John 5:12. These verses, the two men pointed out, were given by God so an individual could become a member of God's family and know, for certain, that he was ready for heaven.

The Beaver Club was nearly empty as DeMoss closed his New Testament. More than two hours had gone by. Amazement had replaced the puzzlement on Blount's face.

"Where did you go to school?" Blount asked, relaxing back in his chair and eyeing DeMoss with respect.

"I have an engineering degree from Rensselaer Polytechnic Institute in Troy, New York."

"Did they teach you the Bible there?"

"No, I've been reading the Bible for more than twenty-five years, since I became a Christian; this is how I learned a little about God's Word."

"You know, I believe you know more about the Bible than my preacher does," Blount said, straightening up and leaning forward. "Mr. DeMoss, eternal life is the biggest thing in life. I believe there is an eternity to be reckoned with, but a deal as big as this must have an awful lot of fine print. Fellows, I just wish I could believe it is all that simple!"

The hard-bargaining man from Steamtown was not to be sold in a day. He had to hurry to the airport and head back to New Hampshire before night closed in. DeMoss volunteered to fly to Nelson's home later to talk further, but Nelson declined. If he wanted to know more, he would possibly drop in on DeMoss in Chattanooga sometime.

Back at Staghead Farm, Nelson Blount tried to look up some of the verses DeMoss had shown him, but being the average churchman that he was, he could not find his way around in the Bible. He talked to several people, including his pastor, about salvation but got no satisfactory answers.

A letter from Ted DeMoss encouraged him. He noted from the letter that Ted was praying for him, and to Nelson's delight, Ted had included references to the salvation verses. However, in all of his busyness involving Steamtown, he did not reply to Ted's letter, nor to another that came. A Christmas card was the only clue he gave Ted that he was still thinking about their conversation. "Best regards, Nelson. Might be seeing you soon," he scrawled.

On Friday evening, March 2, 1962, the Blount automobile drove into the DeMoss driveway in Chattanooga. A letter and a phone call had preceded Ruth and Nelson's arrival. He had indicated to Ruth that his primary purpose for coming south was to find a locomotive that had vanished, along with the man who had taken his deposit of $1,500. The FBI and postal investigators had tried to locate the man but had failed. Nelson was taking matters into his own hands. He and Ruth were stopping to see the DeMosses en route to New Orleans, where the engine was when he negotiated its purchase.

After greetings had been exchanged, Nelson announced forthrightly, "Ted, I've come here to get saved. I have thought over and over about our discussion and I have talked to other people around my area and none of them seem to know the way to heaven. You act like you know. I can stay just a day—only till sometime tomorrow. Start talking."

"Why do you have to leave so soon?" Ted asked.

Nelson explained the problem relating to the locomotive swindle. He wanted to spend the following week on the matter.

"What's one more engine in the light of your salvation, Nelson? Stay till this thing is settled."

"Look," Nelson chuckled, "if you can't sell me on it in ten hours, you're not going to sell me on it if I stay here for ten weeks!"

"I forgot to ask you one thing up there in Montreal, Nelson."

"What's that?"

"Do you believe in prayer?"

"Yes, I believe in prayer, not that you can ask for just anything and get it, but I believe in prayer."

Ted ushered Nelson into a bedroom, and Ted got on his knees beside the bed. Hesitantly, Nelson also knelt. Ted began to pray. There was nothing stuffy or flowery about the prayer. He was talking to God as if he were talking to a good friend. "Lord, help this man. Let him see in Your Word, the Bible, how he may know You personally and have his sins forgiven." He said more, but that was the gist of the prayer.

Then there was silence, and Nelson knew that Ted was waiting for him to pray. Praying aloud was new, but Nelson plunged in. "Lord, I don't know how to pray. I don't know what to say, but I wish I could understand this the way Ted does. I don't want to be a hypocrite. I'm not against Christ, but all this seems too easy. I want the truth, so help me. Amen."

Afterward, the two men continued talking until about midnight.

The next morning, Ted slipped out early to a Saturday Christian Business Men's Committee (CBMC) breakfast meeting, where he asked for special prayer for Nelson and Ruth.

Later, at home, he and Nelson were chatting again when the phone rang. Ted answered. Neil Queen, a Chattanooga contractor and CBMCer, had a line on some old engines that he thought Nelson would want to see.

"We don't have time to go look at locomotives, really, Neil."

Hearing the word *locomotives*, Nelson broke in. "Ted, get the address; you can preach to me on the way."

In Daisy, on Highway 27, north of Chattanooga, the two men looked over the engines. They met the owner, a Mr. Stone, and soon he and Nelson were talking locomotives.

"You know," Stone said, "I know where there's an engine you ought to have for that collection of yours; this is a classic."

Nelson's face brightened, and he became more excited as Stone showed him a picture of it. It was a picture of the *Albert*, a classic 2-6-0 three-foot-gauge engine, much like the 4-4-0 standard-gauge engine Nelson was hunting. But what was more interesting to Nelson was that the man who owned the *Albert* was the very man for whom Nelson was searching—the man who had vanished with his deposit and the 4-4-0 engine!

Seemingly on the verge of accomplishing his stated purpose for coming south, Nelson relaxed and agreed to visit with Ted until at least Sunday. (Ultimately, he put the swindling matter into the hands of a lawyer. But in 1966, four years later, Blount still had not seen the engine or his $1,500.)

While returning to the DeMoss home that Saturday afternoon, Nelson and Ted continued talking about promises in the Bible relating to God's way of salvation. It was the same way to God that Billy Graham had talked about on the television program months before.

Finally, back at the DeMoss home, Ted asked Nelson once again to join him in prayer. First, Ted prayed, and then he asked Nelson to talk to God in a very definite manner. "I'll pray in short phrases a simple prayer, as though I were a lost man, and you repeat after me, but only if you mean it. We're not playing games."

Ted began, "Dear Lord, I know I'm a sinner."

Nelson repeated the phrase and continued throughout the prayer: "I know I'm a sinner. I understand according to the Bible that Jesus Christ is Your Son and that He died for me and that if I earnestly and sincerely want Him as my Savior, that You'll cleanse my soul if I'll put my trust and dependence upon Him. I trust You now; come into my heart. In Jesus' name. Amen."

They got up from their knees.

"Nelson, has anything happened?"

"Honestly, Ted, I don't know." Nelson had been sincere, but he had no special feeling and had not heard any voices.

"Let me show you a verse of Scripture." In his New Testament, Ted thumbed to Romans 10:13. He asked Nelson to read it.

Silently, the locomotive collector read: "Whosoever shall call upon the name of the Lord shall be saved."

Suddenly his countenance beamed. "I see it; I see it!" he said. "Why didn't you show that to me before? According to that, I'm a child of God."

Quietly Ted said, "Nelson, if I were to give you something worth a great deal of money, what would you say?"

"I know what you mean. I ought to thank God." Then, in a simple way, he prayed aloud, "Lord, thank You for saving my soul."

Nelson Blount had, by faith, been born into God's family. God had planted a bit of His own nature into Nelson's heart (2 Peter 1:4). Then, as if blown there by a gentle wind, thoughts came one after another. "Lord," he said, "You've got to save Ruth, Teddy, Carolyn, Bob, Billy, and Steve." He also named his mother and father, brother, mother-in-law, Fred Richardson, and others.

When he finished praying, Ted observed, "I believe with all my heart that you've been saved."

"Why do you think so?"

"All of a sudden, you're concerned about the salvation of others."

That evening at a CBMC banquet in Athens, Tennessee, Nelson Blount gave his first public utterance concerning the experience that later he was to recount to large audiences across the United States and Canada. His eyes brimming with tears, he stood and managed, "The Lord tonight—just tonight—saved my soul."

The next morning, with Ruth remaining behind because she was not feeling well, Nelson accompanied the DeMosses to Highland Park Baptist Church. While reading the church bulletin, Nelson nudged Ted. "Look at this, 'Rock or Sand' is the sermon topic. Jesus Christ must be the Rock, and sand must surely be what I've been building on all these years."

In the service, with a warm feeling in his heart, Nelson sang lustily with the congregation, "Blessed Assurance, Jesus Is Mine!" and "O Jesus, I Have Promised to Serve Thee to the End."

Before the Blounts left Chattanooga that Sunday afternoon, Ted talked privately with Ruth. "Ruth, you may not understand this, but last night, I believe with all my heart your husband became a new creature in Christ; he was saved, and now he's a true Christian. Before you leave our home, I'd like to know if you're a Christian."

"I think I am," she said. "If it hadn't been for my faith in God, I wouldn't have gotten through the accident."

Moments later, Nelson himself told her, "Honey, I don't know a finer woman in America, in all the world, a better mother, a better wife than you've been, but I've found out since coming here that it isn't being good that gets you to heaven, but receiving Christ to take away our bad."

Ruth rejoiced with Nelson that his spiritual search seemed over, that he had found the peace he had been looking for. But little did he or she realize that their trip and the decision that Nelson made would ultimately revolutionize their entire lives, and those of their children, as well as the lives of countless others. The effect was to be felt singularly back in Dublin. The lovely, New England, community church would all but rock on its foundation, and the townspeople were going to be divided sharply over Nelson's enthusiastic stand for Jesus Christ.

And, of course, Steamtown would never be the same now that the boss had a love for God that surpassed even his affection for steam engines. Nelson made this clear in a letter to Al Weaver, dated April 2, 1962, a month after his Chattanooga experience:

> A new fullness of life has come into me since our meeting in Montreal last fall. I am still interested in fulfillment of a lifelong ambition, namely the preservation of the steam locomotive, but now with God's help, the museum is second to that of living for Christ and helping others find this new "Joy of Life" that I have found! I am frank to admit that I see things in a new and better perspective and feel peace of mind in my everyday problems ... Thanks again for taking time out for me and getting me on the right road for God's glory.

Chapter 11
A Family Affair

THE FAMILY GATHERING in the big, red house of Staghead Farm on March 26, 1962, two days after Nelson and Ruth returned from Chattanooga, seemed routine—at first. The children, Carolyn, Bob, Steve, and Billy, came obediently when the booming voice of Daddy rang out with a summons to gather for a briefing session. Ted, then eighteen and the eldest, was away at the time.

"Now I want you to listen, kids," Nelson began, flashing a smile at Ruth, who was by his side on the couch. "Something happened to your dad that I want you to understand. I've tried to be a good father to you and have given you practically everything money can buy. You've probably got more than you really need. But I have failed as a father. I have failed to put you in touch with God. We've gone to church as a family, yes, but it hasn't meant anything."

He began something like that and continued to relate the details of his life-changing encounter with Jesus Christ.

The looks on the children's faces said that they did not like the sermon.

"Jesus Christ can change your life if you will but believe on Him," Nelson explained.

The gathering was not long—twenty to thirty minutes—but it probably seemed like an hour to the children.

Carolyn went to her room, with its nautical decorations, and turned on a twist record. The loud, discordant noises rang across the house.

Billy and Steve were again playing with their electric train. And Bob, with a milk bucket, headed for the big, red barn. Raising a prize heifer and milking were the important things to him at that moment.

Ted, who heard about Dad's new way of life later, in a man-to-man session, sort of shrugged it all off.

Ruth, alone, thought she understood Nelson. He had gotten an extra big dose of religion, and it would not hurt him. He needed a settling influence, something to live for. After all, hadn't they moved from Rhode Island to Dublin to begin a new kind of life? Nelson now had a faith that would be a goal for him and bring more satisfaction in his pursuits, Ruth believed. He would live for God in a greater way and, therefore, make a greater contribution to his community and nation. Technocracy had once seemed to be the answer to Nelson's longings and dreams for a better world. Now his hope was in Jesus Christ. This was fine, Ruth told herself. Nelson would just naturally be a better husband if he could emulate Jesus and learn to live more in line with His principles.

But some of the things Nelson said, and the way he looked at her, made Ruth feel as if she was on the outside looking in. Hadn't she gone to church all her life? And hadn't faith in God helped her through the months following the accident? She had tried to be a good wife and mother, a good neighbor. Hadn't the Bible had a part in governing her conduct, giving her high ideals? Yet there was this feeling that Nelson was a different kind of Christian. He was one brand, and she was another. But how could that be?

As the family, particularly Carolyn, chafed at being pushed into what seemed to be Daddy's new mold, Nelson's best friend, Fred Richardson, was also becoming more and more vexed at the new Nelson. It was all right when Nelson returned from Chattanooga toting a Bible and puffing a cigar. But the unrest he was causing at the plant was not good.

On an auto trip, Nelson turned to Fred and said, "You know, Fred, we're going to have to do something about the condition of your soul. Look, you're my best friend. I don't want you to go to hell."

That hit Fred like an unexpected uppercut. Fred himself tells the rest of the story:

> Nelson told me about what had happened to him in Chattanooga, but it didn't make much sense to me. I was a natural man and didn't understand spiritual things. I didn't think it was necessary for me to fall into the same pattern as his. I was a churchgoer, believed in God. I felt my good works would outbalance my bad ones.
>
> But Nelson continued to work on me. I did honor his sincerity, for I was genuinely seeking. Nelson eventually saw he wasn't getting through to me, so he arranged a meeting with a friend he thought would overpower me with the logic he could see.
>
> Contrary to what Nelson thought, he didn't say much to me about the Lord. He did say one thing: "I know where I am going when I die—to heaven." I didn't have this assurance.
>
> Two weeks later, in the summer of 1962, while attending the World's Fair in Seattle, I heard my name called. Some friends of my wife's had seen me, and they told me about an exhibit called Sermons from Science. I went to see it, wondering if there I might get some sort

of spiritual help. At Sermons from Science, they passed electricity through a man's body. I'm not a scientist, but I was well satisfied with the explanation they gave. Then the emcee said, "You can see how important it is to follow God's physical laws. But it's much more important to follow God's spiritual laws."

This was a new thought to me. When they asked those that wanted to know about the spiritual laws to come into a room for counseling, I joined about half a dozen others. For the first time, I heard the claims of Christ explained clearly. Nelson had tried, but he was a babe in Christ and couldn't give me a clear explanation. I went to the program several times after that. The next day, I received Christ as my Savior. It wasn't any great emotional experience with me, but it was my start with Christ.

Fred Richardson's encounter with Christ in Seattle made a vast difference in Fred and Nelson's relationship. They had been the best of pals as they chased about the country caressing old steam engines. Their close relationship had put Fred in a place of leadership at Blount Seafood Corporation, but being brothers in Jesus Christ had introduced them to a fellowship that was closer still.

Both Fred and Nelson prayed fervently for their families after Fred came to the Lord. Fred's wife, Penny, had become a Christian when she was sixteen years old. As Fred walked closely with Christ, Penny began to grow as a Christian and started a woman's Bible class in the Richardson home. The two Richardson children, George and Ruth, came to Christ a few weeks apart, in late 1962. George later served as a student missionary under the Pocket Testament League in Brazil, and Ruth worked with Campus Crusade for Christ.

Nelson saw the first evidence of God's working in the lives of his children in November, when he took Carolyn to a Boston Youthtime rally. Carolyn herself recalls that experience and the subsequent happenings:

> The first few months I was away at school (Cushing Academy, Ashburnham, Massachusetts), I thought about what had happened to my dad. Finally, one Saturday night, he took me to a youth rally in Boston, where I heard the gospel preached for the first time in my life. Six men from West Point gave their testimonies and told how Christ had changed their lives. I thought that was good and fine—they had the same thing my dad had.
>
> Then a man read Romans 3:23 and expounded upon that—how we are all sinners. I just burned inside, because I didn't think he had a right to say I was a sinner, even if the Bible did say it. All I could think of as a sinner was someone who had murdered or stolen. I just ignored the whole message and convinced myself that I was all right.
>
> However, at the end of the service, the speaker said, "I want to ask you a question. If you should die before midnight tonight, do you know where you'd spend eternity?"
>
> That question tore at my heart, because I didn't know. Ever since I was a child, I'd been afraid to die; right then, when I realized I had no assurance of heaven, I knew that I needed a Savior. The great transaction took place as I received Christ as my very own Savior.
>
> I began to read the Bible, and it was so real and wonderful as I began to see what had happened to me. Time wore on, and the Lord opened the door for me to go to a Christian school for the next year (Glen Cove, Maine). A few weeks before I was ready to leave, the most evident change in my life took place. The Lord spoke to me about complete surrender to Himself. I thought it might mean Africa or maybe even dying. I just couldn't say, "Yes, Lord, You can have my life." I put up a real

struggle, but finally, I got to the point where I wanted Jesus as my Lord in everything.

Every day after that, I found Jesus so much more precious. I felt so burdened for fishermen and a compulsion to bring them the gospel. I had always loved the ocean but had never considered being a missionary to its people before. I was thrilled with what God had put on my heart.

Thus Carolyn became as fired up for the Lord as her father, sharing the good news with any who would listen, especially fishermen on her beloved Martha's Vineyard. In the summers, she became known to the men of the sea as the gal with a Bible.

While she was carrying her Bible one morning, on her way to a quiet spot by the sea to have her personal devotions, Carolyn heard a voice call out from a group of fishermen: "Hey, come preach us a sermon!"

Though the challenge was in jest, Carolyn turned aside with a smile—and her Bible—and walked over. In her girlish way, she said, "All right, you asked for it." For nearly three hours, she talked about the wonders of salvation as described in the Word of God. A few men drifted away before the "sermon" was over, but two stayed to the end, showing appreciation all the way.

Like her father, Carolyn learned lessons of faith as she studied her Bible and listened with her heart for God to speak to her. At Glen Cove, she spent many happy hours by the ocean, reading the Bible as if it was a personal message to her. "I always felt as if we were walking together, and God would just listen while I'd plead with Him to win the fishermen to Himself," Carolyn later recalled.

The younger Blount children—Bob, eighteen; Billy, thirteen; and Steve, fourteen—made decisions for Christ quietly, at home. Billy and Steve overheard Carolyn and

Nelson praying for a friend of Carolyn's. Later, in their bedroom, in separate, unrelated conversations with God, both boys confessed their need of the Savior and committed their lives to Him. Bob became concerned about his spiritual state and settled matters in his room, subsequently making a public profession of his faith in a Youthtime rally in Boston.

Ruth Blount had quietly gone along with Nelson's new beliefs from the time they returned from Chattanooga. But at the convention of Christian Business Men's Committee International in Miami, in October of 1962, she surmised that her good works and church attendance were not enough. The speaker at one meeting urged Christians to rededicate their lives to Christ, and Ruth suddenly realized that since she had never dedicated her life, she could not rededicate it. It was alone in her and Nelson's hotel room that she asked the Lord to come into her life.

At home later, after Carolyn had come to Christ in such a forthright manner, Carolyn and Daddy became concerned about Ruth. She had not told them of her decision in Miami.

"Daddy, I don't think Mother is saved," Carolyn said one evening.

That night, Nelson gathered the family for a Bible study and then sent the children off to bed.

"Mama," he said as they relaxed in the living room, "when did you make your decision for Jesus?"

"Last week," she said. Then she told Nelson about telling the Lord she wanted Him to have her life.

But to the deeply concerned Nelson, Ruth did not seem sure of her relationship with God. So like a hound after prey, he pursued further. "Why don't you say the sinner's prayer right now and let me be your witness? Just tell Him you are a sinner and to save you for Jesus' sake."

Shaken by his persistence, Ruth began sobbing and ran from the room into their bedroom. Nelson waited a few minutes and then went to her. "Honey, I don't want to make you cry. I want you to be saved, and I want you to know you're saved. I know what the old devil will do. He'll tell you you're all right, but if you're ashamed to confess openly the Lord Jesus Christ, the Bible says you can't be saved."

She didn't want to talk more about it then, so they both went to sleep.

After the children were off to school the next morning, to erase all doubt, Ruth said, "Honey, I'll say that prayer." And she did, in bed, with Nelson at her side.

When thinking back on that incident, Nelson recalled, "That was the end of all the shame. She started going out and witnessing and telling other people of the new joy in her life. She's even spoken in gatherings. She's a good speaker."

Acquainted with the Bible as they are, both Ruth and Nelson made family devotional times rewarding, as each evening the Blounts gathered to pray, read, and discuss a Scripture passage. Sometimes the discussion centered on a lesson that could be applied to one's daily life. Another time the topic would be a basic doctrine. Once a week, the Blounts held a prayer session in which they did not ask God for anything. They simply praised Him. The idea for this weekly "thanksgiving day" came to Nelson when he visited a Christian family in Rockland, Maine, who conducted their prayer time in a similar fashion.

The Blounts had an unwritten list of people for whom they prayed regularly, particularly those who had not encountered Christ. Ruth's mother, Mrs. John S. Palmer, and Nelson's father, Willis E. Blount, were among the relatives for whom they prayed that have come to experience personal salvation.

Willis E. Blount, an honest, rugged hard worker during his active years, had settled with Mrs. Blount in Florida in 1944. As early as June of 1962, Nelson began sharing the gospel with him. Nelson's mother told him that she had made a decision for Christ in her childhood, and she believed she was ready to meet God. However, Father Blount wanted none of Nelson's religious talk.

"I don't know why you keep jumping on me. You'd think I was a heathen," he would snarl. "My grandfather was a deacon, my father was a deacon, and I've been a trustee of the church. What more must one do to be right with God? I'm your father. I sent you to Sunday school. This bothers me. This hurts me—your coming around and telling me all this stuff."

"Dad, I didn't ask if you were a Methodist or a respected person," Nelson countered. "I asked if you made the decision which casts you from death unto life. Have you been born again? You don't even know what the words mean. You haven't read the Bible. You don't know anything about these things. You went to church, gave your money, went to trustee meetings, but that isn't being saved."

Still, the old gentleman would shake his head sadly with hurt and bitterness in his eyes. Deeply concerned, Nelson asked a minister, on a visit to Florida, to stop in and chat with his father. He did, but nothing happened until after Nelson got a phone call from his father, summoning him to the bedside of Mother Blount. A heart condition had put her on the critical list.

When Nelson went in to see her some hours later, his mother could hardly speak. She whispered that she did not want to die until Nelson's dad had committed his life to Christ. "I want my husband with me," she said.

Father Blount made his decision during those anxious hours. Calling himself a sinner before God was a difficult thing, he tearfully admitted to Nelson. But once he did, pride vanished.

"He's the most down-to-earth, humble, soft-spoken guy you've ever met in your life. He's a real prayerful guy—likes to have prayer meetings and read the Word. He's now eighty—saved at seventy-eight. I've never seen anyone grow like my father; he's on fire for the Lord," Nelson said proudly in 1966. "He has been quite ill for the past months. Mother recovered from her attack, though she is not really well."

Getting his family on the "gospel train" was a series of adventures for the Man from Steamtown. But there was one adventure that perhaps stood out from the rest. It was a high-flying drama involving Nelson's eldest—quiet, thoughtful Ted, who for some time, felt his father's ideas on religion were too old-fashioned for a young man planning to make his mark in the Space Age.

In the meantime, the quiet New Hampshire community of Dublin was being divided.

Gibbs family homestead. Nelson Blount sitting in the first row, second from left. Lakeville, Massachusetts.

The old Blount home at 11 Wheaton Street, Warren, where Nelson got his first glimpse of steam from a second-story window.

Nelson in front of his father's icehouse in Barrington, RI.

Nelson hauling ice for his father, Willis Blount, Barrington, RI.

The Man from Steamtown

Nelson and Fred posing for a photo to be used in their book "Along the Iron Trail".

Barrington Ice Man and the girl from Poppasquash.

A Family Affair

Nelson and the kids in New Hampshire.

Family gathering, Christmas, 1966: Carolyn and Ruth seated, standing, left to right, Steve, Bobby, Nelson, Teddy and his wife Judy, and Billy.

THE MAN FROM STEAMTOWN

Nelson Blount, aided by Staghead Farm employee's children, pouring sap into the boiler. Staghead was one of the largest producers of maple syrup in southwest New Hampshire.

Dublin Christian Academy, formerly Staghead Farm, Dublin, NH.

Business Meeting (clockwise; starting lower left): Dalton Stratton, comptroller; J. C. Milne, purchasing agent; B. B. Blount, vice president; Nelson Blount, president (all of Blount Seafood Corporation); W. L. O'Neill, R. G. Foster, of Campbell Soup Company; Fred Richardson of Blount.

Sixty-four-foot, all-steel clipper, the "F. Nelson Blount", owned by the Cape Cod Tuna Corporation. Circa 1963

THE MAN FROM STEAMTOWN

Aerial view of Blount Seafood, Warren, RI. Circa 1949.

Aphrodite at Blount Seafood, with the F/V Whitecap
bow on left and shell pile & building in background

Nelson Blount with another large swordfish on the original Aphrodite

Nelson Blount with 800-pound bull woodland caribou brought down with three arrows in White Bear Bay area Newfoundland.

Gun room and den at 1 Manor Road, Barrington, RI.

Aphrodite II soon after she was built in June, 1957.

Nelson in his favorite aerobatic biplane,
a 1937 Waco ZPF-7 biplane fighter.

Shucking (and sampling) Quahogs at Blount Seafood in Warren, RI. circa 1950's.

A Family Affair

Blount with Industrialist Harold Fuller of the National Railroad Museum, Green Bay, Wisconsin, prior to their ride in cab of the "Flying Scotsman," Queen of British Steam, owned by Britain's ace train fan, Alan Pegler.

The Man from Steamtown

Scene of the North Walpole, NH yards with the Repton in the foreground and the Union Pacific "Big Boy" in the background.

Getting ready for a ride at North Walpole.

A Family Affair

Tens of thousands throng to Edaville during the Christmas season to see perhaps the most extravagant display of lights in New England.

In 1956, the Boston & Maine Railroad donated an entire 1900-era train to the Edaville museum – Blount's first standard gauge equipment. The nearest standard gauge track was six miles distant, so equipment was hauled on flat-bed trucks. Mogul-type locomotive is being unloaded at the narrow-gauge engine house.

Christmas Double Header at Edaville.

At Brockway Mills, Vermont, No 89 pauses at old covered bridge.

A Family Affair

Photo By Donald Robinson

Canadian Pacific 4-6-2 No. 1293 steams north out of Bellows Falls in 1964 on an excursion run. When this section of the Rutland Road was incorporated as the common-carrier Green Mountain Railroad in 1965, 1293 could no longer be operated under her Canadian certificate.

Photo from Beverly Historic Society

Billy Graham and Cliff Barrows pay a visit to Steamtown. So enthusiastic was Dr. Graham that he spent part of the excursion trip at the throttle of No. 15. Nelson and Fred also pictured.

Nelson standing on the North Walpole, NH yard "turntable".

Artist's conception of Steamtown of tomorrow featuring museum of stationary stock (center). Later plans were made to include a 42-stall roundhouse, trolley line and steamboat landing in 1890 town complex with river steamer of that era. Total cost would exceed $2 million, and plans called for completion of the project in 1970, which would never be built.

A Family Affair

Photo run by on the New Haven railroad tracks
in southern New England circa 1966.

Steam excursion on New Haven tracks circa 1966.

The Man from Steamtown

A doubleheader steaming toward Summit. Train will split at Chester, 13 miles from Steamtown, and No. 15 will continue to Summit (20 miles farther), with half of train returning to Steamtown with No. 1293. Donald S/ Robinson Photo.

Photo run by for a steam excursion trip in Vermont.

Nelson and son Ted at Edaville in South Carver, Massachusetts.

Ruth Blount Birthday party 2011, Barrington, RI.

Blount family photo at Ruth Blount memorial service,
Dublin Christian Academy, July 28th, 2012.

Blount Fine Foods ever-growing soup plant in 2010,
Fall River, MA.

A Family Affair

Photo Courtesy of The Times-Tribune, Scranton, Pa
Grand Opening of Steamtown National Historic Site, Scranton, PA.

The Man from Steamtown

Photo Courtesy of Steamtown National Historic Site

The "Canadian National" #3254 in the center of our "Core Complex." The turntable and roundhouse area were considered the "Core" of a Steam Railroad Yard. In this photo the "Core Complex of Steamtown National Historic Site."

Left of turntable: Working Roundhouse
Center: History Museum
Right of Center: Theatre
Right behind Caboose: Visitor Center
Technology Museum: The area where the photo was taken.

"Canadian National" #3254 leaving with a long Excursion Train and "Canadian Pacific" # 2317 pacing with a short Excursion Train.

Photo Courtesy of Steamtown National Historic Site

A Family Affair

Photo Courtesy of Steamtown National Historic Site

"Canadian National" #3254 being rotated on the turntable at the end of the day for park visitors. It will proceed into the roundhouse to be serviced and to undergo it's daily inspection.

THE MAN FROM STEAMTOWN

Photo Courtesy of Steamtown National Historic Site

In July of 1995, five operational Steam Locomotives posed in the evening at the turntable to provided an opportunity for visitors to take photographs. From Left (Steamtown National Historic Site's operational Steam Locomotives)
"Baldwin Locomotive Works" #26 an 0-6-0 Switch Locomotive with a Sloped Back Tender (built in 1929)
"Canadian National" #3254 a 2-8-2 built in 1917
"Canadian Pacific" #2317 a 6-6-2 built in 1923

Also shown were two of four other visiting operational steam locomotives:

"Reading and Northern" #425 a 4-6-2
"Lowville & Beaver River" Shay

The "National Park Service" and specifically "Steamtown National Historic Site" celebrated the Grand opening of the Museum Complex in July of 1995.

A FAMILY AFFAIR

Photo Courtesy of Steamtown National Historic Site

A view of the "Steamtown National Historic Site" (one of 397 National Park Sites) located in the former "Delaware, Lackawanna & Western" Railroad Yards. The yards, which date back to the 1850's, are located in Scranton, Pennsylvania. "Steamtown National Historic Site" encompasses approximately 65 acres.

Photo Courtesy of Steamtown National Historic Site

"Canadian National" #3254 just completed it's 13 mile climb from Scranton up to Moscow, Pennsylvania. Once the guests disembarked the Excursion Train at the Moscow Station, the Steam Locomotive backed west out of view, and than proceeded east at track speed putting on a show during a photo run-by.

THE MAN FROM STEAMTOWN

Photo Courtesy of Steamtown National Historic Site

"Canadian National" #3254 Operating during 54 mile a winter excursion to Tobyhanna, Pennsylvania.

Photo Courtesy of Steamtown National Historic Site

"Canadian Pacific" #2317 (a 4-6-2 "Heavy Pacific" Type Locomotive / built in 1923) operating an Excursion in November.
This was the first locomotive that arrived from Steamtown U.S.A.

Photo Courtesy of Steamtown National Historic Site

"Canadian National" #3254 (2-8-2 "Mikado" Type Steam
Locomotive / built in 1917) Hauling a Fall Foliage Train.
This Locomotive was not part of the collection when
it moved to Scranton.

Chapter 12
A Town Steams

THE LATE A. R. "Happy Dick" Brothers, probably best known of all engineers to pull a throttle on the Seaboard Airline Railroad, earned his nickname in the 1930s and early 1940s in towns and over the rolling farmlands of eastern and central North Carolina. A thoughtful man, he concluded that the usual shrill warnings from his steam whistle disturbed patients in the Ellen Fitzgerald Hospital in Monroe. So he began tooting a cheerful little tune as his train approached a crossing near the hospital.

He regularly saluted the patients and people at other points along his run with a combination of musical-like toots that sent these words tumbling into the minds of many: "Happy day, happy day, when Jesus washed my sins away!" They were from a gospel song that expressed Engineer Brothers's own experience.

Although Nelson Blount did not return from Chattanooga by train to the quiet, little New Hampshire town of Dublin, he was blowing the same happy, little tune. Like Happy Dick Brothers, Nelson was busting to tell the whole world the good news of his "happy day" and of the Bible's offer of an absolutely free ticket to heaven. He shared the good news with his own family, employees at Staghead Farm, store clerks, executives, maids and their wealthy employers, the poor, and the rich.

Nelson floundered for a time, not knowing quite how to tell outsiders of his new faith or how to get started in a walk toward Christian maturity. Being a newborn child in the family of God was one thing; growing up as a strong follower of Christ was another. How could he get hold of the truths and principles of the Bible and become a person who could help others, as Ted DeMoss had helped him?

Nelson had already discovered that the Dublin Community Church he had joined in 1954 was in reality a Unitarian church. Sermons preached there were aimed at inspiring a better life, without a transformation in the lives of hearers. Jesus Christ was presented as a model to follow, but the man in the clerical gown in the pulpit did not uphold Him as God manifested in the flesh. This was a fact that bothered Nelson considerably. The pulpit did not believe the Bible to be the inerrant Word of God but rather a book containing bits of ancient wisdom that could inspire and elevate a man closer to God.

It was in June that Nelson got a call from the Rev. John DeBrine, who identified himself as pastor of Ruggles Street Baptist Church, Boston. He invited Nelson to appear on *Song Time*, his network radio program, to answer questions regarding his spiritual experience. After they met and Nelson appeared on the broadcast, DeBrine, an astute man in his late thirties, sensed Nelson's need for guidance in understanding the Bible and other matters relating to spiritual growth. As a result, along with Fred Richardson, they met each week for some months, as schedules allowed, to pray and to read and study the Bible. DeBrine taught

Nelson and Fred elementary truths from the Scriptures and then, as time went on, began sharing more weighty doctrines. He emphasized the importance of daily talking to God and studying His Word, and then sharing Jesus Christ with others.

But even as he was getting established in Christian truth, Nelson ran into snares. For example, he tuned in to a West Coast radio preacher who spoke with such apparent authority that Nelson sent for his literature. To Nelson's surprise, he taught a lot of things that differed from DeBrine's teachings.

One day he phoned DeBrine, to share with him a "revelation." Nelson said, "You know, John, I've discovered through this radio preacher that the doctrine of the Trinity cannot be proved."

DeBrine sighed as he listened. He knew the man only too well, as far as his message was concerned. He was a self-styled prophet, who thought all other preachers were of the devil and only he was right. The new Christian would listen to his broadcast, feeling that here was a man of God worth following, and fall easy prey to one who was preaching a salvation based on human works and not on the merits of the atoning sacrifice of Jesus Christ.

Later, Nelson Blount junked all of that man's literature, as DeBrine showed him that the Bible presents three Persons in the Godhead—the Father, the Son, and the Holy Spirit—yet reveals that these three are one God, the same in substance, equal in power and glory.

In these early post-conversion days, Nelson was like a country boy at a world's fair. As he read his Bible, there was magnificence on every page and wonders beyond his wildest imaginations. This was no longer the dust-covered, stodgy, old Book of former days; instead, it was the most modern, up-to-date Book in existence. Though written and compiled over many centuries, and recording historical events from the beginning of time, this Book spoke with authority about events to come. In it, the eternal God, who cannot be contained by time—the infinite Creator, who knows the end from the beginning—hinted at events that would mark the end of time.

This, to Nelson Blount, was even more thrilling than being an engineer on a great Iron Horse, barreling across country, pulling a dozen gleaming, yellow cars jammed with excursionists. That he, a mortal speck in the universe, should share the thoughts of the Almighty in relation to future events delighted him no end.

A completely new world was opening up to him: "I had never known anything up to then about the antichrist, that man of sin who will rule the world during the tribulation, when disaster and suffering will plague mankind as at no other time in history. I had never been taught anything about the rapture, when all believers suddenly will rise from the earth to be with Christ. All of this, of course, precedes the antichrist and the tribulation, I believe."

His interest in those subjects set him to reading various books on prophecy. "When I read about these things and heard about them, this really shook me," he said, "and it did plenty to spur me on to help other people find the truth as I had found it."

To help Nelson redeem the time and saturate his mind with Bible truth, DeBrine introduced him to the tape-recorder method of getting the Word into him. With Nelson's money, the Boston pastor purchased a tape recorder and had it installed on the floor in the front of Nelson's car. He loaned him tapes of Bible lessons and sermons by some of the outstanding evangelical Bible expositors of that day. "Now let the Holy Spirit teach you as you drive along," DeBrine challenged.

Thus, over the months, Nelson got into the tape-recorder habit instead of automatically flipping on the radio when he got in his car. For hours at a time, as he drove along the highway en route to a speaking engagement or a business appointment, a Bible teacher rode along (on tape): Dr. Lehmann Strauss, Dr. Doug McCorlde, Dr. Charles Woodbridge, Dr. M. R. DeHaan, Dr. J. Dwight Pentecost, Dr. John F. Walvoord, Col. Robert Theime, General William K. Harrison, to name a few.

Over the months and years, he continued the habit and collected well over 200 tapes of his own.

The more he studied and understood the Bible, the more Nelson became indignant toward ministers he knew were failing to communicate the truth of salvation that had transformed his own life. Some, he realized later, were exposed only to liberal thinking and, therefore, could not be expected to share the truth. They were sincere but sincerely wrong. Others were simply preaching about "helping our brothers" and about the "birds and the bees," as Nelson termed it, because they just happened to choose the ministry as a profession.

"Nelson, you're taking this thing too far," Dr. Claude Canfield (pseudonym), his young minister, commented one day when Nelson remarked that he had talked to a hitchhiker about making a decision to receive Christ.

Later, Nelson invited Dr. Canfield to his home and pinned him down concerning his personal beliefs. Jesus Christ, the young minister admitted, was, in his opinion, a Prophet, a wonderful Man whose teachings have done much to help mankind, but "I could never bring myself to believe that He was God or the Son of God." The Bible could not be taken literally.

As the conversation continued, Nelson lost his patience. "Claude, you're simply hoodwinking people; those who sit under your ministry are on their way to hell, and you stand there and feed them a bunch of baloney."

Nelson opened his Bible and showed Dr. Canfield condemning scriptures: "Many deceivers are entered into the world who confess not that Jesus Christ is come in the flesh. This is a deceiver and an antichrist ... He that abideth in the doctrine of Christ, he hath both the Father and the Son. If there come any unto you, and bring not this doctrine, receive him not into your house, neither bid him God speed: for he that biddeth him God speed is partaker of his evil deeds" (2 John 7, 9–11).

There were more scriptures. The young minister blanched. "You know, I never realized that those things were in the Bible. I don't think I ever read that," he said in substance.

Later, the young minister resigned his pulpit to do further study.

Characteristically, Nelson shocked many people of the area when he recounted his discussion with the minister on a radio broadcast from station WKNE, Keene. He did not name the pastor, but from remarks Nelson made, he left little doubt in the minds of listeners as to the pastor's identity:

> "I've got to tell you people that you're either saved or you're lost; you're either in the body of Christ by making a decision for Christ and meaning it, or you're going to hell," he thundered. "I don't care whether you are a Catholic or a Protestant, or what church you go to. You better get with this thing and look into it."

The more than 350 residents of Dublin knew for certain what Nelson Blount believed.

Ultimately, Nelson decided that he and his family had no business attending a church where Unitarian doctrines were taught. God, he believed, was leading them to the Troy Baptist Church in Troy, New Hampshire, twenty-two miles from the Blount home.

As the weeks and months passed, Nelson shared his and God's good news with one individual after another. A certain prominent, wealthy citizen of nearby Jaffrey invited the Blounts to a gathering of other area residents. As guests chatted and sipped cocktails, the hostess slipped over to Nelson and sweetly asked, "Well, Nelson, tell us what this is all about that you now believe."

For three-quarters of an hour, he spoke informally to the entire gathering, recounting his experience and explaining that money and good works will not gain anyone entrance to heaven, that the only way is a personal, sincere decision to commit one's life to the Lord Jesus Christ.

The story of how Jack Boardman (pseudonym), an employee of Staghead Farm, made an about-face is a classic.

Nelson began talking to his help at the farm about salvation, once bringing a group together and talking to them for about two hours. Afterward, their reaction seemed to be: "Now we've heard it. It's fine. Now leave us alone." But Nelson continued to talk about Jesus Christ.

One day, Jack Boardman came to the boss. "Nelson, is there anything wrong with my work for you?"

"Absolutely not. I think you're a terrific guy. Why?"

"Well, I just want one thing understood: leave me alone, because if you don't, I'm going to quit. I'm not going to stand for being preached to anymore. Is that understood? The other guys feel the same way and haven't the guts to tell you."

Nelson's face clouded. "All right, Jack, I'm glad you told me. I will do no more talking to you at all. The Bible says, 'Cast not your pearls before swine.' I won't talk to you, but I'll pray for you."

"Don't even pray for me. You leave me alone!"

Nelson did not press Boardman further, even though he itched to do so. He prayed against Jack's wishes, however. Finally, one day in March, as Nelson and the farmhands were making maple syrup, visitors came—a well-known stockbroker and his wife.

The woman asked as they watched, "Nelson, what's this I hear about you becoming a preacher?"

Nelson explained that he was not exactly a preacher, but he, as a layman, had been talking a lot about a wonderful message. He pulled out his Bible and began an impromptu exhortation on salvation. Out of the corner of his eye, Nelson noticed Boardman nearby, listening. So he preached on. Nelson later said that he was "really talking to Jack but in appearance talking to her."

The couple left, and he put his Testament back in his pocket and said no more.

About half an hour went by, and then Boardman blurted out, "Show me in the Bible where it says ..." (He asked for a specific verse Nelson had mentioned to the woman.)

Nelson read the verse to him and then thrust the Testament into his hand and said, "Here, read it; ask the Lord to show you the truth."

Boardman changed the subject, pushed the Testament into his pocket, and that was that.

The Blounts prayed for him a lot in subsequent days. Then one day, Boardman asked, "Nelson, what do you have to do to be saved?"

"Confess with your mouth the Lord Jesus and believe in your heart that God raised Him from the dead. Then admit to God that you are a sinner and tell Him you want to be saved. Romans 10:9–10. Look, if you want to pray, I'll co-witness."

Boardman said he did not want to; he just wanted to know what the "deal" was. Nelson told him how to pray and suggested that he let his wife be the witness.

One morning, about nine o'clock, Boardman came over to the main house at Staghead. He was troubled. "You told me if I confessed with my mouth and would believe in my heart and say the sinner's prayer in the witness of my wife that I'd be saved."

"That's right; if you meant it," Nelson replied.

"I'm no more saved than the man in the moon. At four this morning, I got up and woke my wife and said that prayer, and I'm worse than I was before."

"Satan is telling you that, Jack. The Bible says, 'Whosoever shall call upon the name of the Lord shall be saved.' Do you think God's a liar? From this point right on, will you do one thing for me? Will you right here and now take this Testament, and any time something is bothering you, will you please look up Romans 10:9–10?"

Once again, Boardman tucked the Testament into his pocket.

"He nearly wore out that page the next few months," Nelson later recalled. "Riding on the tractor—anywhere he was—he'd pull out the Testament and read that verse of assurance. He witnessed to his brother and, after that, had people in town laughing at him and saying he was Blount's rubber stamp, but he stuck to his convictions and became a tremendous witness for the Lord."

In due time, most of the citizens of Dublin began to place themselves into three clear categories concerning salvation. Nelson put it into these terms: "There are people who know and have received the truth. Some are growing; some aren't. There's a second group who don't want to commit themselves; they know in their hearts what is right, but they don't stand up to be counted. It's great for someone else, but they don't declare themselves. The third group is the real Unitarian element—people who absolutely decry anybody like me coming up and talking about salvation from such a terrible place as hell when, as they say, there is no such place and that everybody is all right as long as he seeks after God in his own way. They despise me for breaking up our wonderful community spirit and bringing all this dissension."

A composite of two quite similar cafe sessions—one in the spring of 1965 and the other in early 1966—dramatically illustrates how some townspeople felt about the new Nelson. He walked into the little, white-front restaurant on Highway 101, smack in the middle of Dublin, and ordered coffee at the counter. When he spoke to two men seated in a booth, one sneered, "Well, if it isn't the preacher!"

Nelson ignored the remark, and as he chatted further with them, he indicated that he would pick up the tab for the coffee-break refreshments.

One thing led to another, and then the man who had called Nelson "preacher" gave Nelson a cold, calculated look. He was a man of about thirty-five and had the wind-burned face of an outdoorsman. "Nelson," he said with seething deliberation, "I wish I had a million dollars. If I did, I'd spend every cent of it fighting you; I hate everything you stand for. You keep all of that Bible stuff to yourself and quit cramming it down everybody's throat!"

The verbal attacker's friend fingered his coffee cup, half embarrassed.

"The Bible was written thousands of years ago," the other man continued. "It's not for today. Forget it, Nelson, and quit trying to make everybody live by it."

Nelson, his gray-fabric hat pushed back on his head, allowed that he believed in the Bible and wanted everyone to personally meet the God of the Bible, but he was not making anybody do anything. He calmly sipped coffee as the man in the booth continued his onslaught and took each blistering remark as if it were meant for someone else.

He kept a friendly tone to his voice as he sparred with his attacker, using bits of logic and Scripture that this irate man twisted and cursed.

"God is all right—sure, everybody needs a little bit of God, that I'll admit—but not to the extent that you go, to become a fanatic like you are, Nelson," the man slugged on.

The second man, who had remained silent, spoke. "Look. I believe just as Nelson does, and he has guts enough to stand up. Well, I want you to know I've got guts enough to stand up too. I agree with him. There is a God, there is a Jesus Christ, there is a heaven and hell, and I only hope that I'm in that camp with Nelson and not in your camp."

At that point, the coffee-break session ended, and Nelson bade the two men a cheery farewell as he paid for their coffee and doughnuts. The cafe counterman, who had silently listened to the diatribe, smiled and rang the cash register.

Blount stock went up a few points with some townsmen the day in 1965 that Nelson was seen chumming with Evangelist Billy Graham and his song leader, Cliff Barrows. They had come for a two-day visit with the Blounts and to ride an excursion train. If Blount's brand of religion was the same as Graham's, then maybe Nelson wasn't so nuts after all.

It was not only in Dublin that people began to wonder about Nelson and his complete turnabout. Employees at Blount Seafood Corporation also began to ask one another if the boss had gone off his rocker. There were rumors that he was giving money away like a madman to Christian causes. The Christmas party was cleaned up and given a spiritual emphasis. Word spread that the boss might become a missionary to some foreign land. Maybe the company would soon be liquidated.

There was perhaps some foundation for the unrest at Blount's in Warren. For, large sums were, in reality, now

A Town Steams

being given by the boss to causes he felt would get the gospel to others. And the missionary story was well founded. Feeling that perhaps God would have him leave friends, relatives, houses, and land to go to a far country with the Truth, Nelson prayed for guidance. Even if he were too old for mission boards, he could pay his own way.

He accompanied Jack Wyrtzen, New York's widely known Word of Life evangelist, to South America on a speaking trip. As Nelson spoke to large audiences through interpreters, he realized extensive language training would be necessary for effective work abroad.

Back in the United States, Nelson felt the restraining hand of a wise minister on his shoulder. "That's a very fine ambition, and I'm sure the Lord will honor you, but it is better for you just to wait on the Lord. Find out for sure what He wants you to do."

Before the matter was resolved, Fred Richardson tried to bring Nelson back to earth. "Nelson, you don't know what you're doing to our employees," he admonished. "They all think you're off the deep end, and now they are wondering if they're going to be out in the street after working for you all their lives. 'If that's Christianity, I don't want any part of it,' they're saying."

Nelson pondered the problem and consulted Christian leaders, including John DeBrine. The consensus of their advice concurred with the earlier counsel. "Nelson, instead of your telling the Lord what you're going to do, why don't you let Him tell you what He wants you to do. Be quiet, get in the Word, sit around a while, and let God talk to you. He's in no hurry."

Morale at the plant improved over the next months as Nelson followed this advice. The business grew stronger under Richardson's able leadership. And as time went on, Nelson began to recognize that his mission field was definitely at home—among his friends, at Steamtown, and elsewhere in the United States.

There would be many indications of God's blessings on his decision to stay home—more than he could have dreamed of then.

Chapter 13
Reluctant Teddy

THE DAY TEDDY Blount left for Boston University in September of 1962, he had reason to breathe a sigh of relief, for at last, he could begin living his own life. For one thing, Dad was on a religious kick, and it would be refreshing to get away from the old-fashioned ideas he was preaching. But more than that, Teddy would be a hundred miles from Dad's dominating ways. To be sure, there was not a greater guy anywhere than Dad, but there were so many times in his growing-up years that Teddy had heard, "You're a Blount, Boy! You've got to be a success!"

Teddy could remember going through the motions of taking piano lessons as a youngster—because Dad thought he ought to. He had made little progress, but Dad had kept pushing. "I had a teacher once who thought there was no music in me, but I kept trying, and I'm glad I did. There's music in you, Son; you're just a chip off the old Blount block," the refrain had gone.

Teddy had practiced for seven agonizing years, until finally even Dad had conceded that maybe music was not really Teddy's forte.

The Boston U. freshman could remember other similar situations—studies and athletics, for example. A tall, gangling kid, he had tried hard in both. After all, he was a Blount; success was the goal. Yet, to his consternation—and Dad's disappointment—he was not always the best in math or history, the best batter on the baseball team, or the flashiest back on the football squad.

On hunting trips that made other fellows envious, Teddy went with Dad as far away as the Canadian Rockies for big game. But even these times brought tense moments. "Teddy, a Blount simply has to handle a rifle like an expert."

As they flew in Dad's private plane, Teddy often had the thrill of handling the controls. Few had the touch for flying that Dad had. Someday Teddy himself would perhaps develop into an accomplished pilot. At least, Dad hoped so.

No, Teddy would not have traded places with any other boy when he was growing up. But as great and wonderful and bighearted as Dad was, he did have that one annoying trait: if not in words, he said it by showing Teddy how to do things, by just the look in his eyes or the tone in his voice: "Son, you're a Blount; never forget it. You're destined for success."

When Teddy was twelve, he developed a speech impediment. "Certain pressures" had caused it, doctors said.

At Boston U., Teddy Blount chose aerospace engineering. He went out for crew and was on the varsity crew his last three years. He met a girl to his liking named Judy Richard, a cute brunette. His slight speech problem did not bother her. Soon they began going steady.

When Teddy continued hearing little sermons from his father on weekends about Jesus Christ, it was not exactly

Reluctant Teddy

surprising that he stood to his full six-foot-three height and brushed off Dad's attempts to convert him to his new faith. He was a college man. He would think about this when he was ready.

But as Dad saw it, this was a matter of life or death—there were eternal implications. Somehow Teddy had to understand that this was not simply another follow-in-my-footsteps thing.

Deep furrows lined Nelson Blount's brow as he told the dramatic account of how the Holy Spirit finally caught up with Teddy. Occasionally he flashed a smile as he reached back in time for the details that included a near airplane tragedy and a hunting trip:

> Teddy applied at a lot of colleges and wound up at the U. That's Boston University. About this time, I made my decision and accepted Christ and became much concerned for Teddy, knowing a bit about what was going on in universities in general.
>
> One day I went down there to pick him up. I arrived an hour or so before he got out of class. So I went to his room in Myles Standish Hall to wait for him. He was rooming in a suite with five boys, and these boys apparently were agnostics or downright atheists.
>
> In his room, I started gabbing with his roommates. The guys started to chide me about being a preacher. "How can you, a solid businessman, go for all that baloney?" one asked sneeringly.
>
> "In other words, you don't believe in God?" I asked the boy who said this.
>
> "This is my god," he said, pointing to his guitar.

"I don't believe that," I said. "You can say that laughingly, but when you get in a mess, you won't say that."

He told me very frankly that the Bible was as old-fashioned as Carrie Nation [According to Wikipedia, Carrie Amelia Moore Nation (November 25, 1846–June 9, 1911) was a member of the temperance movement that opposed alcohol in pre-Prohibition America. She was particularly known for promoting her viewpoint through vandalism. On many occasions, Nation would enter an alcohol-serving establishment and attack the bar with a hatchet.] He told me he was a Catholic from New York City.

Actually, in the discussion, there was a Jew, a Catholic, and two Protestants. All had departed from the faiths of their fathers. The four of them began to debate me openly while I was waiting for my son. Finally, I went over and grabbed a volume of either the Britannica or Americana Encyclopedia, and I started to thumb through it. I said to the boy who at that moment was giving me a real hard time, "You're a pretty smart chap. You have all the answers. I just wonder what percentage of all the knowledge you think you have."

He would not answer me.

"Do you think you know 50 percent of this?" I said.

He said, "Well, no."

I said, "Twenty-five percent?"

I finally got him down to where he admitted he did not even know 1 percent. "This is a very wise statement, because you don't," I said. "Now isn't it possible that you could be mistaken about Jesus Christ?"

Before I got through with them, they were arguing which religion was the best—Jewish, Catholic, or Protestant. It shows they were searching for the answers, did not have them, but had settled on this attitude only because they absolutely wanted nothing to restrict them. This was much the same as my own testimony, and I told them so.

Then my son came in, and he was upset to some extent that I had talked to his roommates the way I had. Oh, he didn't get after me, but I think it bothered him some.

A few weeks after that, I could see him getting further and further away in my discussions and talks with him. The more I tried to get him to make a decision to accept Christ, the more he seemed not to want to do it. I could see my free will was not his free will. The only thing I could do for him as a father was to pray, and I got every Christian I knew to pray for him.

It wasn't many weeks after that when Ulric Jelinek, president of the Severna Manufacturing Company, well-known scientist and inventor, came to Boston to the Boston Museum of Science for a lecture. I asked Teddy to hear him, and Ulric really challenged him. Ulric is a real Christian. But Teddy wasn't ready to be pushed into conformity. He hadn't seen the necessity at this point to give up known things for unknown things.

Well, I had all my friends praying for him, and I didn't say much to him. Teddy and I had hunted a lot as he grew up. He had his own .30-06 Remington Gamemaster rifle after he was ten. Well, he suggested one day that we go hunting like old times. I was delighted. Of course, I had an ulterior motive. I was hopeful that during this time we could talk about some truths of the Bible. So I began to bone up on things that I felt would be good.

A week before Thanksgiving, 1962, we left on this trip to British Columbia. At the New York airport, we got on a jet, but then they took us off for some reason and roiled up an old, four-engine, pro-driven DC-7. We were the last ones on the plane—we had the last two seats, right by a wing. It was about eight at night when we took off. They kept the lights on until about midnight, and I was reading the Bible.

It got to be about two in the morning, all the lights were out, and everyone had gone to sleep. The plane was drumming along, and I noticed that the starboard, inboard engine was running rough. I mentioned it to Teddy.

Suddenly the engine came to a grinding stop and burst into flame, lighting up the cabin. The fire encompassed the engine on both sides.

The stewardess came down and was looking out our window when all this panic was going on. Earlier I had told her I was a pilot, and now she asked me what it all meant. I said, "It means we're not going to make it. He's not going to put that fire out with carbon dioxide because the fire's outside as well as inside."

She was panic-stricken, along with everyone else. Here I was faced with the fact we weren't getting where we were going, my son wasn't saved, and we were about to face death. I was very shaken. I had been in a similar situation once on my way to Europe, but the plane landed safely. This time I wasn't so much worried about myself, but I had my son with me. I don't think he said anything to me.

Finally, the crew put carbon dioxide to the engine, and the inside fire stopped. But outside it was still going. The aluminum skin had melted from the heat, and the pilot had all but shut off the engine; we were almost in a stall. We were flying at 22,000 feet. Then the fire went out. I still can't understand why. Neither could the crew. All I know is I really prayed during this time—over about fifteen minutes. I asked the Lord why He was doing this to me. Maybe, I reasoned, this was the thing Teddy needed to bring him to the understanding that life is uncertain.

A few minutes after the fire went out, the pilot came out and told us they were trying to go back to Minneapolis. They would make it about dawn and land by daylight, because a storm raged below us, and the wing was too badly melted to risk landing in it. We landed about dawn at the Minneapolis airport, and everybody rushed out of the plane—nearly ninety people. The interesting thing is they got another plane a little later, and there were only a handful to get on that plane. The others must have gone to the *Empire Builder* or a bus. There were only five or six of us, that's all.

Teddy and I continued on to British Columbia, and we went hunting. I never did really do the things I had planned to do. I remember reading the Bible a great deal. I recall shooting a big buck on a mountaintop; Teddy heard the shot and arrived about twenty minutes later. By this time, I had dressed the deer and was sitting on a stump, reading my Testament.

About the closest I got to talking about truths in the Bible was on Thanksgiving Day, when we were invited for dinner by this guy who was hunting with us. He was a Mormon, and we got into a lively discussion about the Mormon faith. While Teddy didn't listen a great deal, he heard a little. It wasn't witnessing; it was more a theological discussion.

Well, on our way home, we had more engine trouble and landed at Great Falls, Montana. We had to get off the plane for four hours, and they gave us meal tickets and told us to go downtown for dinner. I rented an Avis car, and we invited a lonely soldier to go with us.

We had dinner in a hotel, and the soldier told us the story of his life. He was being transferred to Germany, and he wasn't very happy about life in general.

I gave him my own testimony and a few things about the Scriptures, and he became interested. About this time, Teddy said to me, "There's a Walt Disney animal movie on across the street at the theater; I'd like to see it."

I was torn between whether I should keep talking to the soldier, or go with Teddy. I don't advocate movies, but I wanted to be with my son, and this was an animal picture. So I asked the soldier if he wanted to go with us.

He said, "No, I'm going out to buy a Bible and read about some of these things you've been telling me."

So I gave him the keys to our Avis car, and he went out and bought a Bible.

When we got back, he was sitting in the car with the light on, reading the Bible. The interesting thing is we got on the plane and I witnessed further to him, and he accepted the Lord. We left him in New York and got another plane to Boston. I took Teddy to his room and came home. I was discouraged; I had helped the soldier, but Teddy seemed as unmoved as ever.

The next Sunday I was asked to speak at Ruggles Street Baptist Church, which is a couple miles from Boston University, and Teddy apparently knew that I was going to be there; he hadn't said anything to me as such, but he came.

I was speaking, and it suddenly hit me when I saw him that he had come to hear me, and all the time before that, when I tried to speak to him, he wouldn't listen. So I started to cry; I really fell apart. I bet I couldn't talk for a full sixty seconds. After I silently asked the Lord to give me strength, I finally got control of myself. I finished talking and sat down. I felt bad; Teddy would be so ashamed of me, he'd never listen.

But John DeBrine, the pastor, got right up and said, "Now you've all heard Mr. Blount, and I'll ask you a question. Is there anyone here who is not sure where he is going to spend eternity and wants to accept Christ as his Savior?" He invited others to give themselves wholly to Christ.

As he was talking, Teddy got up and walked down to the front, with others who came for dedication. I couldn't talk. Teddy's girlfriend, Judy, had been sitting with him; she stayed in the seat, and she was crying.

I didn't talk much to Teddy that night, only enough to know that he had made his decision for Christ.

He took Judy to her dorm at Jackson College, part of Tufts. Apparently, she noticed something had happened to him, and she didn't know what to do. She talked to Teddy on the telephone, and Teddy said later she was almost incoherent. So he sent over the man who had counseled him at the church—John Weliczko, a ministerial student. Judy couldn't make a decision for Christ; yet she didn't want to be separated from Teddy.

She finally wrote me a letter. She loved Teddy and wanted to marry him, but he had changed, and she couldn't understand him. She thought she was all right—she went to church, and so forth, and she just couldn't understand this thing. "Will you help me?" she asked.

I was going to Maine, and I couldn't go to her right away. So I got hold of John DeBrine. Actually, John Weliczko, in the meantime, had been asked to go over to her dormitory at Jackson, and he had already spent several hours with her. She finally accepted the Lord through Weliczko's counsel.

Judy and Teddy have been married since. She graduated from Jackson; he graduated from Boston U. the summer of 1966 as an aerospace engineer, and they're going to Conservative Baptist Theological Seminary in Denver, to be really grounded in the Word of God as they try to find the direction of God for their lives.

One interesting thing, when Teddy was baptized, he had to give a word of public testimony. Tension worsens Teddy's speech problem. But, you know, he spoke for perhaps five minutes and had no difficulty whatsoever—not a sign of his impediment.

Those were memorable days in the Blount household. God had made the family circle complete. As Nelson often said, God doesn't do things halfway. He does "exceeding abundantly above all that we ask or think" (Ephesians 3:20).

During those days, God was also bringing about other changes at Staghead Farm. Not only were revolutionary transformations going on within the hearts and lives of the Blounts, but also Staghead Farm was going to become converted!

Chapter 14
A New Owner for Staghead

THE MECHANIC IN the white coveralls at the airport in a Massachusetts city said he had known Nelson Blount for eighteen years, beginning as an apprentice, when he helped work on Nelson's planes. A Roman Catholic, he obviously was impressed with the change in the life of the Bible-quoting, flying industrialist.

"He used to be a real hell-raiser," he told me, as Nelson checked with another mechanic regarding the Cessna we had left to be serviced. "When he came in with his loud talk, punctuated by words not appreciated by a couple of the girls, the gals would go to the washroom."

Confronted later with this comment, Nelson honestly could not remember it being quite that bad. "Men, yes! But very seldom did I swear in front of ladies," he said.

Be that as it may, he had his mouth washed out—with God's soap. The airport mechanic went on to testify to me. "Something's really happened to Nelson. I think it's great," he said thoughtfully. "He's got me believing too."

This was more evidence that the encounter Nelson Blount had with Jesus Christ did more than make an evangelist of him. When the Holy Spirit benignly invaded Nelson's life, a new seed was planted, imparting to him God's nature. It not only guaranteed him heaven and gave him the desire and ability to fellowship with God in this life but also built in a new potential for righteous living. Radical upheavals began; old, undesirable habits shook loose and fell away, and, just as vitamins make for a healthier body, the divine nature improved and affected such areas as Nelson's temperament.

The words of Paul were coming true: "If any man be in Christ, he is a new creature: old things are passed away; behold, all things are become new" (2 Corinthians 5:17).

It was not that Nelson suddenly became perfect; he had not and would not in this life. He constantly had to battle the old nature, and it was disappointing every time he slipped. However, at the outset of his new life, he learned how to restore his fellowship with God (not that he was ever out of God's family, but when he sinned, he simply knew he was not on good terms with his heavenly Father). From memory, he knew the remedy: 1 John 1:9, "If we confess our sins, He [God] is faithful and just to forgive us our sins, and to cleanse us from all unrighteousness."

Thus Nelson Blount had a good beginning in the Christian life.

However, he continued to have a somewhat brusque manner. He was overheard telling an employee who had been touching up a locomotive with paint: "You didn't get much paint on there—whatever you used. I could get more on with a toothbrush!"

However, associates generally agreed that, though still a hard-nosed employer, Nelson was easier to live with than before he met Christ. One of his Steamtown secretaries said,

"If an (employee) isn't doing his work properly, he will get a good talking to, but very rarely does anyone get fired."

This was a switch, of course, from the old days, when Nelson fired and rehired one particular employee "every week."

Happily, there was a certain grace creeping into Nelson that might be identified as a humility that was missing before the divine invasion.

In an informal evening church service, a teenager quoted a Bible verse that had been a blessing to him: "Seek ye first the kingdom of God; and all these things shall be added unto you."

Mr. Blount immediately rose. "That's fine, but I would remind the young man that he omitted the most important part of the verse: 'and His [God's] righteousness.' I heard a message on this recently, and without God's righteousness, we have no hope of finding the kingdom ..." He went on to preach a little sermon as the embarrassed boy stalked out of the service.

That evening after church, Nelson made a discovery: the verse the boy was quoting was Luke 12:31, that had no mention of the phrase "and his righteousness," which was contained in a similar verse, Matthew 6:33. With his three boys, Bob, Steve, and Billy, and his wife Ruth, in the living room, he freely admitted he had been wrong. "I shouldn't have done it that way. I'm absolutely wrong, and I'll apologize to the boy."

Another incident involving Mr. Blount occurred in a small gathering of businessmen. A minister made several remarks that reminded Nelson of the pious platitudes he had formerly heard on Sundays. With the impulsiveness of Simon Peter lashing out with his sword, Nelson leaped from his seat and openly scolded the speaker for not taking a clear-cut stand on the Scriptures. "If you believe that the

Bible is the Word of God, come right out and say so, and preach it." Nelson was totally unacquainted with the man, and when a close associate suggested that he had been tactless and without Christian grace, Nelson phoned the minister and apologized.

In his pre-conversion days, a pipe marked Nelson as a man at peace with the world (though he was not), and a cigar marked him as a hard bargainer (which he was). There were times he made halfhearted efforts to give up smoking. Perhaps with a struggle, he could have, but somehow he never quite mustered up enough willpower. He did not even try to conquer the habit after beginning the Christian walk. Actually, he was too busy with Steamtown and reading his Bible to give it special thought.

The day he went to Gordon College, near Boston, to fill one of his first speaking appointments after his commitment to Christ, Nelson was puffing a stogie. He snuffed it out as he entered the building. In the meeting, a man testified that after he had begun following Christ, he had admitted to God that he simply did not have what it took to quit smoking, even though he had realized it could be hurting his body. At this point, he said that he had relied on the power of the Holy Spirit to help him lick his habit, and it had worked.

Immediately, a Bible thought occurred to Nelson: "I can do all things through Christ which strengtheneth me" (Philippians 4:13). He thought about his own battle with tobacco. He bowed his head and prayed silently, "Lord, I've been trying to do this on my own, and I haven't been able to quit. I want You to take it from me right now. I never want to smoke again."

At home a few days later, Ruth noticed that Nelson had not been smoking and commented on it. His leathery face brightened. "You know, Mama, I hadn't even thought about it. The Lord has given me victory." He soon disposed of his collection of pipes, tossing his cigarettes and cigars away with them.

Though Nelson's new nature within him was pulling him in the right direction, it took nourishment for him to grow and receive God's power to throw off the old habits and traits. Nelson found this out early on. He grew because John DeBrine got him into the Bible in those early months of his new life.

"The new convert should read the Word, live the Word, and he'll begin to love the Word," said Nelson. "I can't seem to get across to people that this isn't an automatic thing. God really wants you to dig; He doesn't reveal everything to a Christian at once. 'Study to show thyself approved unto God, a workman that needeth not to be ashamed ...' The Bible has a great deal in it, but things come only as a result of real intensive search.

"I advocate that new Christians get in fellowship with old, seasoned Bible teachers, as I did, or take a Bible study course. If you get off the track, the Lord straightens you out, provided that you observe three things I see as most important: (1) Keep yourself clean (1 John 1:9); (2) read the Word, which keeps you on the straight and narrow path; and (3) pray regularly."

Nelson quickly realized that his wealth was not his to hold selfishly. Hugh Downs asked Nelson on the *Today* television show how it was that he could be a millionaire and a Christian at the same time. Had not Christ told the rich, young ruler to distribute his wealth and follow Him if he wanted eternal life?

Nelson quickly reminded Downs that the story of the young ruler does not really teach that one must be materially poor to be a follower of Christ. The Bible also has a lot to say about being a good steward, he pointed out. Actually, as Nelson saw it, what he had, in reality, belonged to God;

A New Owner for Staghead

Nelson was primarily a servant working for God. Since they had become Christians, he and Ruth had given substantially of their income to ministries whose primary aim was to proclaim the gospel. In addition, Ruth continued to support an "adopted" Indian boy. ("This boy was saved before we were, showing God's foreknowledge of our family all being one in Christ," marvels Ruth.)

Some people who heard of Blount and his wealth concluded that since he was an enthusiastic, new believer, he also would be a soft touch. One man, a retired minister, after hearing Nelson on the *Today* show, wrote him concerning a project he wanted to start. He was so sure that Nelson would finance it that he enclosed a check filled out for $50,000. All it lacked was Nelson's signature. The check never became negotiable.

To be good stewards, both Nelson and Ruth agreed that their living standards needed adjustments. Though little by little, they trimmed here and there and generally reevaluated their way of life, God did not seem to be calling them to live like paupers. All they had, in reality, belonged to God, they were learning.

It would seem that the fact that Nelson sold their beloved *Aphrodite II* meant that it was too much of a luxury. Yes and no. God gave no certain command about the boat. In 1966, Nelson and Ruth, not being legalists, felt that if they really needed it, they would still own the yacht, for both still enjoyed fishing. They agreed on its sale since Nelson had less and less time for sea vacations, being tied up with Steamtown during July and August (the best swordfishing months) and often traveling for the Lord in speaking engagements.

The sleek yacht had given them so many adventures and pleasurable vacations. After it was sold, when the family spent a vacation at Cape Cod, Nelson chartered a boat, or they used one owned by his brother, Luther, or a company tuna clipper. So they still had their fun.

The member of the family who shed the most tears when *Aphrodite II* was sold, was Carolyn. She still had salt water running in her veins. Her bedroom still had a sea motif, with a fishing net and pictures of colorful Cape Cod vacation spots on one wall. There were also two life preservers from *Aphrodite*, along with a model of the family yacht of yesteryear.

A burden on the hearts of Nelson and Ruth for the establishment of a Christian school in southern New England brought about the most radical change in the Blount economy in Dublin. In 1963, Carolyn was a junior in the Christian high school in Glen Cove, Maine, operated by Christian Schools, Inc. The school was crowded, and the Blounts and other Christian friends began praying for suitable facilities for a similar school in the Dublin area. The George H. Gentsches and the Blounts looked at several prospective sites, but the cost in each case was prohibitive.

The more he looked, the more Nelson prayed. "Lord, You know the big problem. Kids are being taught secularism, and atheistic materialism is creeping into the public schools. We need a Christian school, where kids can learn under Christian teachers and become grounded in Your Word as they receive their education."

As Nelson prayed, thoughts of turning Staghead Farm into a Christian school began to haunt him. "Lord, our place would make a wonderful place for a school, but this is our home; Lord, You don't want this place."

One evening in late spring of 1963, Ruth said, "You know, Daddy, this would make a wonderful place for a school, right here, where we are."

"I don't know what you're thinking," Nelson countered, "but are you thinking the same kind of stuff I've been thinking?" A smile played momentarily on his face. "If that's the case, we ought to give Staghead Farm to the Lord."

They called a family council and discussed the matter with the children. All agreed that if the Lord really wanted Staghead, He could have it.

The next day, Nelson phoned Harold Duff, president of Christian Schools, Inc., in Glen Cove, and asked him to come to see him.

Later, in the spacious living room of Staghead Farm, Nelson came to the point. "Harold, we feel there should be a Christian school in this area. Would you people be interested in running it? You, of course, have several schools now." Nelson went on to offer Staghead. The biggest problem was leadership and a faculty.

Duff replied, "We'll pray about it, Nelson. I don't really know. It's a wonderful offer, and I'm sure the Lord will honor you for your offer."

When Duff returned to his office, he picked up a letter that had just arrived. It was from a Florida pastor named Mel Moody, who felt God was calling him into Christian education in the New Hampshire area. Did Duff have any openings?

"That hit Harold right between the eyes," Blount later recalled. "He got on the telephone, and within a few weeks, the school agreed to at least sponsor the project. They came over and looked into the matter further. Meantime, Moody came up and agreed to be director of the school. Within a couple of months, the whole organization was put together."

Thus, in May of 1964, such headlines as these hit area papers:

STEAMTOWN OWNER GIVES FARM AWAY
DUBLIN MAN DONATES PROPERTY TO SCHOOL

An *Associated Press* news dispatch, datelined Rockland, Maine, began:

> Industrialist F. Nelson Blount has given his $350,000 estate in Dublin, N. H., to Christian Schools, Inc., of Glen Cove. The school trustees voted Wednesday to accept the one thousand-acre estate, and said they would open a Christian high school on it ...

The school was dedicated in late summer of 1964, with some 400 people present. Harold Duff led the service and accepted the gift of the farm from the Blounts on behalf of the board of directors.

Twenty-eight students from seven states enrolled and were on hand for classes when Dublin Christian Academy opened in September. Included were Carolyn Blount, who entered as a senior, and Bob Blount, a sophomore. (The second year, Dublin Christian Academy enrolled thirty-six students, and in September of 1966, it opened with fifty. In 2011, it had graduated over 700 students.)

With a growing burden for the Academy's double-barreled program of academic and Bible training, the Blounts did not stop with giving the farm. They continued to give generously to support the school.

Giving their home away in May so that it could become a school in September caused the Blounts to have to make some fast decisions. Where were they going to move? Should they build or buy? What type of house?

The Blounts decided to build on thirty acres of property they kept a quarter of a mile west of the farm. The building site was perfect for a home. It was on a hill overlooking Dublin Christian Academy, with majestic Monadnock guarding the location to the west. Between the site and the mountain, there was a wooded valley with a network of meandering streams and animal life.

A New Owner for Staghead

Because of Ruth's knee and hip problems resulting from her highway accident, the Blounts planned a long, one-floor, frame, ranch-style house. It would be far less pretentious than Staghead Farm's seventeen-room main house.

The contractor pushed the construction hard, but houses generally are not built in a short period. So as August rolled around, the Blounts were looking for a temporary place to live, in order to allow the academy to move in and get the big house set up for classroom use.

The George Gentsches, of nearby Hancock, New Hampshire, invited the Blounts to live with them in their spacious, four-bedroom home. Not wanting to crowd the Gentsches, the Blounts declined, accepting instead the offer to occupy a two-bedroom, furnished apartment that was also owned by the Gentsches. Nelson and Ruth, with their three younger children, moved in on August 18, 1964, and occupied the apartment for three months, until their new home was ready.

Though it was only a humble cottage compared to their former home and other fashionable mansions in Dublin, their newly-built gray ranch house with its white shutters offered a lot of comfortable living. There were five bedrooms, a spacious living room, an efficient kitchen, a dining room, and a den. In the living room on a winter's evening, a warm fire crackled in the fireplace, and Smoky, a black and brown dachshund, snoozed in the dancing shadows.

On the outside wall, separated by picture windows, hung large oil portraits of Ruth and Nelson, painted fifteen years before. A library occupied the wall opposite the fireplace, and a glance told you that Nelson—or somebody—was a steam fan. There were literally scores of books relating to the Steam Age, including of course, *Along the Iron Trail* by Blount and Richardson. In addition, there were, to be sure, books by great Christians of yesterday and that day, plus a library of the taped sermons and lectures that Nelson listened to in his car or at home.

The den featured a chair carved in the form of a grizzly bear, and you could sit in his lap. On a wall behind was a mounted deer head with ten-point antlers. In the corner was a piano, at which you might find Nelson after dinner, playing and singing some of the songs that he had learned in the past few years—"How Great Thou Art," "To God Be the Glory," and a host of others.

In front of the Blount home, Nelson's 140-yard asphalt landing strip sloped away into a grassy hillside. Nelson took off in his Cessna 180, and the hill literally dropped from beneath the plane. There was a 2 percent drop to the strip, and the field sloped even more. The hill, he felt, was perfect for sheltering him from a strong head wind whenever he came in low to touch down well below the asphalt strip.

Only once did the front-yard airstrip cause Nelson anxious moments. But the incident, a near tragedy, had a happy ending. Nelson told about it in these terms:

> I was flying a preacher's daughter to Word of Life at Schroon Lake, New York. She weighed about 140 pounds, and with her bag and all, I guess I was hauling 200 pounds besides myself and what I had. I had a different plane, a high performance job, with flaps that would even get out better than the 180 I have now. We took off and got off all right, but a short time later, we ran into fog. So I recognized I couldn't fly safely in that stuff. I turned her back, and we landed and waited around for two hours.
>
> Suddenly the wind shifted, and it got real windy from the north, making it foolhardy to take off downhill. So, even though there are trees up ahead, we proceeded to take off uphill. We were airborne quickly, but at the top of the hill, we got into a downdraft and lost altitude, and the engine began losing power at the same moment.

I recognized we weren't going to clear the trees, and I dropped the plane down. We went over a stonewall and took the undercarriage off and continued on into the trees, going about sixty miles per hour. We mowed down some small trees and came to an abrupt stop, where our home is today. Neither of us was hurt, but the plane was a total wreck.

We had prayed, thanking the Lord we weren't hurt, as people from all around came running to our rescue. I had heard a sermon a few days before by John DeBrine, saying a Christian is never the victim of his circumstances. So I said to the girl, "I can't understand this, but the Lord has some reason, and the airplane is insured; there's nothing detrimental here."

I called a friend of mine and asked him to loan me a plane. In two hours, up he came, and he had the plane I have today, a plane that had just been traded in by a bank for a twin-engine plane; he told me to use it for a month. So I used the plane. We took off and went to Word of Life. I did some of the talking, giving my testimony. I was OK except for a black eye.

Later, an insurance adjuster came and settled the airplane thing. He gave me enough money for the plane to buy this new plane I have and have money left over, so I actually came out better. This airplane is older—six years old—but it had fewer hours on it and has an automatic pilot and two radios and other things that the plane I cracked up didn't have.

But I kept asking, "Lord, there must be a reason for this accident. What is it?" One day the adjuster called. I had given him my testimony. He wanted me to speak to his men's club in his church and give them my story.

Well, this church was liberal; they didn't have a minister and were in the middle of a real change in the church. I spoke and gave an invitation, and, as I recall, over thirty men made professions that night. The insurance adjuster himself made a decision for the Lord.

One of the men that sells me paint, who had made a decision for Christ in my office, came and brought his brother-in-law, and his brother-in-law made a decision for Christ. Since that time, they have both really gone on for the Lord. So many things have come out of that accident.

Weather permitting, Nelson flew to work at Steamtown as routinely as other businessmen drive to their offices from suburbia. It saved him more than an hour a day, which was important to a man as busy as Nelson. He especially appreciated the timesaving factor during the hectic days of the Steamtown fracas in New Hampshire and as he began to build the new Steamtown—a time when he was, in his own words, "architect, building engineer, contractor, and expediter." The fact that he never gave up is undoubtedly one reason L. G. Bucklin, executive vice president of the Rutland Railway Corporation, once said of Nelson, "In railroad lexicon, 'he's a good runner.'"

Chapter 15
HIGHBALLING IT TO VERMONT

IN LATE 1962, Steamtown edged toward fulfillment in New Hampshire, even though several state newspapers still insisted that the Granite State, whose number two source of income was the tourist business, had no right to spend one million dollars on an amusement project. Crusading newsmen, such as, Paul Cummings, Jr., editor of the *Peterborough Transcript*, and William Loeb, publisher of the *Manchester Union Leader*, continued to rebuke the governor and his council, who had approved the Steamtown idea "in principle" nearly two years before, claiming that the men in Concord were tax squanderers.

But even so, around Keene especially, hopes remained high that Steamtown would move from North Walpole to the $100,000 site the city had set aside for Nelson Blount's greatest steam show on earth. Nelson himself was not quite as hopeful. He was fed up with insinuations and outright accusations. His offer of equipment for a steam museum had been with sincere motives, he insisted. He was not making the donation simply to make another million on his excursion line, which would be tied in with the museum.

As a new Christian during those days of being misjudged and unappreciated by many, Nelson felt much like the Psalmist David, who also ran up against a few enemies in his day and wrote:

> Make haste, O God, to deliver me; make haste to help me, O LORD. Let them be ashamed and confounded that seek after my soul: let them be turned backward, and put to confusion, that desire my hurt.
> —Psalm 70:1–2

About this time, Nelson was admiring the scenery in the state of Vermont and telling civic clubs and other groups that, all things considered, Steamtown just might locate in the Green Mountain State. It appeared the Rutland Railway would go out of business, and perhaps steam excursions could be run on a stretch of Rutland trackage.

But New Hampshire Steamtown enthusiasts felt the steam show would surely become a Granite State project, especially when the B & M agreed to sell Blount the Keene-Walpole trackage, subject to ICC approval.

Eyes were turned toward Concord. The Steamtown project depended on the governor and his five-man, executive council, plus a final OK on Blount's getting the Keene-Walpole line from the B & M. Time was becoming more and more a factor. Outgoing Republican Governor Powell was welcoming into office a Democrat, John King, whom he supported, and King had appeared friendly toward the idea of Steamtown. Which governor would get the final report on the issue was a question that had everybody wondering.

As time grew near for Governor Powell to leave office, along with four of the five councilors who had "in principle" favored Steamtown, another voice was heard. John Rowe, commissioner of the Department of Resources and Economic Development, proposed that the state—not Blount—purchase the B & M trackage and right-of-way and operate steam excursion trains. "We feel the state should own the whole works," said Rowe.

But in February of 1963, the advisory commission of Mr. Rowe's department turned thumbs down on Steamtown by a vote of five to one. It did not have enough Granite flavor. That was the death rattle for what had been an exciting, live issue. Death came a short time later, when Governor John King's executive council voted three to two against the state owning Steamtown.

Yankee conservatism, in effect, was telling Blount, "Go blow your whistle somewhere else."

Keene's mayor, Robert Mallat, Jr., moaned that the decision was one of New Hampshire's "biggest mistakes."

Just how certain it seemed that Steamtown would become a state project was indicated by the fact that a state tourist map for 1963 listed "a live museum of the steam locomotive era" as coming to Keene.

Nevertheless, steam excursions ran in New Hampshire in 1963—from North Walpole south to Westmoreland. But any possibility of Blount's buying the line vanished when the B & M decided, upon pressure of the state, to continue freight operations on the rails.

In the meantime, the steam show itself remained in the yards south of the Walpole roundhouse, fearful that at any moment the state might cut through the property with its new highway project. But the equipment was to remain there until 1967.

Over in Vermont, the new democratic governor, Philip Hoff, watched television as a newscaster told of Steamtown's heave-ho from New Hampshire. The Steamtown project had been a subject of interest in Montpelier for some months, ever since Nelson Blount discussed the matter with Hoff's predecessor, Governor F. Ray Keyser, Jr. A phone call from Hoff to Blount indicated that the Green Mountain State definitely would like the steam spectacle. Yes, there was a chance that Blount could have a piece of the Rutland. No, a bond issue was out of question, for Vermont and its 389,881 residents could not afford to make Steamtown a state-run project. But otherwise, Vermont would be willing to bandage the wounds Blount had suffered in New Hampshire.

In the meantime, Blount set up a foundation—Steamtown Foundation for the Preservation of Steam and Railroad Americana—and donated twenty engines and other steam equipment, promising more, year by year. It was expected that eventually, the foundation, which received contributions from those interested in preserving the Steam Age, would own all of Blount's collection.

Nelson Blount was listed as founder and chairman. Other trustees included such names as: Lane Dwinell, former governor of New Hampshire; William B. Murphy, president of Campbell Soup Company; E. Spencer Miller, president of Maine Central Railroad; Nelson's old friend, Fred Richardson; and his "spiritual father," Ted DeMoss. (Others who were later on the board of trustees of the Steamtown Foundation were: Thomas P. Salmon, municipal judge, Bellows Falls; Robert L. Mallat, Jr., mayor of Keene; Edgar Mead, partner, Haas and Company, New York City; Richard Morehouse, partner, Morehouse and Chesley, Lexington, Massachusetts; Emile Bussiere, attorney, Manchester, New Hampshire; Nathan C. Hubley, Jr., president, The Carter's Ink Company, Boston; David Williams, Jr., president of the Association of Holiday Inns of America, Orlando, Florida; Tom Willey, vice president and general manager of The Martin Marietta Corporation, Orlando, Florida; Andrew

Hughes, treasurer of Rheem Manufacturing Company, New York City; Dr. James Humphries, chief physician, Home Life Insurance Company, New York City; Robert Gilmour LeTourneau, president of R. O. LeTourneau, Inc., Longview, Texas; Dalton K. Stratton, vice president of Blount Seafood Corporation; and Frederick Nelson Ted Blount.)

With headlines blazing across New England papers that the steam orphan was looking for another home, Blount got invitations from thirty-six communities in various sections of the United States. Orlando, Florida, offered $250,000, 100 acres, and a minimum of a one-million-dollar development fund. Oneonta, New York, produced an attractive sixteen-page brochure, urging him to bring Steamtown there.

However, Nelson began to spend more time in Vermont, keeping in touch with officials in Montpelier. All concerned were waiting for further developments involving the wonderful, old Rutland that had sputtered along for 119 years, plagued by strikes, bankruptcy, seizure, and other ills.

Its recent history had gone something like this: The colorful road appeared to be returning to good health in 1957, when William I. Ginsburg assumed the presidency of the line, bringing with him solid business experience and respect as Vermont chairman of the Democratic Party.

However, thunderheads gathered as employee morale declined and the operation was plagued by other problems, including rising prices and loss of business to trucks. Then, ultimately, lightning struck—four brotherhoods walked off their jobs on September 15, 1960.

Vermonters wept when Ginsburg applied for abandonment of the 333-mile line. The Rutland simply could not die; it was needed. Businessmen rose up with a Save-the-Rutland campaign, but it lacked the fervor of the button-wearing, banner-waving demonstration of 1938, when a similar situation existed.

Finally, with weeds growing five feet high between the Rutland's rusty rails, the ICC agreed with Ginsburg. In a fifty-seven-page document, ICC said the overall odds were against successful operation of the road, and the 119-year-old Rutland could, with government permission, lie down and die.

Then, in May of 1963, with Governor Hoff spearheading the move, the state purchased 180 miles of the Rutland track for 2.7 million dollars, with the view of leasing it and restoring rail service. It was a move that would ultimately prove to be the first time a defunct road had been revived to live for more than two and a half years.

Jay Wulfson, former operator of the Middletown and New Jersey Railroad, leased the Burlington to Bennington stretch of the Rutland and organized the Vermont Railway, leaving the fifty-two mile stretch between Bellows Falls and Rutland for someone else. (After two years, Wulfson was in the black, averaging some 700 cars a month and serving over 100 shippers.)

About the time Wulfson made his bid, Blount tossed in his engineer's cap, bidding for the trackage between Bellows Falls and Ludlow, about halfway to Rutland to the north. He added that eventually he would be interested in the track all the way to Rutland, if studies showed that a short-haul freight railroad would be feasible. And, of course, he had to prove to ICC that freight service was actually needed. Brightening his prospects was the assertion of a lime-plant operator, who said he would have to leave or go out of business without rail transportation.

Actually, Blount's primary purpose for wanting the Rutland track was twofold: He could simultaneously operate his excursion runs and a year-round freight-passenger line, enabling him to keep skilled employees and other workers throughout the year, without the layoffs after the tourist season.

With the 1964 excursion season approaching, Nelson had to act swiftly. He could not use the B & M trackage from North Walpole to Westmoreland again; the solution seemed to be the Rutland trackage. Vermont gave him the green light, without his signing a formal leasing agreement, but he ran into a roadblock. The B & M refused him permission to use its trackage to get his rolling stock out of New Hampshire and across the Connecticut River, into Bellows Falls, to the Rutland trackage.

With the tourist season near, Nelson became anxious, for prospects for an early settlement with B & M seemed slim. It was not surprising. In recent years, Blount and B & M had grown farther and farther apart, even though it had been a B & M gift that had launched him into collecting standard-gauge equipment.

Could word have leaked back to B & M brass that certain bondholders had courted Blount a few years before, with the view of putting him in as president to set the B & M house in better order? At the time, Nelson had seemed willing enough, even to the extent of taking a big pay cut, if necessary—for, after all, railroading was in his blood.

But Nelson was not interested in being president of anything except Monadnock Northern, and as that road's chief executive, he wanted to highball it to the Green Mountain State. He and his family talked to God about the matter for some days. God, they had learned, was interested in every phase of a Christian's life. "Lord," Nelson would pray, "the B & M has me trapped; what are we going to do?"

For the rest of his life, Nelson believed that it was an answer to prayer the day an official of the dying Rutland called him with a solution. In effect, he said, "Nelson, we've been reading about what the B & M is doing to you, and we think it's a rotten deal. I have a plan. The state hasn't officially taken over, and they won't until the governor signs the deed of sale, so we still own the rights. We have the right to come right over to your engine house, use your turntable and everything. We have one locomotive left—we'll send it down any time you say, preferably early in the morning, and we'll haul all your stuff over to Vermont. Once you're over in Vermont, you can tell B & M to go fishing."

Not wishing to cause Rutland officials further weighty problems, Nelson questioned his caller: "You're sure this isn't going to get you into a mess?"

"Absolutely not. We've got all the working agreements; the B & M has overlooked canceling them," came the voice on the phone. "We'd better get this show on the road before their attorneys wake up and cancel the working agreements."

"OK, I'm for that," Nelson said. "Come down at four o'clock in the morning."

Thus, in the early hours of May 28, 1964, a Rutland diesel crossed the diamond in the B & M yards. The signal was not operational, so a man flagged. A short while later, rolling stock that Nelson needed to begin his excursion run moved into Vermont, over B & M tracks.

During those days, Blount and his excursion associates had been talking with the B & M people about a working agreement, but as far as Blount was concerned, B & M had a cold firebox. So it was that the Blount boys and certain B & M brass were meeting on the matter in Boston the very day the excursion stock moved into Vermont, courtesy of the all-but-dead Rutland.

As a secretary brought a message in to a B & M executive, Nelson smiled to himself. The scarlet that crept up the official's neck verified for Nelson what the message said.

The B & M man exploded. "They have just crossed our main line without notifying the dispatcher. We won't even talk to such people. Gentlemen, let's return to our office and forget this whole thing." These, in substance, were his words.

A lawyer turned to Nelson, stunned. "What on earth have you done?"

"Sit tight. They're the ones in trouble—not us." Nelson went on to explain that in overlooking the working agreements with the Rutland, B & M had left a legal loophole for the Blount steam stock to roll over B & M track into Vermont. The agreement had been made a century before by B & M. The Rutland had priority in crossing a B & M line; in the absence of signals, a man would flag manually. Thus the Rutland line, in one of its last acts, legally had hauled the equipment into Vermont. The B & M, Nelson concluded, had abandoned the signals, and there was no man to signal manually as prescribed by the agreement. So, it was the B & M that could get into hot water, not Blount and company or Rutland. The B & M had jumped the gun; they had considered the Rutland dead when there was still life in the old road.

Back in Bellows Falls, villagers who knew what had happened were chuckling. But B & M still could not quite see the humor of it, evidenced by the charges it filed with the ICC against Blount. Later, the railroad dropped the charges.

Nelson began operating his 1964 excursion runs from a "cow pasture" two miles north of Bellows Falls, even though he was still steaming about the indignities he suffered at the hands of the B & M in their not allowing him to originate his runs from the Bellows Falls station. The pasture was not only inefficient and expensive, but also it was bad public relations with tourists who traveled miles to ride the steam trains.

From the pasture, named Riverside, Monadnock Northern trains puffed between the improvised terminal and Chester Depot, thirteen miles to the north. A Canadian Pacific 4-6-2, *No. 1293*, thrilled steam buffs during September and October. This engine joined *No.15* on doubleheader runs. Meanwhile, another Canadian National engine, 2-6-0, *No. 89*, was being readied.

Though Nelson had leased the Rutland trackage in 1964 in the name of the Green Mountain Railroad, ICC approval on the common carrier line did not come through until March of 1965. Though he was not a diesel fan, the owner of the new road purchased the one remaining Rutland diesel, *No.405*, and the first freight train rumbled along the track on April 3.

For a time, Blount again battled the B & M regarding freight rates, and B & M slapped an embargo on the new road at Bellows Falls, leaving Green Mountain with no connecting line. The B & M finally ordered the embargo lifted in February of 1966. After that, Green Mountain remained an important link between Bellows Falls and Rutland, fifty-two miles, connecting with Wulfson's Vermont road and the Delaware and Hudson to the north, and the B & M to the south.

There was at least one train a day on the Green Mountain—actually, a mixed train that was hauling freight and passengers. In some instances, passengers rode in the caboose and enjoyed some of Vermont's most scenic country while playing conductor. The line originated 180 cars a month, servicing eight major firms, including Johnson & Johnson's talcum powder plant. A salesman was even added to drum up new business and take some of the area shipping off the highways and back to the rails.

In 1966, Green Mountain—completely separate from Monadnock Northern, though both used the same rails—had two diesels, three steam locomotives, twenty-five freight cars, and ten passenger cars. Blount was ready to add more rolling stock when business warranted it.

Interestingly, Green Mountain rented equipment to the excursion line, and Monadnock Northern paid Green Mountain for the right to use its rails. And since the excursion line operated on common carrier tracks, Monadnock rolling stock, as well as Green Mountain equipment, had to be maintained according to ICC specifications.

In 1965, approximately 48,000 people thrilled to the "All aboard" of Monadnock trainmen and rode off into yesteryear behind the sound of steam. Most overlooked the cow-pasture look of Riverside. Nelson was the person bothered most by it. He felt he had let the public down. But he had high hopes and big plans of making things up to steam buffs and other tourists in the future.

Chapter 16

MAGNIFICENT STEAMTOWN, 1967

OLD *NO. 89*, A 2-6-0 MOGUL, looked as spirited as she must have been the day the Canadian Locomotive Company gave her a christening pat in 1910 and sent her away for her first run. There at Riverside she sat, purring, with thick, black smoke billowing from her stack and wisps of steam playing about her six great drive wheels. Behind her in her tender, destined to produce more black smoke, was ten tons of oil-treated coal.

From high in the cab window, Engineer F. Nelson Blount waited, squinting as crowds of tourists scampered toward the half-dozen, bright, yellow, wooden coaches and other excursionists purchased tickets at the picturesque, little, red-and-green-trimmed station. Blount looked like an engineer should: face tanned by wind and sun; faded, blue overall jacket; and a navy blue, corduroy cap with the brass emblem, "Chief Engineer, Green Mountain Railroad." But that day he was working for the Monadnock Northern, which he usually did when he was in the area during the excursion season.

Magnificent Steamtown, 1967

With most of the passengers in their seats, Conductor Louis Dion, a grandfatherish, retired B & M road foreman, looked at his gold pocket watch. "All aboard!" he cried, and stragglers rushed to the ticket window.

As the last passengers climbed on the train, a man in a tall, white chef's hat and white apron walked toward the station from the open-air restaurant, where he had been barbecuing chicken. The man, Ralph Hogancamp, picked up a microphone and, in a friendly voice, addressed the passengers in the waiting coaches:

> Good afternoon, ladies and gentlemen, boys and girls. It's my pleasure to welcome you here to Steamtown, USA and let you know that we are pleased you came. We hope to bring a bit of pleasure to you.
>
> The trip you are about to take on the former Rutland Railroad and now the Green Mountain Railroad is entirely in the state of Vermont. You're going to travel along the Connecticut River for a little distance. You'll note the river is very much like a lake at this point, and that is because of the hydroelectric dam at Bellows Falls, which sets the water back forty miles.
>
> As you leave the Connecticut River Valley, you will be going under a high viaduct, the bridge that carries Interstate 91. And from this point on, you will be in the Williams River Valley—that river named after the Rev. Williams, who was the first Christian minister to preach the gospel in this part of North America. He preached up here at the mouth of the river, not only to the early white settlers but also to the Indians of whom he was captive at the time he was marched northward from the Deerfield Massacre in Massachusetts toward Quebec. Those were rugged days.
>
> You're going to cross the Williams River seven times between here and Chester. One of these crossings will be over a spectacular gorge. Then you're going by two

covered bridges; on your way back, you'll stop at one of the bridges and go very slow over the gorge. Both of these occasions, of course, are for your enjoyment of the scenery and picture taking.

I think you'd be interested to know that you're going to climb 298 feet from the time you leave this station until you arrive at Chester Depot, and that is cause for the fireman to have a busy job on the way up. The train of yellow cars—built in the car shops at Laconia and Concord, New Hampshire, at the turn of the century—with our engine *No.15* (currently in the roundhouse), was in the motion picture *The Cardinal* some years ago ..."

Hogancamp, still at the mike, gave more details about Steamtown, inviting passengers who had not seen the stationary exhibit to visit the museum area upon their return.

Then, as the conductor gave the signal, Engineer Blount tooted the whistle, released the brakes, and pulled the throttle forward gently. Seconds later, steam power seized the drive wheels, and the old Mogul huffed and puffed; the train was leaving Riverside on a ride into the nostalgic days of yesterday, when Steam was king.

In the cab of the engine, a gleeful, chunky passenger settled down for a rollicking ride. He was a United Air Lines flight engineer from San Francisco and had paid double fare to ride up front.

Soon, they were rocking along, cinders flying and trees along the right-of-way only a green blur. Over the rumble of steam at work, the UAL man, jiggling in his seat on the fireman's side, yelled to the engineer, "Clear air turbulence, eh, Captain?" He had flown hundreds of thousands of miles on jets; this trip on an engine, his first for twenty years, admittedly gave him a greater kick than his routine flights.

On the trip to Chester, the passenger in the cab was dazzled by what he heard and saw. To keep the boiler pressure up to 160 pounds, Fireman Maurice DeValliere, a graduate geologist captured by the romance of steam, shoveled fast and furiously, his face reflecting the orange glow from the firebox. He seemingly turned a dozen hand wheels and pushed a lever to control the flow of steam.

Like 10,000 horses, the engine snorted up the incline, past the Interstate 91 viaduct, gaining speed as she showed steam buffs with cameras along the right-of-way, what a fancy Dan she was, despite her fifty-six years! *Chug, chug, chug,* her mighty, deep-throated voice echoed importantly through the wooded hills. The engineer pulled heavily on the whistle at every bend and at each crossing—two longs, a short, and a long that faded out across pasturelands like the wail of a banshee, sending black and white Holsteins scattering and skittish horses trotting, their magnificent tails gracefully waving at the passing train.

All too soon, the train slowed down, drifted past a bright yellow tower, and with whistle blowing and bell clanging, eased to a creaking stop at Chester Depot. Passengers piled out to explore the 100-year-old station until it was time for the return trip.

As they were returning to Riverside, passengers in the coaches, again took in all of the scenic beauty along the route. Everyone rushed with awe to windows as the train stopped at the 150-foot-deep Brockway Mills Gorge, and cameras recorded the pause at the unpainted, quaint, covered bridge a few yards from the track. Then, as the train picked up speed, riders munched candy bars and sipped soft drinks purchased from the refreshment vendor.

A few passengers read again the Steam Era "regulations" on their ten-inch-long, orange tickets: "That in the event that brush should happen to grow too close to the cars, the holder will not disturb its continuity through the process of leaning too far out the window(s); ... This railroad shall not be responsible for any delays caused by the presence of any uncooperative cows or other animals on the right-of-way ..." There were smiles, especially at the seventh item on the list: "Diesel proponents may be required to show justification for their patronage."

Back at Riverside, after the twenty-six-mile, ninety-minute trip, passengers detrained to visit the souvenir shop or get a snack from the open-air restaurant. Some carried tape recorders and were happy at having captured some of the wonderful sounds of steam. Camera bugs had pictures of their excursion trip on color film, and a few had the autograph of Engineer Blount tucked away in their shirt pockets. And all had memories that would linger for years and be kept alive even longer by rail books and sounds-of-steam records purchased in the souvenir shop.

"Did you see the engineer get off the engine at the gorge?" someone asked. "I was holding my breath, wondering if we'd ever get back. There he was on the very edge of the gorge, sawing away bushes!" (On the trip, Blount had taken a saw with him to trim away growth that was obstructing the view of the gorge and, with the aid of Fireman DeValliere, had proceeded to accomplish his task high above the churning waters.)

As *No. 89* waited at Riverside for another run, Chief Engineer Blount chatted with train fans. A wealthy, young man wearing a trainman's outfit talked about renting Monadnock equipment for a special excursion run into Pennsylvania, and Nelson assured him there would be no problem. Then, spouting specific details about his steam show and painting a two-million-dollar picture of the future, Nelson answered questions of other fans about particular engines and certain sights and wonders of Steamtown. The average Steamtown visitor listened bug-eyed at such things as, for example, how certain locomotives came to Steamtown.

The 4-8-8-4 *Big Boy*, biggest mobile machine ever built, headed the list of interesting locomotives at Steamtown. Presented to Nelson by the Union Pacific Railroad, it was 135 feet long and weighed 1,189,500 pounds; yet in its heyday, it ripped along at speeds of up to eighty miles per hour. UP paid approximately $265,000 in the early forties for the giant and retired it in 1962, after more than a million miles of freight and passenger service. Steamtown paid a freight bill of about $6,000 to get *Big Boy* from the Union Pacific yards in Council Bluffs, Iowa, to the museum site. En route, *Big Boy*'s tender failed to properly negotiate a curve in Manchester, New York, and three wheels on one side left the track. To remedy matters, railroad workers built a platform for the wheels to move over, and then another engine pushed the tender and *Big Boy* forward as the wheels caught a metal rod that pushed them back on the track.

At that time, there were about fifty steam locomotives at Steamtown, and others were coming month by month. Ultimately, Blount expected to have some 100 engines on display. Among other items, there were eight cabooses, a steam-fire engine, a steamroller, a steam shovel, and steam-traction engines, plus countless smaller items harking back to the Steam Age.

FDR's plush diner-lounge car, *The Mountaineer*, attracted much attention at Steamtown. Even though it was used on excursion runs for a time, it was deemed too heavy and changed to an air-conditioned diner for visitors desiring atmosphere dining. *The Mountaineer* was built in 1930 by the Pullman Standard Car Company for the B & M. It was formerly called the *Maine* and traveled several times next to the Presidential car, the *Magellan*, when Roosevelt made trips to his summer retreat in Maine. The interior of the car was well-known for its colonial period decor. One of the doorways in the dining room section was said to have been copied after a famous New England house.

In addition, there were two other private cars on exhibit.

Nelson Blount talked about gathering rail equipment as casually as a rancher might speak of rounding up cattle. For example, he said:

> We bought two engines recently from Louisiana that were built in 1870 and 1880. I have four engines sitting down in the Everglades right now. I have two American engines on the way from Brazil, where I discovered them when I was there with Jack Wyrtzen. I'm bringing the Queen's locomotive over from England. Through a friend, General de Gaulle is giving a locomotive from France, and I'm dealing also for other engines in Europe. I try to get various types of everything.
>
> I have a couple of trams coming from Europe—France and Germany. A tram is like a streetcar with a boiler on it. The boiler made its own power and people sat alongside the boiler and the tram ran down the streets just like a streetcar.
>
> I brought home three steam carousels from Europe—one went to California, the other to a tourist resort in New Hampshire, and I'll keep the other. These particular carousels originally ran by horse power—a horse ran on a treadmill. They were converted to steam and then later were electrified. I'm keeping the one operated by steam.

To be sure, there were a number of places throughout the United States where steam hobbyists kept the Steam Age alive, exhibiting a few pieces of rolling stock and/or featuring excursion runs. But Steamtown was a five-ring Barnum and Bailey big top compared to the rest. And whether people liked him or not, knowledgeable steam fans thought of Nelson Blount as Mr. Steam.

Like fabled trains of yesterday that could be stopped by nothing short of slides or high water, he had steamed on through not only the storms of New Hampshire but also past roadblocks and political fog in Vermont to make Steamtown a reality. After he was pushed into the cow pasture north of Bellows Falls, he finally purchased the ninety-acre tract for $20,080, under the name of Green Mountain Railroad. (The property served both Green Mountain and Steamtown, with the latter paying rent to the railroad.)

Immediately, as earth-moving machinery (operated by a small company in which Nelson bought interest) leveled out the land, Nelson began wondering why the Lord ever let him get into the pasture, which was part swamp. The hydroelectric dam had backed up water and eroded some twenty-five acres. He had personally invested more than $150,000 in the project. *But why*, he asked himself. Words in Nelson's Bible described his feelings: "Save me, O God for … I sink in deep mire, where there is no standing." (Psalm 69:1–2).

One morning, he prayed out by the Connecticut River and talked over his problems with God. It was 9:30 when he finished. At 9:45, as he walked into his office in the North Walpole shop, the telephone rang. Rutland Railroad, still maintaining an office, wondered if he had any use for a contract that specified that the New England Power Company, upon demand, would bear the cost of raising the level of the property seven feet. The contract had been signed with Rutland, which owned the land when the hydroelectric dam was built.

"Can you think of a more direct answer to prayer?" Nelson later said. "Here we were, sinking a big sum of money just to push dirt into the area to make the swampland usable."

In late 1966, New England Power Company settled the matter, paying Green Mountain Railroad a sum to cover costs on work already done in raising the level of the land and, in addition, giving thirty-five additional adjoining acres of property.

Blount often wondered just what had happened to the red carpet in Vermont. The state ended up being only slightly more receptive than New Hampshire. Despite studies that showed that the turnstiles at Steamtown were turning faster by the year, the state was not being very cooperative. For one thing, the highway department harassed him about directional signs along the highway. He had to remove a sign at the turnoff to Steamtown, resulting in confusion to tourists and even leading to accidents.

When he was trying to get the Vermont project off the ground, Steamtown needed about $130,000, but those who went to bat for Blount struck out. He told a newsman, "You know, we're not asking the town or the state for any money. We merely wish to take out a regular business loan, which we'll pay back in three years or less. But the local area will be the one to benefit. Tens of thousands of tourists will pour through here, on an even greater magnitude than previous years. Merchants will gain up to twelve dollars a day per person for each day of our season. That's a good slice of money!"

As an individual, Blount had the assets to back up the sizable loan he wanted, but Steamtown's only assets were steam locomotives—and a bright future.

In late 1966, Mr. Steam at last found a sympathetic bank in the Vermont Bank and Trust Co., and the needed money was about to be made available.

Still, despite his trials, Blount was happy to be in Vermont. The scenery was great, and there had been helpful people at Montpelier, such as Ernest Gibson, Public Utilities Commissioner. So prospects for a full-scale Steamtown spectacle were growing with each passing month.

In 1967, the museum stock was scheduled to be on display at Riverside, bringing together Steamtown, USA and its sister company, Monadnock Northern, the excursion run. The display would include a turntable capable of switching engines to forty-two tracks. All of this was Stage One, Blount said, and would cost about $250,000, including the preparation of the land and landscaping.

Stage Two was a museum, roundhouse, and a side-wheeler steamboat. The museum, of course, would house much of the stationary equipment. The side-wheeler, which was specially designed by Blount, would "lend an atmosphere of romance and authenticity as it takes visitors on excursions along the Connecticut River," said the Steamtown founder.

Nelson frequently told people of the historical significance of the river. "John Fitch designed the first steamboat that plied the Connecticut River at Bellows Falls long before Robert Fulton's *Clermont* was in operation. Fitch's boat ran in 1787 and Fulton's in 1807."

Stage Three would complete the two million dollar Steamtown complex that Blount and other trustees had planned. It would include a New England village of the 1890s, when steam was reaching its prime, that would feature stores where visitors could shop, a small electric trolley line, and a sparkling white church with a towering spire where gospel services would be held regularly. There also would be a neat, orderly version of a typical late nineteenth century rail yard.

Steamtown's Blount hoped that all of the plans would become a reality by 1970.

In the meantime, during 1967, he expected over 100,000 visitors to check in at Steamtown and 90,000 passengers to ride excursion trains.

That year, Nelson Blount's newest brainchild, the Gospel Special, was featured a number of times. Interestingly, Gospel Specials grew out of Nelson's reading a Vermont law that was passed in 1840 and was never repealed. The law directed conductors on passenger trains operated on Sundays, to read from the Bible to passengers.

"We tried several Gospel Specials last year," Nelson said. "We never used to run excursions until early Sunday afternoon, so we wouldn't compete with church. People put pressure on me to change this, since so many people wanted to ride on Sunday mornings. So we decided to run a trial Gospel Special to Summit, leaving at eleven. I announced to passengers that we would be holding a service, that they could attend or simply explore the area, whatever their desires. Most of them came to the service.

"I started out the program by telling them what the Vermont law states. A hundred years ago, I told them, God wasn't dead—and I told them that God isn't dead today either. I went on for more than half an hour, reading the Bible and explaining it, and telling them what God has done for me."

For the 1967 season, Blount planned to invite various laymen to conduct services and share their own stories of how their faith in God changed their lives. But there was also a certainty that the man from Steamtown would himself be the engineer and master of ceremonies on the Gospel Specials. Like railroading itself, this matter of sharing the good news with others was in his blood.

Chapter 17
WHISTLE-STOPPING FOR THE LORD

WITH A CASCADING stream of double-talk that has no sure source of reference, and which the layman cannot truly comprehend, even if his life depended on it, theologians of the modern God-Is-Dead cult attempt to bury historic Christianity. Fortunately, as F. Nelson Blount, Monadnock Northern's chief theologian, asserted, no one's life depends on digesting this unbiblical, theological hash. While the cultists of his day talked in vague, mystical terms about taking a step "toward life when one truly acknowledges that God is dead," Blount blew the whistle vehemently on such nonsense and talked in plain, certain terms about taking a step the Bible's way, toward the living God, to find peace of heart and mind—and eternal life.

This tried and tested way, Blount reminded people, has its own element of death—the death of Christ, God incarnate in human flesh. But God the Son did not remain dead, and that makes all the difference in this world and the next. Blount said, "First Corinthians 15:3–4 sums it up. 'Christ died for our sins according to the scriptures ... was buried, and ... rose again the third day.' That is the gospel. When you truly believe it and accept it in a personal way, it transforms. Christ bore the penalty of your sin—*death*—opening the door of heaven to you. His resurrection guarantees it and, furthermore, makes it possible for a *new* you to exist here on earth. It's the most amazing news of all time; yet for more than thirty years in my church, I missed it."

Because he knew that God was alive and still interested in human problems, Engineer Blount was constantly whistle-stopping for the Lord. He shared the news of free salvation with tens of thousands across the United States and Canada.

At the drop of his corduroy engineer's cap (and even without dropping it), Blount would preach to small or large gatherings. Or he would spend an hour with an individual, be he a tired street sweeper, wound-up executive, or frustrated millionaire—as he himself once was—just telling him from the Bible how he too could dial God's number and get in personal touch with Him.

"Satan has a lot of numbers you can call; just be sure you dial the same number I called," was the gist of Nelson's challenge. "Jesus said, 'I am the way, the truth, and the life; no man cometh unto the Father, but by me.' That's from the Bible; there is no other way but through Christ, and don't let anybody tell you anything else—not even an angel!"

Blount spoke to gatherings hundreds of times a year, sometimes as many as six times a day. One evening, he might have driven to a country church in downstate Vermont and spoken to as few as thirty-five; the next day he might have flown to the Midwest and addressed 2,000 in a convention. As a CBMC (Christian Business Men's Committee) member, he spoke at numerous CBMC functions far and wide and shared his story with railroad groups and civic gatherings. In 1965, for example, he shared his story at the annual

Kiwanis convention. He also was on coast-to-coast radio and television several times.

By his own admission, he got more of a thrill in sharing what has been termed the "Old, Old Story" than in running on a full head of steam along the old Rutland track. As a result, he was home less than when he was flying about the country solely for pleasure.

Despite his rugged constitution, Nelson knew he should slow down. But he didn't. Like a Paul Revere, he raced against time. Death was coming, and men needed to be ready to face the living God. Christ commanded His disciples to go all over the world and preach the gospel. Nelson was a disciple and simply obeying his Commander.

"I have strength and power that most guys don't have," 224-pound Nelson explained. "One thing that the Lord has given me is strength. When I fulfill a long speaking mission, I fold up like a tent, charge my batteries, and I'm ready to go again. I have a tendency toward high blood pressure, only when I'm really pushing. Actually, it's been too low, up until now."

For months in 1966, Nelson battled a virus. Once or twice it had him down, but when a speaking engagement came, he would pull himself together, ask the Lord for strength, and be on his way.

In April, Ruth wrote a note to a friend: "Nelson is off to Alabama, still carrying the old virus with him. Hated to see him go in that condition, but know the Lord is able and will provide for him."

During this period, when he became especially tired, his hearing would suddenly leave him but would return when he had "charged his batteries."

In one month, Nelson and the virus traveled more than 30,000 miles, mainly by commercial airliners, and he spoke some fifty times.

In one day, in California, he spoke at a prayer breakfast, at an evening banquet, at nine o'clock in a servicemen's center, and appeared on three television programs, including a midnight interview show. In each instance, he shared his story of finding peace and security through Jesus Christ.

After the midnight program, at 1:00AM, a station official said, "Mr. Blount, may I talk to you?" Nelson went aside with him, and the television official revealed that the recent death of his mother had shaken him. She was a Christian. Nelson's comments had convinced him that he needed to put his trust in Christ and follow his mother's faith. When Nelson left him at about 1:45, the man had committed his life to Jesus Christ.

The next morning, Nelson appeared on an early broadcast and hurried from the station to speak at a church service.

Nelson felt he could not maintain his fast-paced schedule without his Cessna 180. "God has blessed me with material goods and has given me this plane," he said. "So naturally I put it to use for Him."

He gave this example: One afternoon, he finished his excursion run at Bellows Falls at about 4:00PM. He immediately went to his plane, which was in back of the Monadnock Northern station, and minutes later, he was winging his way toward Ocean City, New Jersey, some 300 miles away, where he was to speak that evening in a CBMC conference.

He landed at Atlantic City. And while he waiting for his friend Bob Woodburn to pick him up and take him to Ocean City, Nelson engaged a man in conversation. Soured on life and skeptical of religion, the man listened to Nelson's testimony and clear-cut presentation of the gospel. Before Woodburn came for Nelson, the man had professed faith in the Lord Jesus Christ.

The next morning, Nelson attended the conference until midmorning and then departed. He flew back to Steamtown to climb into the cab of *No. 15* and head up Williams River Valley on another excursion run to Chester.

And so it went—Nelson Blount had a testimony and would travel.

Countless people, like the television official and the man at the Atlantic City airport, acknowledged Jesus Christ as their Savior in man-to-man conversations or gatherings where Nelson spoke. This step of faith, Blount believed, was merely the beginning of a wonderful, new life for all who would stay in the Word and go on to get to know God better in daily fellowship. Nelson knew that God's love would begin to fill that life, and God would give wisdom and prudence in life's decisions and problems.

Nelson's speaking ministry started soon after John DeBrine interviewed him on his *Songtime* network radio program in 1962. That appearance resulted in several invitations for Nelson to share his story in churches and elsewhere. He told his story with the fervency of a Billy Graham, pulling no punches, making no apologies, and emphasizing, "This is what the Bible says."

In person-to-person discussions, Nelson would all but overwhelm his counselee with his enthusiastic presentation, sparring with illustrations, hammering home key Scripture verses by the dozen, and generally crowding his listener into the ropes, seeking an early decision. If time permitted—and it usually did, for Nelson seldom was in a hurry if he had the ear of someone needing the gospel—he would sometimes launch into a lengthy summary of the Bible, from Adam to Christ.

His fervency was like that of the atheist who said if he believed the gospel, he would "crawl on broken glass across England, if need be," to share the message with others.

Nelson was like a man with a cure for cancer, earnestly sharing the secret.

"Nelson went all out in chasing and collecting steam engines, old cars, guns, and a host of other things," Ruth Blount related in 1966. "He's all out for the Lord, and I'm sure he always will be."

At Steamtown, Nelson spent considerable time just counseling mixed-up visitors. Once, in 1963, he asked an assistant, Bob Adams, to keep people away while he finished his income tax; it was just before the filing deadline. "You know, that's the first return I ever had difficulty with—the IRS audited it and had me haul out all my records," Nelson pointed out. "That taught me a lesson: never be too busy to talk with anyone for the Lord."

In his dingy, eleven-by-ten-foot office in the shop at North Walpole, scores of people made professions of faith in Christ. In addition, many others were counseled by a small staff of ministers, including Bill Matson, Nelson's secretary, usually after seeing and hearing the film story on Nelson's life in the bright yellow railroad coach Steamtowners called the Gospel Car.

There was no sign that said, "Gospel Car." But a sign on the side of the car did invite visitors to see and hear a fifteen-minute film on the life of the Steamtown founder. Nelson was interviewed on the film and made the point that one cannot have real peace of heart and mind without a personal encounter with Jesus Christ.

As the lights went on in the darkened coach, a young man would step forward and ask any who would like to know more about God's plan of salvation to remain. When visitors filed out, each was presented a tract, giving the testimonies of the ex-train chasers, Blount and Richardson.

Those who remained for counseling were ushered into a caboose coupled to the Gospel Car, and there, the counselor and counselee looked into a Bible for promises concerning salvation.

As might be expected, some patrons were offended, and a few stomped out of the Gospel Car before the film's conclusion. One man objected so strongly that Steamtown refunded his money at the gate—money he had not paid; he had been seen slipping in without paying.

From all indications, those who appreciated the film greatly outnumbered those who resented it. In many instances, even those who did not agree with Nelson's view that Jesus Christ was the only way to God, indicated that, nevertheless, their fifteen minutes were well spent. They realized Nelson's sincerity and said the presentation added to their education.

Almost daily during the Steamtown season, when Nelson was there, visitors looked him up to talk about their spiritual needs. He pushed work aside and often counseled a visitor for an hour, often showing the person underlined verses in his New Testament.

Nelson believed that the Word of God, written centuries ago, was the very word of authority man needed in the twentieth century (and he would say that for people in every century). People who sat in his office, he found, were seeking truth amid a bedlam of error. They wanted to know what life was all about. They wanted answers to questions: Who is God, and what is His relationship to man? What happens after the incident called *death*? Everyone wanted to know the truth about himself, life, God, and destiny.

Entire families sometimes came seeking help or to see the millionaire who dogmatically said that he had found the answer to life. Bill Matson told about some visitors from Miami: "They were amazed that a millionaire would take his time and talk to anyone who came along. These people—a mother, father, two teenage children, and another teenager—all received Christ here as they talked with Nelson. We've heard from them since, and from every indication, they're active in things of the Lord in Miami."

There was no systematic follow-up of people Nelson introduced to Christ. All who made professions got a gospel of John (or, in later days, a pocket New Testament) and were advised to get into a church that was faithfully preaching the Word of God. Blount said, "The Holy Spirit takes over from there; I have faith that He will continue the work."

Numerous people wrote to thank Nelson for his counsel. Some indicated the delight of being sure that God had removed their guilt, and many told of the thrilling new life they were enjoying. Many of these letters were stuffed into drawers and files in the Steamtown office.

One day a letter came to Nelson's office from a retired Catholic priest, who was known around Steamtown as "Father Choo-choo" because of his interest in old locomotives. He had been delighted with Nelson's gospel presentation and later brought several nuns with him to meet Nelson and also to hear his testimony. Since his last visit, Father Choo-choo had been in an automobile accident and lost his sight. The letter was a thank-you note for Nelson's continued interest and letters of encouragement. It was another indication that the Man from Steamtown had a love that extended to those of other faiths.

Some friends insisted that Nelson did not always know when to quit talking, when he was presenting the gospel to a person. One man said, recalling an FBI radio program of some years ago that all but jumped out of the radio as it came on the air, "He comes on like *Gangbusters*. He usually gets attention, but I've seen him continue talking when the person mentally has turned him off."

One day at Steamtown, a local businessman seemingly had tuned Nelson out. The man had come to the office on a business matter, but before even finding out what he wanted, Nelson got onto the subject of the man's relationship to God. Nelson appeared to be overselling, especially when he got into a lengthy dissertation regarding the highly involved angel rebellion and the doctrine of man's free will, all to show the visitor why, according to the Bible, he was on Earth in the first place.

God's Spirit must have been in command, however, for all of this broke down the arguments the man weakly put forth. God, Nelson pointed out, had created man to love Him and fellowship with Him; sin had broken this relationship; and God had given Christ to redeem man and restore the relationship. Words came at the man like machine-gun fire—volumes of words, with a ring of authority.

A lull came when the man, half slumped in a chair and fingering his hat, tried to speak and choked up; something obviously was bothering him.

Nelson spoke understandingly, but he firmly maintained that the visitor's only hope for peace in this life—and heaven in the next—was a personal commitment to the Lord Jesus Christ. Then suddenly, as if on impulse, Nelson scrawled words on the back of an envelope and gave it to the man. "Which statement will you sign? It's one or the other; there can be no middle ground."

The man squinted nervously at the words:

I hereby accept Jesus Christ as my personal Saviour. Signed:
I hereby reject Jesus Christ as my personal Saviour. Signed:

That day, the visitor made an indication of his acceptance of the Son of God into his life. Months later, the report was that it had "taken" and he was "coming along."

After that, Nelson had "accept/reject" cards printed up and usually carried several with him.

One card actually haunted an executive for days. It started this way: President of one of the largest industrial firms in New England, Mr. Fisher, a man in his eighties, contacted Nelson and told him he had heard about his new religious convictions and wondered what it was all about. They met, and Nelson shared his story.

Mr. Fisher professed that he did not believe in the deity of Christ and that he was of Unitarian persuasion. Conversation revealed, however, that Mr. Fisher's father had been a believer in the "old-fashioned religion."

Nelson beamed knowingly and chortled, "Now I know something; he prayed for you! Like many young people, you must have rebelled. God is still trying to reach you because of your dad's prayers."

Finally, Nelson gave the industrialist the printed "accept/reject" card. The elderly man refused to sign either side, but he put it in his pocket. Finally, they parted on a friendly note and had subsequent discussions.

Then on Good Friday in 1966, Mr. Fisher phoned and asked Nelson to meet him for lunch. After the meal, the man pulled out the "accept/reject" card. "Nelson, this thing bothers me!"

Before they parted this time, the executive had professed faith in Jesus Christ and signed the "accept" side of the card.

Nelson found even the engine cab a place to work for God. Maurice DeValliere, Nelson's fireman, who quit a geology job to work on the railroad, made a clear-cut decision to follow Christ as he worked alongside Nelson. Maurice said there were other conversions on excursion runs—at least there were conversations that started amid the almost overwhelming noise in the cab. The transactions came later, perhaps at a picnic table at Riverside.

Employees at Steamtown and at Blount's in Warren all had clear presentations of the gospel. A number of Nelson's employees professed faith in Christ, including Clyde Sessions, Green Mountain chief engineer, who for a couple of years as the report goes, considered Nelson a nut.

A Massachusetts mink rancher, who had observed Blount in action among his employees commented, "He knows the spiritual situation of almost everyone. He'll introduce you to a group and say, 'This is Joe—he trusted the Lord last month; this is Jerry—he knows what it's all about and won't give in, but he will; this is Bill—he says he trusted many years ago, but he needs to get in the Word and get the Word into him. I've been telling him ...'"

Nelson did not add notches to his gospel gun for every person who professed Christ; he was simply proud that they made a commitment to Jesus Christ. They were just evidence that a businessman who dares to open his mouth and let the Holy Spirit use him can have thrilling experiences in soul-winning.

Prayer, Blount asserted, releases God's power in a manner that produces fruit, which would not otherwise be plucked. The entire Blount family prayed as fervently for the souls of people as the average Christian family prays for loved ones who are sick in body. At a given time, the Blounts' prayer list might have included friends, relatives, casual acquaintances, certain Blount employees, and people who had heard Nelson speak and then had shown an interest in the gospel.

At one period, the family members were praying together for the salvation of an alcoholic whom God had laid on their hearts. In storybook fashion, the telephone rang, and the caller proved to be the very man for whom they were praying. Previously, he had been urged to get in touch with Nelson should he desire spiritual counsel. Now, a sudden urge had come on him to bring God into his life. Nelson invited him to come to Steamtown the next day. There he presented Christ to the man and heard him make a profession of faith.

But things went from bad to worse with the man. Up to early 1967, Satan and alcohol still controlled his life, even though Nelson worked patiently with him, even to the point of sending him on two occasions to a Christian center for alcoholics. Needless to say, the Blounts continued praying fervently that the man would give himself wholly to God.

Some incidents in Nelson's activities in introducing people to God border on the unbelievable, unless you know the ways of God and the work He was doing through Nelson Blount. The following episodes serve to illustrate:

The Would-be Suicide

Jack Hillman (pseudonym), an official of a New England state, phoned Nelson in desperation at about four o'clock one morning. "I've got a real problem. My brother Phil in New York just phoned me, saying he's going to take his life. I don't want this to happen. He's my brother. All I could think of was you."

Nelson had presented the gospel to the caller a year before, and he had made a profession of faith in Christ.

Quickly, a phone call was put through to the New York man, and Nelson reasoned with him and invited him to Staghead Farm. Phil arrived about three that afternoon. His eyes were bleary, and he was unshaven; one glance indicated that he was troubled.

Nelson took him into his study. Mere Phil poured out a sordid story of infidelity; his wife had finally left him, taking their children. His world had been blown to bits. He had called his brother to say "good-bye."

Nelson discussed promises from God's Word. That evening, Nelson took Phil to a church program, where he heard Nelson's testimony and message. He brought Phil home and prayed for him, but Phil would not pray.

The troubled man wanted to retire, and Carolyn ushered him to a guest room. She gave him her own Bible, saying, "Everything I have underlined in red tells of God's salvation. If you so desire, you can read some of the verses. If there's anything you want, awaken us."

For the better part of an hour in the living room downstairs, the Blount family prayed for their upstairs guest.

At 5:00 AM, Carolyn awoke and again began praying for him. Ruth and Nelson also awoke and prayed for him.

Unknown to them at the time, Phil had awakened and was reading the Bible Carolyn had given him.

Before breakfast, Carolyn heard Phil calling her. She put on her robe and went to him and talked to him for nearly an hour. She explained the verses underlined in red. God, she said, could transform his entire life if he would only open his heart to Christ.

At breakfast, Phil made the announcement to the family: "It's settled; I made my peace with God. If you don't mind, I want to say a prayer." He prayed and thanked God for the testimony of the Blounts to him.

The episode did not end there. He went to see his brother and asked forgiveness for a matter that had stood between them. Later, Phil returned and spent a week with the Blount family, getting a better grasp of basic Bible teachings. As this book was first being written, he was about to get back together with his wife—a happy ending indeed for a would-be suicide.

The Bible Salesman

As told by Clarence P. Morrill, West Yarmouth, Maine
(This story was added to the updated
edition of this book in 1988.)

My first involvement with Nelson Blount was shortly after he moved his Steamtown operation to Bellows Falls. As an advertising specialty salesman, I had called on him several times in regard to a proposed Steamtown calendar for the gift shop. In my conversations with him, it became obvious that he was what I termed a "religious" man, so when my company added an attractive, large family Bible to the executive line, Nelson seemed to me to be a likely prospect.

One day in April, 1964, I walked into his office with the Bible. His interest was immediate—not in buying the Bible but in whether I knew its basic message. Having attended church and Sunday school from childhood, I was acquainted with some of the verses he began to read, but not many, for, to my knowledge, I had not heard a clear presentation of the gospel.

Nelson proceeded to explain to me the way of salvation as he paged through the Bible. And then he asked me if I would like to receive Christ as my personal Savior. I agreed, so he produced a tract, "Are You on the Right Track?" which he had composed and had printed. The sinner's prayer was the last item on it. I prayed the prayer in faith and was baptized by the Holy Spirit into the body of Christ.

I had little idea of what was happening to me, but I felt as though something inside me was dying, and it didn't seem to matter. Things that I had observed every day seemed brand new to me, and I developed a thirst for reading God's Word.

Later, I took a junior high Sunday school class in the church my wife and I had been attending for the past three years. But soon I was told that what I was teaching was not acceptable. We then began attending a Bible-preaching church, where I taught Sunday school, eventually became a deacon, and was very much involved in church activities. This spilled over into my becoming involved as a board member and accountant for Monadnock Bible Conference in Jaffrey, New Hampshire, and a board member of two other Christian organizations.

After retiring in 1981, and moving to Cape Cod, I became acquainted with John DeBrine, president of *Songtime*, Inc., through a Bible study he was conducting. He expressed a need at *Songtime* that resulted in my setting up an accounting system on my computer and keeping the records and paying the bills for about six years. I also became a *Songtime* board member and held the office of treasurer. Because of physical problems, I had to resign my position in February, 1988, but am still very much interested in *Songtime* and other Gospel ministries.

In retrospect, I can see that through my visit to Steamtown with the Bible one day back in 1964, the Lord was preparing to fill a need at *Songtime*, as well as many other areas of service along the way. And through the years, He was slowly changing a man who had been a poor, lost Bible salesman into the likeness of His dear Son, all because of the willingness of Nelson Blount to be used to convey His message.

In July of 1967, a month after the first edition of this book was published, Nelson was invited to the White House. In January, he had received a phone call from Liz Carpenter, Lady Bird Johnson's secretary. Mrs. Johnson was planning a trip related to her "Beautifying America" campaign. Could Nelson, right away, go up to the roundhouse in Bellows Falls and start up one of the engines to test it for possible use on Lady Bird's trip? Nelson's response was, "No," not even for the President of the United States. It was a stormy, snowy day, and you simply couldn't, in such a short time, fire up an engine that had been cold for the winter season. However, Liz Carpenter said that she, her secretary, and David Rockefeller would come to Dublin to talk it over. Tentative arrangements were made, but Nelson was leery of the whole idea; use of the engine would require security, strengthening bridges, and much time and money. The trip was finally cancelled due to a new grandchild that Lady Bird expected about the time of the proposed trip—much to Nelson's relief.

In appreciation for the time he took, the White House invited Nelson to come to Washington for a luncheon. When he arrived in the White House dining room, he found himself the only outsider in the midst of cabinet members. When someone asked who he was, Nelson quipped, "Oh, just a nobody."

He had brought with him a marked Bible to give to President Johnson, but because of the Six-Day War in Israel, Mr. Johnson was called out several times. The Bible was given to him later.

However, Nelson captured the ears of the men at his table, telling them that the land that troops were fighting over really belonged to Israel. He opened his Bible and read them many passages, making the butler quite nervous because no one was eating, and he wanted to serve on time. The men listening to Nelson were amazed at the information Nelson was getting from the Bible and invited him to someday return to discuss the matter further.

What was the secret of Nelson Blount's uncanny ability to help others place their faith in Jesus Christ as Savior? He had a vital relationship with God, a grasp of what God said about salvation in the Bible, and an all-out dedication to let the Holy Spirit use him.

Nelson, himself, occasionally put it in these words: "I'm not paid to do it; I'm just a satisfied customer."

Nevertheless, his fervency did embarrass some Christians. Indeed, a friend who went with him on a trip to England, at times, wished Nelson would cool it. After all, they were there to see and ride a very special locomotive—not to evangelize.

Chapter 18
CABOOSE

BROAD SMILES WREATHED the faces of the Man from Steamtown and his American companion, industrialist, Harold Fuller, on that January, 1966, day in Doncaster, England, as the *Flying Scotsman* glided into the station in her green finery, at the head of the Fenland Pullman. This was the Queen of British Steam that they had come to see and to ride. It was reputedly one of Britain's fastest engines, which held the record for the run from London to Leeds, a blistering two hours, thirty-one minutes, fifty-six seconds, set five years before World War II.

News photographers shot pictures of the locomaniacs from America, along with the Scotsman's owner, Britain's ace train fan, Alan Pegler, chairman of the Ffestiniog Railway Company. British writer, Richard Clark, reporting for the Yorkshire Life, moaned that he could not understand "the fascination that grown, sensible men can display for oily, noisy steam engines." But as he looked over the sleek Scotsman and rubbed shoulders with Blount, Fuller, and Pegler—not to mention other railfans who came for the occasion—Clark began to get the fever himself. As he concluded his article, the writer said, "And now, the mystery to me is how this seductive Queen of Steam managed to woo and win even me after just one morning meeting on a draughty and far from romantic station."

Jolly, mustached Alan Pegler, dressed in his policeman-like trainman's uniform, took his American guests on one of the wildest rides of their railroading days. Forty guests, most dressed in faded overalls, rode behind the engine in Pullman cars. (According to Wikipedia.com, in the United States, *Pullman* was used to refer to railroad sleeping cars, which were built and operated on most US railroads by the Pullman Company [founded by George Pullman] from 1867 to December 31, 1968.) Pegler's passengers enjoyed the touch of luxury that once characterized British rail travel.

In the cab, Blount, wearing his Green Mountain chief engineer's cap, bantered and exchanged rail chitchat with Fuller and Pegler, who was determined to show his American friends what the forty-year-old Queen could do. He had bought her for 3,000 pounds (roughly $8,400), three years before, to prolong her reign, and now she was strutting her stuff for the two prominent American rail enthusiasts. All signals were "go," and she shot past small village stations and streaked through busy railroad yards with breathtaking speed. On one hill, the Americans clocked her at over eighty-five miles per hour.

For Blount and Fuller, it was a glorious five hours. The *Scotsman* whipped through Lincoln, on to March in Cambridgeshire, and back to Doncaster again through Peterborough.

Someone wondered if Blount might be trying to pocket the wonderful engine for Steamtown. Diplomatically, he crooned, "All the dollars in America couldn't buy the *Flying Scotsman*—she's too much of a beauty."

However, Blount and Fuller did talk with the *Scotsman*'s owner about his showing off the fabled engine in America.

Though he did not try to bargain with Pegler, Nelson Blount did leave some American cash on the cowcatcher of another famous British engine—the locomotive that once pulled the Queen's train. In Nelson's mind, he had bought the Queen's engine, but delivery at Steamtown depended on certain signatures that would allow it to leave British shores for a foreign land.

While in Britain, Nelson, as usual, carried on his program of personal evangelism—sometimes to the embarrassment of his somewhat roundish, mustached friend Harold Fuller, president of Green Bay Steel Tube Corporation and former chairman of the National Railroad Museum in Green Bay, Wisconsin. Fuller and his son had visited Steamtown in 1965, heard the way of salvation from Nelson, and both professed trust in Christ. Later, in October, Fuller and Nelson struck a bargain: Fuller agreed to attend the international convention of the Christian Business Men's Committee in San Francisco, if Nelson, in turn, would go with him to England to visit Mr. Pegler and ride his *Flying Scotsman.*

Thus Fuller had come to England an admirer of Nelson's deep faith, but he wished he were somewhere else when the Steamtown man turned on the steam and forthrightly "preached Christ" to dignitaries. It was not so bad to tell rail workers with Beatle haircuts how to get on the right track, but one simply did not talk like that to highly proper lords and ladies. Blount was simply too blunt at times for the man from Green Bay.

"Look, Nelson, please promise me one thing," Fuller said one evening as they prepared to go to dinner with

Sir John Ratter, a member of the British Railway Board. "Don't start preaching."

Nelson smiled, a twinkle in his eye. Though he was Fuller's "spiritual father," Nelson was some six years his companion's junior. "OK, Harold, I promise not to say a word, but if the occasion arises, naturally, I can't sit and remain silent. You know, the Holy Spirit often opens up opportunities."

"All right—but only if Sir John brings it up himself."

Nelson asked Fuller to join him in praying that the Lord would lay it on Sir John's heart to inquire in his own way.

After the Americans were served dinner in the finest British style that evening, they sat chatting with their host. The Briton, a man of about sixty, lit his pipe and thoughtfully asked the Americans if things were falling apart morally in the United States as they were in Britain.

Yes, they were, Blount replied, and he knew why; and, what was more, he had the remedy.

Fuller, knowing what was coming, could have wished, just then, for the Flying Scotsman to roar through, but to his relief, the Briton entered right in, questioning Nelson further about his beliefs. As a result, the evening's discussion centered on the Bible. Moreover, Sir John invited his Steamtown guest to have breakfast with some of his underlings to share his thoughts.

When Harold Fuller returned to Green Bay, he read a "thought for the day" in the *Green Bay Press-Gazette* and recalled his bit of foot-dragging as Nelson freely shared his faith with others. Remorsefully, he clipped out the quotation and mailed it to Nelson: "'For I am not ashamed of the gospel of Christ' Romans 1:16. How difficult it is for us to stand up for our convictions in the presence of people who we think are looking down on our beliefs. Yet we, like the Apostle Paul, must not be ashamed of the gospel."

Thus, it was little wonder that the man from Green Bay referred to the Man from Steamtown as a "modern St. Paul of Tarsus—a great evangelist."

While Blount was grateful for the bouquet tossed by his sidekick of the *Flying Scotsman* trip, he asserted that he was not worthy to carry St. Paul's sandals. He suggested that, if comparisons were to be made, he would have qualities more like Peter's when he was starting out with Jesus—blunt, impetuous, outspoken. "Like Peter, I have a habit of opening my mouth too often at the wrong times; I admit it," Nelson said.

Nevertheless, certain interesting comparisons can be made between Blount of Steamtown and Paul of Tarsus. Both met Christ in life-changing encounters. Paul met Jesus on the Damascus Road while he was "breathing out threatenings and slaughter against the disciples of the Lord." Nelson met Jesus on the road to New Orleans, steaming to get his legal hands on the locomotive swindler. Both men, despising reputation, "straightway ... preached Christ ... that He is the Son of God."

Though Nelson was never beaten, stoned, or shipwrecked, as was Paul (Nelson was not even train wrecked!), in a twentieth century sense, he too took "pleasure in infirmities, in reproaches ... in persecutions ... for Christ's sake."

Besides ducking occasional verbal brickbats and going on his missionary journeys in 1966 when a virus all but had him down, Nelson did carry burdens that would have been too much for him if he did not remember and believe the words of God that were recorded by the man from Tarsus: "My grace is sufficient for thee: for my strength is made perfect in weakness" (2 Corinthians 12:9).

In the case of Ruth's health since the fateful highway accident in 1959, it took a lot of God's grace for both the Blounts, Ruth especially. But it was not at all easy for Nelson to see Ruth continuing to be in poor physical health. By 1966, she'd had four major operations and internal problems that were not directly connected with the accident. Despite her uncomplaining attitude, Nelson disliked leaving her so often as he traveled on his gospel journeys. When he was asked by a friend why he did not forthrightly trust God to heal her, Nelson said, "We are trusting Him for everything. However, it seems every time she's in the hospital, someone in the hospital with her gets saved or at least hears the gospel!"

Business problems—usually steamy ones—plagued Nelson. If it wasn't the ICC or B & M, he was battling red tape in Rhode Island or Vermont. "With all I'm involved in, I have all sorts of problems. Unlike the average guy's, mine are big ones. But I don't let them get me down; I don't brood on any one of them—I just go from one to another," Nelson said with a chuckle.

At one point, as if to test his patience, the Internal Revenue Service had him haul out enough personal records to fill a gondola car—almost. Finally, after three days, the investigator said there was nothing wrong, but then he moved on to go over the records of the Monadnock Northern excursion line. Was it a hobby or a true business? The IRS contended it was a hobby. Nelson contended it was enjoyable, to be sure, and grew out of a hobby, but in reality, it was no more a hobby than the Boston Patriots professional football team was to its owners.

Win or lose, Nelson was committing the matter to the Lord. Before going into an all-day session with the IRS, he prayed simply and pointedly about the problem. Lose and it could be a big setback to Steamtown plans. But God knew all about it. Nelson would leave it in His hands and try to learn whatever God had to teach him from the experience. When Nelson came home, he was weary but in good spirits. There was a kiss for Ruth and a brief but cheerful report: The situation seemed to be brightening.

Further evidence that Nelson kept a song in his heart during this pressure period was seen on workday mornings. Prior to departing for Steamtown, while waiting for his plane to warm up, he'd sit down at the piano in the den. And with the deer head on the wall seemingly cocking an ear, he'd play and sing such favorites as "Amazing Grace" and "How Great Thou Art."

Only now and then was it evident that he was under unusual stress. Or perhaps it was that, like the average person, he was a tiny bit absentminded. For example, on a bright September morning, his engineer's cap on his head and a preoccupied look on his face, he kissed Ruth "good night" as he left home for Steamtown!

Perhaps the strangest of Nelson Blount's trials—of the lighter variety—came one Sunday in Boston. He and his family had attended the morning service of Ruggles Street Baptist Church to hear John DeBrine preach, and afterward, Nelson invited bachelor DeBrine to join the Blounts for dinner.

"All right, Nelson, but for once, let's do it up right—not a hamburger joint this time," the preacher pleaded in mock seriousness.

The party found themselves eating an hour later in a fashionable restaurant on the outskirts of Boston. As the meal progressed, DeBrine noticed the Blounts whispering to each other.

Shortly, the truth came out: Nelson had not brought enough cash to cover the check. Fortunately, the pastor bailed him out.

If there was any marked similarity between F. Nelson Blount and the Apostle Paul, recalling the comment of Harold Fuller, it had to be their all-out dedication to bringing people to Jesus Christ. Paul asserted that he would give his very life, if necessary, to see his beloved Israel saved. Without doubt, Nelson had a similar heart concern for people of his day.

However, as Nelson went about his business for God, he often was wearing his familiar blue corduroy engineer's cap and faded, blue overalls. He continued to keep his hand on the throttle and his eye on the rail, like the engineer of the age-old song, for after all, he still had that consuming desire to keep the glorious Steam Age alive for generations to come.

Once a steam fan, always a steam fan—this Man from Steamtown.

Appendix One
An Update, 1988

SINCE THE PUBLICATION of this book in June of 1967, much has happened regarding the ongoing story. This special section, first published in the 1988 version of this book, relates to the sudden loss of Nelson Blount in late 1967, what has transpired in the lives of his family since his passing, and how a new home was found for his marvelous Steamtown. Other than some technical edits, this section is unchanged since 1988.

Nelson's Last Run

At about 5:00 on Thursday afternoon, August 31, 1967, three months after the publication of the first edition of this book, Nelson Blount called it a day at Steamtown in Bellows Falls. Being tired and with his head aching, he swallowed a couple of aspirins just before Steamtown associate Bob Adams drove him to his new, two-seat, red and white Maul Rocket to fly the thirty miles to his home in Dublin. The craft had only thirty hours of flying time on it, and Nelson was elated to have new transportation. He had been under heavy pressure for the past weeks, caring for countless details at his beloved Steamtown, serving as engineer on steam excursion runs, and traveling widely to share his Christian testimony in speaking engagements.

After a brief preflight check of his plane, Nelson was soon airborne, intending, it is believed, to stop by the Keene airport for gasoline before flying home. But seemingly, he forgot that the plane was low on fuel, and only minutes from home, the engine began to sputter and then cut out. After switching from one fuel tank to another, he must have realized that his fuel was gone.

In his years of flying, Nelson had been in trouble before. But from all indications, what he had to do, he had to do quickly, for the plane was at a relatively low altitude, and he could not hope to glide much farther to find a truly suitable landing spot. Just ahead, he saw an open field, with the east end nearest to him sloping sharply toward the center, and the opposite end forming a rather steep incline. He quickly maneuvered his small craft into the hill, much as he did in landing on his home strip, on a slight slope.

But, as the plane touched down, the left landing gear strut evidently buckled. Then the plane swerved, bounced forward a couple hundred feet, touched down again, and then slammed into a large pine tree near the top of the hill. Perhaps the pilot was trying to stop the craft between two trees, an old trick simply to shear the wings in an effort to survive a crash landing.

At home, Nelson's wife, Ruth, listened vainly for the sweet drone of his plane as the evening progressed, but she wasn't unduly concerned when darkness fell and he hadn't arrived. She figured he had decided to sleep overnight at Steamtown, and in his busyness, he had neglected to phone her.

An Update, 1988

The next morning, at about 9:00, Ruth stiffened in alarm when Nelson's office manager, Bill Matson, called to ask why Nelson had not arrived to take out an excursion train. Later, as she talked silently to the Lord while preparing lunch for her two youngest sons, Steve and Billy, a radio newscaster reported that a wrecked, single engine plane had been found by two young girls earlier that morning near Dublin. The pilot, he said, was dead.

Ruth's first thought was a familiar Bible verse that she quoted to her two young sons: "For we know that all things work together for good to them who love God, to them who are the called according to His purpose" (Romans 8:28).

Later, Ruth recalled, "A surge of inner strength and grace gripped me at that moment. I found the real meaning of God's abiding peace that passes all understanding, as described in Philippians 4:7. I knew then that I had an inner resource of wisdom and strength to handle whatever was ahead of me, though I did shed tears that night."

Humanly speaking, it was difficult, in the days and weeks ahead, for all of the immediate family to begin to grasp just how "good" could come from the death of their much-loved husband and father.

Prior to the plane crash, Nelson, as a man who took his signals from his Bible, may well have been thinking that God was about to call him home to Himself. In Nelson's New Testament that was found in the wreckage, he, apparently a short while before, had underlined James 4:14: "Whereas you know not what shall be on the morrow. For what is your life? It is even a vapor that appeareth for a little time, and then vanishes away." In the margin, Nelson had scrawled: "Time is short."

An autopsy indicated that he had met death instantly from a fractured skull and other injuries.

Nelson's funeral was termed by Ted DeMoss, the man who led Nelson to Christ, as a "graduation exercise, a thrilling example of the wonderful, matchless grace of God." Approximately 500 people gathered in the National Guard Armory in Peterborough, New Hampshire, on Monday, September 4, 1967, to pay tribute to Nelson. At 1:30 PM, there was a moment of silence as, in the distance, a locomotive whistle sounded.

The entire immediate family exhibited a joy not found at many funerals. The older members were especially radiant. Their prayer was that many in the audience would sense their need for receiving Christ and experiencing new life as Nelson had done five years before. Later, there were indications that several had been touched in their spiritual lives.

The Rev. John DeBrine, then pastor of Ruggles Street Baptist Church and still the director of the *Songtime* radio broadcast, conducted the service. He put Nelson's death in perspective, saying that it wasn't how much time one put in on earth, but how he put in his time—and that the Lord had to leave many of us on earth for years before anything was accomplished. Nelson, DeBrine pointed out, had spent his time well since he had come to Christ, winning countless individuals to his Savior and Lord.

Even today, the vital message Nelson so diligently shared, is chiseled boldly on his tombstone for passersby to read: "Believe on the Lord Jesus Christ, and thou shalt be saved" (Acts 16:31).

In the months and years that followed, the Blount family—Ruth and the five children, Ted, Carolyn, Bob, Steve, and Bill—proved the sufficiency of God's grace in their lives and increasingly saw God's hand in action, making "all things work together for good" for His own honor.

An Update, 1988

A New Home for Steamtown

The sudden death of Nelson Blount presented an unusual challenge for the remaining trustees of Steamtown. Essentially, Nelson had been everything from chairman to gandy dancer at Steamtown, the motivating force that had made his creation one of Vermont's chief tourist attractions. Now not only were his guiding hand and hard work missed but also, equally important, his financial resources that had repeatedly kept the venture solvent when gate receipts and other expected income lagged. Other than the collection of locomotives, Nelson left no bequests of cash or securities to assure the continuation of Steamtown.

The problems of his estate were quite complex. Everything was eventually resolved with this overriding thought in mind: "What would Nelson wish to have done?"

One result was that Green Mountain Railroad was sold to Bob Adams and other key employees for a nominal sum. Steam excursions continued, even though Steamtown realized no profits.

Shortly before his death, Nelson had seriously considered stepping down as Steamtown chairman to nominate Edgar T. Mead, Jr. to the position. Fred Richardson knew this and therefore, recommended to the board that Mead become chairman. Nelson's thought had been that Mead was well qualified to set up a program to raise several million dollars to build suitable cover for the valuable Steamtown collection. Some funds were indeed raised but not in sufficient amounts to carry out the master plan and thereby, keep Steamtown in Vermont, where adverse weather conditions were already taking a toll on the engines and other railroad equipment.

In the meantime, William K. Viekman took over the reins as general manager. One of his principal contributions was his working with Fred Richardson and volunteer professionals to produce a film focusing on Nelson's life-changing encounter with Christ. This film was a well-received tribute to Nelson's remarkable career and his Christian testimony. It was shown for many years at both Steamtown and Edaville—appropriately, in specially equipped railroad passenger cars.

In the early 1980s, the Steamtown board began to seriously consider moving Steamtown from Bellows Falls. At the request of the trustees, Don Ball, author of eight popular railroad books and then the Steamtown director, made a study and recommended that a move be made to the historic railroad yards at Scranton, Pennsylvania. Scranton Mayor James McNulty pledged two million dollars over a three-year period to finance the move. The old Delaware, Lackawanna, and Western engine house facilities would provide shelter for the entire collection, which was rusting away outdoors at Bellows Falls. Steamtown would be the crown jewel in the revitalization of downtown Scranton. With twenty million people living within a one-hundred-mile radius, city officials estimated that Steamtown could attract as many as 400,000 new visitors.

Following the announcement that Steamtown would be moved to Scranton, the facility at Bellows Falls enjoyed one of its best seasons, with 60,000 visitors. The "Farewell to Vermont" excursions in October of 1983, were unprecedented successes, each carrying nearly 1,200 passengers aboard a twenty-one-car train. These trips were reputed to have been the longest trains ever operated by Steamtown and the longest passenger trains ever operated on the Rutland Railroad trackage.

On January 30, 1984, the first equipment to be moved from the Vermont site left Bellows Falls for its new home in Scranton. On the afternoon of January 31, a crowd of approximately 10,000 people welcomed Steamtown's

An Update, 1988

official arrival. Old *No. 2317*, a 4-6-2 Canadian Pacific engine, was fired up for a ceremonial "first run" on February 4, chugging a half mile to the recently opened 150-room Hilton Hotel, the completely refurbished, historic Scranton railroad station.

As time progressed, the Steamtown trustees faced disappointments, as certain commitments did not fully materialize. Additionally, some moves made by the board, though made in good faith, were found in retrospect to have been ill-advised decisions. The directors did not want to see Nelson's dream die.

With the extraordinary help of Scranton board members, a plan to donate the collection to the National Park Service was projected. And so it came to pass that Congressman Joseph McDade of Pennsylvania was instrumental in making Steamtown a part of the National Park Service. On October 30, 1986, Congress enacted legislation that created Steamtown National Historic Site "to further public understanding and appreciation of the development of steam locomotives."

A gala ceremony the weekend preceding July 4, 1988, with balloons, fireworks, bells ringing, and a band playing patriotic numbers, marked the official opening of Steamtown National Historic Site. Congressman McDade, National Park Service Deputy Director Denis Galvin, and past Steamtown Superintendent Amos Hawkins cut the ribbon on Steamtown's interim headquarters at the Hilton at Lackawanna Station, inaugurating the fledgling operations at the nation's newest national park. The new superintendent, Dr. John Latschar, was welcomed.

Then came Friday, October 7, 1988. It was a red-letter day in the turbulent history of Nelson Blount's Steamtown, USA. The long planned for National Park Service donation ceremony took place in Scranton, at the historic Lackawanna

Railroad Station, now the Hilton Hotel. Nelson's efforts were well recognized by a lengthy list of distinguished speakers. It was especially appropriate that Ruth Blount was present to witness this significant occasion and to see her son Ted, as Steamtown chairman, officially turn over the unique collection that her husband had so diligently assembled.

Also present for the ceremony were Bill Blount and Steamtown Foundation trustees Steve Blount and Fred Richardson. Chairman Ted Blount especially gave much credit to Fred for his faithful service on the board for twenty-five years and his tireless efforts to find an appropriate new home for Steamtown.

Thus, as of this 1988 update, under the professional sponsorship of the National Park Service, Nelson Blount's remarkable collection will be permanently displayed and given the care it deserves. Cost estimates for construction and restoration of equipment over a lengthy period, run as much as sixty million dollars. The cost to restore one steam engine has been cited at between half a million and a million dollars. Over time, most of the collection will be restored to its historic condition, and some equipment will eventually be fired up for excursion runs, which are expected to begin on Memorial Day of 1989.

The Blount Family—In Their Own Words, 1988

If departed loved ones are aware of what is transpiring on Earth (the Bible isn't clear in this regard), Nelson Blount must be smiling and thankful to God for keeping His loving hand on the Blount family and leading them individually over the years since his death. With his courageous widow, Ruth, giving encouragement and direction, each of the five children, from Ted, the eldest, on to Bill, the youngest, has gone on to follow the Lord and serve Him, and each has been blessed in his or her life pursuits.

Ruth

The first year following Nelson's homegoing was challenging in many respects. There were continual problems with the house; many, many decisions to make; hospitalization for surgery; and my two closest friends moved from the area.

One of the most difficult challenges was coping with the many requests for money. One couple arrived two days after Nelson's service and said that Nelson had indicated he might help them with a Christian ministry. What these and others didn't know was that Nelson had borrowed heavily and owed more money to the banks than ever before.

Gradually, the Lord was stripping away my dependency on people (I had always leaned heavily on Nelson), and He was teaching me to lean on Him and His promises, which I found never failed. Philippians 4:13 became more real in my life: "I can do all things through Christ, who strengthens me."

After all my children had left home, I started praying about moving to Rhode Island. The winters had been rough up on the hill where we had settled, near Dublin; I also wanted to spend more time with my mother and to be near four of my children who ended up in Rhode Island after finishing their college work. After much house hunting, I finally moved in 1975. I am so thankful for the five years I spent time with my mother; the Lord took her home at the age of ninety-three.

My children have been a great comfort and encouragement to me; they keep me young at heart, even though my body says otherwise. I'm an avid fan of the Boston Red Sox and will always be grateful for their participation in the World Series a month after Nelson was taken; it gave me a real change of pace at that particular time.

Dublin Christian Academy, the school that we donated property for, is going well. The Academy now has grades K through twelve.

I am deeply grateful to Fred Richardson and the Rev. John DeBrine for the interest they have shown in the family over the years. And I'm thankful to Ted DeMoss and the late Allan Weaver for introducing Nelson to the Lord and, consequently, our whole family.

With all of the decisions that I have had to make in these past years, I can truly say that the Lord has led me all the way.

Ted

My wife, Judy, and I had hardly arrived in Denver, where I was to enroll in Denver Seminary, when I was told that my father had been killed in a plane crash. We immediately flew home to face a difficult week. Mom encouraged me to return to Denver, which I did, joining my class a week late. We believed it was God's will that I receive training in a good Bible school or seminary.

When we returned home to Dublin that Christmas, so we could all be together as a family, Fred Richardson talked with me about returning someday to Warren to join Blount Seafood Corporation. That was far from my thoughts, but over the next year, the Lord led me in that direction.

Following graduation from seminary in 1970, I started as an assistant manager and, in 1973, became president. Interestingly, George Richardson, Fred's son, joined Blount Seafood as a manager. For forty years, my dad and Fred had been buddies, and now God had brought George and me together. Today George is vice president and has responsibilities that include government relations, shell stock procurement, and personnel.

An Update, 1988

Blount Seafood continues to grow and expand. If Dad were to return to the plant today, he would hardly recognize it. Whereas ninety-nine percent of our business was with Campbell Soup Company when I became president, today we have diversified; though we chose to continue in shellfish.

It was during these first years of expansion that my brother Steve joined us to become general manager of the plant, following his apprenticeship. By 1980, the number of employees had doubled to 125, and sales had grown ten times the 1970 level. The secret to our success was producing quality products and investing our profits back into the business.

During recent years, our expansion has developed into such products as seafood-related soups and several types of seafood entrees, all packaged under the "Whitecap" and "Pt. Judith" labels. During 1988, we formed two companies. The first was New England Seafood Flavors, dealing in natural seafood flavors in powdered form, which other companies used in their products. The other company, New England Mussel Products, a partnership of Blount Seafood Corporation and Great Eastern Mussel Farms, was in Tenants Harbor, Maine. Mussels have been popular in Europe for decades and are just catching on in the United States.

God has blessed Judy and me with three children, F. Nelson Blount II (Todd), a senior at the University of Vermont; Lisa, a freshman at Gordon College; and Courtney, a fourth-grader. Judy and I are members of Barrington Baptist Church and had the privilege in the early 1970s of chaperoning a group of young people to Haiti to help build and paint churches there.

Another item I should mention: At Blount Seafood, we continue the Christmas party tradition begun by my father, devoting time to a Christmas message honoring the Lord. It is usually given by one of our Christian employees. No alcoholic beverages are served at our party, as my father would have had it.

Carolyn

The day following my father's funeral, as I was reading my Bible, just prior to returning to Tennessee Temple College, 2 Corinthians 4:14–15 made a great impact on me. The passage said to me that God had allowed my father's death for a purpose, "for your sake." (Open your Bible and read it, though you may not see the message as I did.) It took me eighteen years to realize God was telling me through the latter part of verse fifteen that my father's Gospel witness would be multiplied; whereas he had reached thousands with the gospel, through the trust fund that he had left, I would someday reach hundreds of thousands with God's message.

Illness kept me from finishing college, and when I recovered, I soon went to work as a cook in a Christian servicemen's center in Newport, Rhode Island. This led to my boarding the fishing boats at the wharves to give fishermen gospel tracts and portions of God's Word. In college, I had prayed for the fishermen, and now in 1971, God was using me to reach them. In a year, I boarded twenty-seven vessels with cakes I had baked and shared Christ with the men. Some of the fishermen called me "the Bible and cake lady," and all treated me with great respect.

A lobsterman named Tony Sousa received Christ through reading a New Testament I gave him, and two years later, he became my husband. Tony still goes to sea for lobsters. We have three children, all who love the Lord: Jonathan, fifteen; Rebecca, thirteen; and Bethany, eleven. We live in Middletown, north of Newport.

About three years ago, God gave me a heavy burden for the people of Mozambique, a communist-controlled country on the southeast coast of Africa. I had heard

An Update, 1988

how Marxist soldiers cruelly persecuted the Christians there. On my knees, I asked God to show me what He wanted me to do. He began to give me a strong desire to go personally to the people of Mozambique with Bibles and to make it possible for godly men to be trained to preach the gospel throughout the land.

I made connections with a black national in a neighboring country who I had heard tell of conditions in Mozambique. With my husband's blessings, a few months later, I arrived at the border to meet a group of Mozambique believers.

Under a work called El Shaddai Ministries, God has supplied money through a number of His people to provide food, clothing, and thousands of Bibles for Mozambique. I have made five lengthy trips, despite returning from one with a severe case of malaria. One or two of my children have accompanied me on certain trips and braved the many dangers there. I have been shot at by soldiers, attacked by robbers, and once was stuck on a mountain surrounded by hyenas.

I believe that God wants me first of all to be a mother to these suffering people. I found that only as they could feel the love of another person could they really comprehend the love of God for them. Many times, I have put my arms about them to show them love. A ten-year-old orphan boy told me he had escaped from his church just before soldiers used grenades to kill the congregation; his parents and brothers and sisters were among them. I comforted him in my arms and assured him that God would be his father. God enabled me to arrange for a friend to take the boy out of the country to care for him. The widows have been heavy on my heart. One woman told me that her pastor husband and son had been killed before her eyes and chopped in pieces because of their Christian faith.

We now have two training centers for pastors and can train as many as 400 at a time. A few months ago,

El Shaddai Ministries sent three Christian laymen to Mozambique to help black nationals get the centers started.

Truly my heart is with these dear people, and through my contact with them, I have learned what it means to suffer for Christ's sake. These people risk death to be Christians, and as a result, they have a power in their lives that most of us here in America know nothing about.

I thank God for the support of my husband in allowing me to make the trips to Mozambique; my children and mother also have been so supportive. I'm so glad that my father had the God-given ability to envision God's plan and to move ahead regardless of obstacles, and I believe God has blessed me with this gift also. I am amazed at what God has enabled me to accomplish in the past few years. Surely we have a great God as we trust Him. Through my experiences, Philippians 3:10 has become my goal in life: "That I may know Him [Christ] and the fellowship of His sufferings ..."

Bob

After my father's death, I left home for a two-year agricultural program at the University of New Hampshire. But I did not complete the program there, for after going to the Inter Varsity Christian Fellowship Urbana Student Missions Convention during the winter break in 1967, I felt led of the Lord to transfer to Bob Jones University to train to be a teacher.

In 1971, I graduated with a B.S. degree in secondary education. The following fall, I taught science at the seventh-grade level in a public school in Hughes, a small community in central South Carolina.

However, I still felt drawn to farming instead of teaching. During the spring break in 1972, I was visiting in Maine, and, though I wasn't seriously looking, the Lord opened doors that enabled me to purchase a farm near Skowhegan. I named it after the family farm in Dublin:

An Update, 1988

Staghead Farm. My brother Steve worked with me for about a year, helping me get established.

Steve and I began attending a good church in Skowhegan, and there I met Susan Gower, who had also graduated from Bob Jones University, with the same degree I had earned. Strangely, we had never met in college. We soon began dating, became engaged, and were married on December 30, 1972.

Susan and I sold our first farm and purchased a larger one near Vassalboro, Maine. We have 540 acres and specialize in breeding registered Holstein cattle. Recently, I was chosen by the Holstein Breeders Association as Maine's Outstanding Young Holstein breeder for 1988.

Susan is busy with a Shaklee business, selling food supplements and helping neighbors and other friends keep healthy.

We have four daughters, Jennifer, fourteen; Loralei, twelve; Melissa, nine; and Crysten, seven. During the summer, the girls operate a roadside vegetable stand.

We are all active members of a church, which honors Jesus Christ. Susan has taught the girls at home for the past six years.

Steve

Just days after Dad's death, I started high school at Dublin Christian Academy. I graduated in 1971 and attended King's College in Briarcliff Manor, New York, for a year and a half, then went to work with my brother Bob on his farm in Maine for a year. In 1973, my uncle Luther Blount invited me to work for Blount Marine in Warren, Rhode Island. Finally, in 1977, I joined Blount Seafood, where I eventually became plant manager.

I met my wife, Cindy (Thornhill), at church, and we were married in July of 1975. We have two children, Stephen Richmond, Jr., ten, and Rachael Elizabeth, eight.

For the past fourteen years, Cindy and I have worked with the youth at our church. This work is a major part of our lives. I also have opportunities through sports to work with youngsters. I play a lot of basketball and softball and coach soccer and baseball teams. Sometimes just having a word of prayer before or after a game with the kids sets the tone.

I know the importance of adults in the lives of youngsters. I myself had a most difficult time adjusting to my dad's death. For one thing, the day he crashed, was the first day I was not with him that summer. We had spent a lot of time together, as he taught me how to hunt and fly. I felt I was robbed of finally spending time with my dad. Years before, he was away so much that we didn't spend much time together.

I am so thankful for a strong, Christian mother, who filled the void, especially during the teenage years. My faith in the Lord has grown over the last twenty-one years, and He has blessed me with a super, Christian wife and two great kids, who also love the Lord.

I am glad to be able to work at Blount Seafood with my brother Ted; Fred Richardson's son, George; and other Christians. I have enjoyed serving on the board of Steamtown, along with Ted and Fred Richardson. I feel that the Lord has used me at work. The Lord has brought me many people; some just want to talk about God, and others may have a problem, and we are able to pray together. I remember that my dad was always willing to talk about the Lord and pray with people. I'm glad the Lord has given me this desire also.

Bill

When my father died, I was thirteen and about to start eighth grade. With the rest of the family, I was traumatized by my father's death. Yet, I must give special appreciation to my mother, who stood strong before all

An Update, 1988

of us. The Lord enabled her to carry on the family with remarkable stability.

She was very much involved in the next major event in my life. I was sixteen when a doctor detected an unusual-looking mole on my left knee. Tests indicated it was cancerous, a melanoma.

As my family waited for the surgery date to arrive, we prayed and called the elders of our church to pray over me. I believed the Lord would be faithful to me. Whether I lost my leg, or even my life, I knew the Lord was in complete control. If my life was spared, that would be confirmation from God that He still had special plans for me.

After the surgery, no further cancer was found, and I knew then that God still wanted me to work for Him in some capacity.

After graduating from Dublin Christian Academy, I attended Philadelphia College of Bible for a year and then transferred to Bob Jones University to major in radio and television production. I remained, following graduation, to take postgraduate courses in business management. Little did I know that God was preparing me to operate a radio station.

When I returned to Rhode Island, through a series of events, I became owner of radio station WARV, operating on 1590 AM, at 1,000 watts daytime, and serving most of Rhode Island. In 1987, WARV gained the authorization from the FCC to increase its broadcast power to 5,000 watts and was granted permission to be on the air twenty-four hours a day.

In early 1982, Blount Communications, Inc. began negotiations for a second station, WFIF, Milford, Connecticut, and I acquired the station in June. The format is Christian, much the same as my first station. WFIF serves the Bridgeport-New Haven area on 1500 AM, at 5,000 watts.

In early 1983, when I was still single and praying to the Lord to lead the right young woman into my life, I met Deborah Cooper, an air traffic controller at the Quonset TRACON facility in Rhode Island. We met in a private home at dinner. Both of us felt the Lord had led us together, and we were married in December of 1983.

In November of 1984, after a difficult pregnancy and an emergency C-section, Debbie presented me with a beautiful son, William Joshua. The Lord taught us many things that first year that bonded our marriage and helped us grow as one.

Debbie and I recently moved into a new house in Exeter, Rhode Island. She does the bookkeeping for our two radio stations, and I continue to manage them. We are active in our local church and involved in the *Songtime* ministry of John DeBrine.

A Bible verse that describes my life is: "Faithful is He who called you, who will also do it" (1 Thessalonians 5:24). I know God spared my life for a reason. Through radio, my wife and I are able to share the gospel with thousands of people every day!

Appendix Two
Another Update, 2012

This section covers where Steamtown and Edaville are today. It also gives another update on the family.

Steamtown National Historic Site, 2012

The Steamtown National Historic Site was fully acquired by 1995, to the tune of sixty-six million dollars. And like everything with Steamtown history, the acquiring process wasn't without a bit of controversy.

Prior to the full acquisition of the park, arguments played out in news articles from the likes of *The New York Times* and *Newsweek*, stating that Nelson's collection was "second rate" at best and not worthy of all the spending it would require. However, a response to one of these scathing editorials in *The New York Times* came directly from governor William Scranton (descendent of the founders of the city of Scranton), which charged that the collection was vital because nineteenth century American history, thus far, had been notoriously underrepresented in the national parks system.

Another supporter jumped into the media dialogue just before the grand opening in 1994. *Rail Fan and Railroad Magazine* editor Mike DelVecchio, who had once been on team Second Rate, changed sides after visiting the site, saying, "When it is finished, Steamtown will be the only place in America that can recreate the experience of mainline steam railroading."[1]

Later, after it was up and running fully as a national park, in November of 1995, *The New York Times* published a favorable review by Linda Greenhouse, a news correspondent who had visited with her family. She said of Steamtown, "The pleasure of the park is to see trains not only as one might see them in a museum but to see them in motion. Steamtown is a dynamic museum, with locomotives moving regularly from the yard into the park's architectural centerpiece, the roundhouse."

Currently, the federal government seems to be honoring its commitment to the park, as it has made a recent pledge to give funds (1.5 million dollars) this year for asbestos removal in several of the cars. The government has also promised to match private funds for repairs and maintenance.

While Nelson's collection is still at the "heart" of Steamtown, several of his cars have been sold, and many more have been added from other collections all over the country. The Steamtown of today resembles Nelson's Steamtown because it has a history museum with locomotives on exhibit and a working rail yard. It offers short excursions on passenger cars as well. However, there's one major difference: there is no Gospel Car.

Ted and Steve Blount were on the board for Steamtown for decades. Their commitment to their father's memory and his love for steam trains was the sole reason. When the national park system took over, both Blount brothers were relieved.

"I was glad because it was a long way away to go out there," Ted says. "Vermont was tough, not in my backyard attitude, no signs on the highway. It wasn't political; they just weren't open to it, didn't really care if we stayed or left and weren't going to help."

Steve commented, "We were going out there probably four or five times a year for meetings and so forth, and there [were] always major things going on. It was always struggling, and by the time [the National Park took over], it was a relief that National Park System was taking over. It was the best ending result."[2]

Edaville Railroad

In 1970, Bartholomew, a former employee of Edaville, who had worked the railroad equipment years before, stepped up and purchased Edaville from Ted Blount, who had been looking for a buyer since Nelson's death. Bartholomew ran the show for two decades, until issues with increasing property taxes caused him to eventually close the doors in 1991. Then the equipment was sold to a party in Maine (Maine-Narrow Gauge Railroad & Museum).

In 1999, the site reopened and ran steadily—becoming known as Edaville USA by 2005. Then, in November of 2010, the operators did not renew their lease. The landowner announced that the site would be shut down for good and converted into housing lots. But by June of 2011, a new operator had stepped up, and as of right now, Edaville will reopen in September of 2011.

In recent years, the park was known for its Day with Thomas rides and Edaville USA's Christmas Festival of Lights.[3]

The Blount Family, 2012

Obtaining an update from Ruth and each of the five children and their expanded and expanding brood (fourteen grandchildren and twenty-nine great-grandchildren as of today), proved to be a challenge. Although their lives have taken them in different directions (only two of the five children work at the original Blount company today), they share a steadfast connection to God and a tenacious work ethic. It is clear that Nelson's legacy continues to live on; beyond the success and good deeds of this family is this continuing, deep connection to Nelson. Each of his children feels that their father has helped to shape their lives, even after he was gone.

Ruth

After living alone for many years on Chapin Road in Barrington, Ruth moved into Steve and Cindy's home in September of 2000. It was becoming more difficult for her to be independent as she needed assistance more often. Her years spent with Steve and Cindy were filled with many family members and visitors stopping by. Of course, she watched all of the Red Sox and Patriots games, which she followed with keen interest. Summers were the best time for her because family barbeques and pool activities brought by many more beloved visitors.

As the years went by, her health became more of a challenge, and in 2012, she was not able to overcome a serious lung infection. After a few short days in the hospital, she went home to be with the Lord on July 16, 2012, at the age of ninety. Most of the families were able to visit with her in those last few days. Even her son Bill was able to make a phone call to her from Alaska. Many of the family members

Another Update, 2012

were at the hospital when she died, and it was a meaningful time of praying and signing. While it was a tearful occasion, it truly was a celebration of her life.

Over sixty-four immediate family members, including many great-grandchildren, gathered for a graveside service in Dublin, NH, where she was laid to rest next to her beloved Nelson. The celebration service took place at The Dublin Christian Academy, where all of her children spoke in remembrance of her. The challenge was clear; the family was meant to carry on this spiritual legacy started by God through Nelson and Ruth.

Ted

Ted and George (Fred Richardson's son) ran Blount for decades, successfully expanding the company's production capabilities to include a wide variety of value-added shellfish products, including IQF chopped clam meat, concentrated clam broth, stuffed gourmet clams, conch, and both condensed and ready-to-serve chowders. As busy as Ted was, he always made time for church and his family.

Today, Ted and his wife, Judy, split time between Florida and Rhode Island, attending Grace Place in Florida and Godspeed in Rhode Island.

Ted's son, Todd, is a deacon at their church in Rhode Island, as well as the founder of a Christian leadership program called Rhode Trip. This is a six-year commitment for young men and calls upon them to devote a week each summer, from grades eight through twelve, to surviving and thriving in the great outdoors. Not coincidentally, Todd founded the program with Lyle Richardson, grandson of Fred Richardson. Steve's son, Stephen, along with Lyle and Todd have also started and led several men's Bible studies tailored for young men in their twenties.

Nelson's influence on Ted's life occurred through the example Nelson set forth. Ted said, "I'm the oldest and the luckiest, having spent a lot more time with him. He was a very charismatic guy and attracted a lot of attention. I'm the opposite of him. I'm more of an analytical person. It was by spending all of that time with him, I saw the things he did well, and I saw the things I could do better. But Dad had excellent character and set a good example."

Carolyn

Starting in 1985, after hearing an African missionary speak at her church, Carolyn, then a stay-at-home mother of three, decided to go into war-torn Malawi to see for herself if the devastation described was true. What she saw changed the course of her life forever.

A self-admitted "girly girl," Carolyn didn't necessarily like the dirty conditions or having to sleep in a tent. "This was not my thing," Carolyn later said. She attributes her continued desire to help the impoverished people of Africa to "mouth telephone." "It means God calls you up and tells you where to go, and you just have to show up." And show up she has continued to do for the last twenty-five years.

Carolyn now has a ministry in Africa called, El Shaddai, where she works with the hundreds of widows in Malawi who have lost sons and husbands due to the long-standing civil war. Her latest relief building in Africa is called the Nelson Blount Center.

Although she does not always have the funds to travel to Africa, "When He calls, I just pack my bags and wait." Carolyn does not let anything stop her commitment to helping those in dire need.

Carolyn's boundless energy and steadfast commitment to helping others come directly from her father. She said,

Another Update, 2012

"I still feel Dad's spirit in me. I do. I've never met another person after or before him that had the passion and vision that he had in everything he did, whether it was in the business world or the Christian thing; it was a light in him, a flame that never went out. He was always driven—but with joy."

Bob

After selling his dairy farm of twenty-four years, Bob started working for a dairy herd management company called, Dairy One, and has been doing that for the past fifteen years. He is a member of the United Church of Christ and was recently elected to the Missions Committee. A mission trip is scheduled for Honduras in January of 2012.

In addition, Bob has been delivering food donations to the local food bank and helping with the local sandwich program that serves meals to the needy. His four daughters have completed many missions to Guatemala with Mission Impact.

Nelson's conversion was life-changing for Bob. He said, "My father's conversion was pivotal. He introduced Christ to the rest of his family, as well as anyone he had come in contact with. I just met a man a few months ago whom he had given a ride to in Vermont forty some years ago, who related to me the story like it was yesterday. He told me how my father had shared the gospel with him and prayed for him. This guy had been hitchhiking on his way to visit his intended wife while he was in college. It blew my mind how these kinds of stories keep surfacing.

"My faith has given me strength in the times I have really needed it. I think faith is what carries us all through life. Dad's influence still is there in all facets of life."

Steve

A few years ago, around 2006, as he began to slow down in his duties at Blount as vice president of procurement, Steve started a house church, Godspeed Fellowship, in Seekonk, Massachusetts. Steve is an elder at the church, where families get together at a public school every Sunday.

Steve hasn't retired, though, and along with Ted, remains at Blount Fine Foods (formally Seafood), sharing the same office on Water Street in Warren that Fred and Nelson shared. Decorating the pine-paneled walls are a picture of the roundhouse in Walpole, the head of a moose that Nelson killed in British Columbia, and a deer head that Grandfather Palmer killed in 1930. Two desks face each other, in the same position that Fred Richardson and Nelson Blount had them. In later years, their sons, Ted and George would sit across from one another, running the seafood business and other Blount ventures. Today brothers Steve and Ted sit at those desks, assisting Ted's son, Todd (F. Nelson Blount II), in running Blount Fine Foods.

In recent years, Ruth came to live with Steve and his wife, Cindy. Her health and spirit were relatively strong, and she continued to take frequent visits from the family. In August (2011), the family celebrated her ninetieth birthday with most of the extended family.

Steve feels his father's death was a pivotal moment for him, and Nelson's legacy was a powerful factor in shaping his life. He said, "When he was killed, I was fourteen, when you are trying to figure out what a dad was supposed to be, so it took me a long time to get over his death. But he definitely influenced my life with Christianity and so forth. I never was like him. He was the dynamic guy to knock people down with the gospel Word. I was more the life-will-show-it kind of person. People were attracted to him. He would come home in the late afternoon, and he'd always have various people straggling along with him. Back then, there [were] a lot of hitchhikers. He would never *not* stop for a hitchhiker! I don't care how full the car was! He would stop for a hitchhiker and tell him about the Lord. That was Dad."

Bill

Bill has created a completely different business from his father's—radio broadcasting. Yet, his path, vision, and drive clearly resemble Nelson's. Today Bill owns and operates six Christian/Talk formatted stations throughout New England, operating in Maine, New Hampshire, Massachusetts, Rhode Island, and Connecticut. His wife, Debbie, daughter, Shayne, and daughter-in-law, Katie, all play an active role in the broadcasting company.

Bill has been very involved with the National Religious Broadcasters organization. His involvement with the organization has allowed him to meet and speak with President George W. Bush at the White House and recently with Israeli Prime Minister Benjamin Netanyahu in Israel.

Bill's mission work with the Bible League has led him all over the world, where he has interviewed many persecuted Christians who have smuggled Bibles into dangerous regions.

Nelson's gift for preaching the Word of God has been passed along to Bill. He said, "God has enabled me to continue the evangelist's vision of my father, by broadcasting the gospel throughout the Northeast and partnering with organizations to reach the world for Christ. Our stations have supplied over 150,000 Bibles to persecuted believers and those without access to Bibles around the world. I've traveled to dozens of countries to interview persecuted Christians and get Bibles into areas where they are illegal or unavailable."

Blount Seafood, 2012

Steve and Ted's children carry with them, their grandfather's dedication to the Lord and also the energy for the Blount business. Several of them are involved with Blount Fine Foods. Both of Steve's children work for the company. His son, Stephen, is in the national sales department, and his daughter, Rachel, works in marketing the company's company stores. Ted's children work in the company too. Courtney is a receptionist in Fall River. Lisa is now home with her children but was a receptionist too.

Todd, who was born months after his grandfather passed away, joined Blount Seafood in 1994, just after completing a Management Trainee Program at NYNEX (later Verizon). Todd took the Blount Seafood to the proverbial next level by focusing on expanding the soup end of their business and going beyond seafood processing. As president since 2000, he has converted the business to a premium prepared foods company, primarily focused on soups for numerous restaurant and retail food companies—big names like Stop and Shop Super Markets, Sam's, and Friday's, under brand names like Blount, Panera Bread, and private label. Todd has tripled the size of the business over the past ten years and increased revenues to over one hundred and fifty million dollars. The company has won many awards, including, the 2010 large business of the year by the Providence Business Journal and the 2012 large business of the year by the Family Business Association of Massachusetts. Todd also won the Ernst and Young regional Entrepreneurial of the year award in 2011. With his love for family legacy, he republished this book for the purpose of passing down the personal and spiritual story that has shaped so many.

Epilogue
A Personal Word from F. Nelson Blount

WHEN I WAS approached about having my story told, I realized that my connection with railroading would interest a lot of people, and that some of my other adventures in life might make an interesting book. But I think I can sincerely say that the primary reason I agreed to the project was to share my spiritual experience and possibly help a few others get on the right track. So for that reason, I have asked for the last word.

You've read my story. You realize that I've been quite a character and have tried all sorts of things, searching for peace of mind and heart. As you've seen, God had to beat me over the head, and a lot of things had to happen to me before I really got serious about knowing Him and becoming a member of His family. I call it "getting saved," for it involves being rescued from the curse and guilt of sin.

In case you missed it in my story, I want to clearly outline how you too can have God's gift of salvation. First, I'll mention a few of the things that will *not* save your soul or put you in right relationship to God: Doing your best doesn't. Neither does church membership (I was a church member for over thirty years before I became a member of God's family). Nor does taking communion, baptism and confirmation, good works—see Ephesians 2:9, just believing in God—see James 2:19 (even devils believe), or gifts to charity—see Titus 3:5. All of these have their place, but none of them will get you to heaven or prepare you to live here on earth.

God has provided only one way to be saved: Jesus said, "I am the way, the truth, and the life: no man cometh unto the Father, but by me" (John 14:6).

The Bible says that as many as receive Him (Jesus Christ), to them He gives power to become the sons of God, even to them that believe on His name (John 1:12, paraphrased).

That's what salvation is all about—receiving the Son of God into your life and trusting Him completely for forgiveness of your sin. That was the very reason Christ died on the cross and shed His blood—to pay the debt of your sin (to die as your substitute). Furthermore, He arose from the grave that you might share His new life (eternal life!).

To obtain what Christ has already purchased for you, take these steps:

1. Acknowledge to God that you are indeed a sinner. "For all have sinned, and come short of the glory of God" (Romans 3:23).
2. Face it—you cannot save yourself. "For by grace are ye saved through faith, and that not of yourselves; it is the gift of God: Not of works, lest any man should boast" (Ephesians 2:8–9).
3. Recognize that God provided only one way for you to be saved—through Jesus Christ, God's Son. "But God proves His love for us by the fact that Christ

died for us while we were still sinners" (Romans 5:8, C. B. Williams translation).
4. Receive Jesus Christ as your Savior and Lord by a direct act of faith. If you now want to personally invite Him into your life, He has given His word that He will come in. "Behold, I stand at the door, and knock: if any man hear my voice, and open the door, I will come in to him ..." (Revelation 3:20). Pray this simple prayer:

> God, be merciful to me, a sinner. I believe Christ died for me and that His precious blood shed on Calvary's cross will cleanse me from all sin. So by faith I now receive the Lord Jesus Christ as my Savior and my Lord, trusting Him and Him only for the salvation of my soul. In Jesus' name I pray. Amen.

Yes, having God as your heavenly Father and possessing His eternal life comes that simply. There's no fine print in the contract. You become God's child through this forthright act of faith. Then you have access to God. The Bible becomes your instruction Book for living, and as you depend on Christ, He gives you power to carry out His instructions for all of life's relationships.

If you haven't taken this step of receiving Christ, I challenge you to do it now. He will transform your life and give you peace of heart and mind. He did it for me. He will do it for you.

—F. Nelson Blount

Endnotes

1. Wikipedia "Steamtown USA" last modified April 14, 2013. http://en.wikipedia.org/wiki/Steamtown,_USA.
2. Condition, a short assessment of its mechanical, and some recommendations. "Steamtown NHS: Special History Study." U.S. National Park Service - Experience Your America. http://www.nps.gov/history/history/online_last accessed September 2011
3. http://members.cox.net/oldedaville/history2.html, Wikipedia "Edaville Railroad" last modified April 26, 2013 http://en.wikipedia.org/wiki/Edaville_Railroad PDF file of The Whistle Volume 2 Number 2 2003

www.ingramcontent.com/pod-product-compliance
Lightning Source LLC
Chambersburg PA
CBHW020357080526
44584CB00014B/1056